State, Democracy and the Military: Turkey in the 1980s

Editors: Metin Heper and Ahmet Evin

State, Democracy and the Military
Turkey in the 1980s

Edited by
Metin Heper and Ahmet Evin

Walter de Gruyter · Berlin · New York 1988

Editors

Professor Dr. Metin Heper
Dept. of Public Administration
Boğaziçi University
80815 Bebek, Istanbul
Turkey

Professor Dr. Ahmet Evin
Deutsches Orient-Institut
Mittelweg 20
2000 Hamburg 13
Federal Republic of Germany

Library of Congress Cataloging in Publication Data

State, democracy, and the military : Turkey in the 1980s / edited by
Metin Heper and Ahmet Evin.
p. cm.
Derived from an international conference on state and society in
current Turkish politics, held Sept. 1985, Hamburg, Germany.
Bibliography: p.
ISBN 0-89925-454-3 (U.S.)
1. Turkey-Politics and government-1960 -Congresses.
2. Turkey-Constitutional history-Congresses. I. Heper, Metin. II. Evin, Ahmet.
JQ1802.S73 1988
956.1'038-dc19 88-15033

Deutsche Bibliothek Cataloguing in Publication Data

State, democracy, and the military: Turkey in the 1980s / ed.
by Metin Heper and Ahmed Evin. - Berlin ; New York :
de Gruyter, 1988
ISBN 3-11-011344-9
NE: Heper, Metin [Hrsg.]

 - Typesetting: Appl, Wemding. - Printing: Gerike GmbH, Berlin. - Binding: Dieter Mikolai, Berlin. - Cover design: Hansbernd Lindemann, Berlin. Printed in Germany.

Preface

Following the general elections of November 1983 that came in the wake of the 1980–1983 military interregnum, Turkish politics has entered into a new phase of multiparty rule. The military has restructured the Turkish polity in such a way that it now has direct access to governmental decision-making through both the National Security Council and the Office of the President. This arrangement allows the military to address the issues which it considers to be critical for the vital interests of the country – primarily law and order, and, secondarily, foreign policy and education. Thus, there seems to be a division of labor between the state elites, on the one hand, and the political elites, on the other.

Viewed from this perspective the transition to civilian politics gains particular significance. Simply put, it is conceived at least by the state elites to be a transition not to unfettered civilian politics but to the type of polity already delineated. However, the present state elites in Turkey give the impression that they are reasonably sympathetic to the free play of politics as long as they themselves have the final word concerning certain areas that they view as being critical.

As for the political elites, except for a few leaders, many are inexperienced, since the military did not allow (until 1987) the precoup politicians to take an active role in politics. The issues facing present-day Turkish politics are whether the critical balance in question can be maintained so that the regime does not drift into a new crisis situation, as happened in the Weimar Republic, and whether a more open *and* viable system can be established in the near future.

Leading students of Turkish politics have addressed themselves to various aspects of this particular issue at an international conference, sponsored by the Stiftung Volkswagenwerk, which took place in September 1985 in Hamburg, Federal Republic of Germany. The present volume derives from their contributions.

Hamburg, 1988 *Udo Steinbach*

Acknowledgements

The editors are grateful to the Deutsches Orient Institut, and in particular to its Director, Dr. Udo Steinbach, who was instrumental in convening the international conference on "State and Society in Current Turkish Politics" as coorganizer. Both the conference and preparation of the manuscript for publication were made possible through generous support from the Stiftung Volkswagenwerk, Hannover.

Istanbul, Manchester, Paris, Hamburg *Metin Heper, Ahmet Evin*

Contents

Part I
State and Society: Theoretical Approaches

Chapter 1
State and Society in Turkish Political Experience

Metin Heper

1 The Theory

The state as well as society's transitions to democracy have recently become important foci of interest. One contemporary conceptualization of the state is political rather than legal. In this case the state does not refer to "human associations that successfully claim monopoly of the legitimate use of physical force within a given territory." The state is not presumed to have final authority, that is, sovereignty as formulated first by Bodin. Consequently, the state is not taken as a basic instrument to be used by elected governments for their own specific political purposes.

Instead, it is noted that the sovereignty of the state varies from one setting to another. The sovereignty of the state vis-à-vis other associations and collectivities is an empirical question for each individual case. Thus, one would come across in different polities or, in the same polity in different historical periods, a greater or lesser degree of "stateness," depending upon the extent to which the major goals of society are designated and safeguarded by those who claim to represent the state, independently of civil society.[1]

The defining feature of the state, formulated in political rather than legal terms, is not the degree of penetration, one of the cardinal features of the traditional approach of the issue of the state, but the autonomy of the state elite from the political elite. In fact, often an inverse relation obtains

---

[1] Pioneering work espousing such a conception of the state is found in J. P. Nettl, "The State as a Conceptual Variable", *World Politics* 21 (1968), pp 559-592. A recent and important work on the state is Peter B. Evans, Dietrich Rueschemeyer and Theda Skocpol, eds., *Bringing the State Back In* (Cambridge, Cambridge University Press, 1985).

between the degree of stateness, on the one hand, and that of penetration, on the other.

According to R. N. Berki,[2] a polity with a certain degree of "stateness" may be referred to as a "transcendentalist" polity, if a nominal meaning is attributed to that term; with transcendentalism reference is made not to a divine phenomenon but to those interests that *transcend* particularistic group interests. Thus, in a transcendentalist polity, in contrast to an instrumentalist one, one comes across essentially a "moral" rather than an "interest community." In a moral community, public interest does not merely delimit but also defines the proper pursuit of individuals. Politics is not taken as the adjustment and reconciliation of various private interests and beliefs, but is viewed primarily in terms of leadership and education.

In this sense, one can talk about the salience of "stateness" in a given polity to the extent to which public interest is defined by the non-elected elite. It follows that there is a zero-sum game between the arena of the "state" and that of "politics."

Historically, in some settings, for example, in the Anglo-American one, the major conflicts have been resolved essentially through resorting to politics. Basically because it was possible to forge a harmonization of the different groups and classes, they could arrive at a dynamic consensus and resolve their differences progressively. Their consensus was dynamic in so far as the ground rules for reaching decisions did not take on primarily a substantive but basically an instrumentalist coloring. The common denominators did not turn out to be certain norms and values, such as, nationalism, étatism, and the like; rather they emerged as procedural rules of the game such as one-man one-vote, majority rule, etc. In another category of settings, particularly in Latin Christendom, a dynamic consensus could not emerge. Instead, there developed a bitter conflict between the kings, on the one hand, and various "orders," on the other. The orders in question organized themselves within the framework of what were essentially legal entities, such as *parlement* or *Stande*. Rule-making rather than politics became the basic means of conflict resolution. The rule-making within *parlement* or *Stande* lacked the flexibility and dynamism of the Anglo-American tradition of common law. The emerging consensus turned out to be static rather than dynamic.[3]

---

2 "State and Society: An Antithesis of Modern Political Thought," in *State and Society in Contemporary Europe*, edited by Jack Hayward and R. N. Berki (Oxford, Martin Robertson, 1979), pp. 2-3.

3 For the crucial distinction between the Anglo-American as against continental polity of estates, see A. R. Myers, *Parliaments and Estates in Europe to 1789* (London, Thames and Hudson, 1975).

In still another type of settings there obtained a third category. It was neither relatively harmonious, operating as associations and collectivities that could resolve their conflicts progressively through forging a dynamic consensus, nor did it have kings and estates in relatively bitter opposition to one another and consequently tending to "salvage" the most conflictual issues from the trials and tribulations of the political arena. In this third type of polities one finds hopelessly conflict-ridden societies, which could not be organized against the center and, therefore, could not pose any countervailing power. Such polities were referred to as patrimonial.

As has already been implied, the capacity of a society to progressively create dynamic consensus as a resolution of conflicts over fundamental claims turns out to be one major determinant of "stateness." To the extent to which a dynamic consensus is not reached, there emerges a state that is sovereign vis-à-vis civil society.[4] Absent in this particular approach is the Hegelian assumption of the inevitability of a benevolent state represented by an "absolute class," or bureaucracy, facing a civil society made up of collectivities that are only interested in their particularistic interests. Rather, both the nature of the state and its locus are treated as empirical questions.

Within the present framework, one dimension of the Hegelian "ideal" model, that is, conflict-ridden civil society with inordinate emphasis on particularistic interests, constitutes one of the four ideal-types (extreme instrumentalism) that may be approximated in empirical reality in different degrees. Extreme instrumentalism, or "debilitating pluralism," implies a levelling political system that is expected to be based on continuing, active, and effective consent of the governed. The *sans-culotte* republicanism of François Babeuf in France is one of the best examples of extreme instrumentalism. Many developing countries today, with their praetorian systems also show characteristics of extreme instrumentalism:

> In a praetorian system social forces confront each other nakedly; no political institutions, no corps of professional political leaders are recognized or accepted as the legitimate intermediaries to moderate group conflict. Equally important, no agreement exists as to the legitimate and authoritative methods for resolving conflicts.[5]

In contrast to extreme instrumentalism, in moderate instrumentalism it is assumed that consensus as progressive resolution of conflicts can only emerge in an atmosphere of civility, or restraint. The "deferential democracies" of the English-speaking countries, which are usually taken as

---

[4] Harry Eckstein, "On the 'Science' of the State," in *The State*, edited by Stephen Graubart (New York, Norton, 1979), p. 16.

[5] Samuel P. Huntington, *Political Order in Changing Societies* (New Haven and London, Yale University Press, 1968), p. 196.

prototypes of moderate instrumentalism, are based on Cicero's plea for a fair balance between right, duty, and office. The society that John Locke envisaged was, after all, composed of independent, but sensible men.

Instrumentalism in general rejects the sole emphasis on government *for* the people. As already noted, in a transcendental polity, the determination of those ends is made independently of the civil society. Just as it is the case in instrumentalism, it is possible to observe the extreme and moderate versions of transcendentalism. The extreme form of transcendentalism may be distinguished from moderate transcendentalism by the fact that, in the former, rulers are under few constraints if any. The Machiavellian body politic, created by force and maintained by force, is the most appropriate example; Italian city-states were polities "devoid of any traditions."[6]

When, however, a set of static norms is imposed upon society, there is a tendency towards moderate transcendentalism. The state is based upon the norms in question. For instance, during the seventeenth and eighteenth centuries such values as order, hierarchy, secularism, and solidarism, gradually turned out to be norms around which the French state[7] was institutionalized.[8]

I have noted above the recent interest in transitions to democracy as well as in the state. In this context, what is not often treated is the particular difficulty that is faced in transitions to democracy in those settings with a state tradition. On a theoretical plane, Bertrand Badie and Pierre Birnbaum have addressed themselves to this issue:

> ... [S]ocieties with minimal states, particularly Great Britain, are still capable of achieving an almost natural compatibility between social function and political function. The political function of the state has been based on an old tradition of safeguarding individual and collective liberties, as is shown by the early development in England of a theory of national sovereignty and by the long-standing tradition of habeas corpus. In contrast, societies on the continent with strong states have been struggling for several decades with the dangers of political destabilisation due to the breakdown of the state model.[9]

---

6 Gerard Ritter, "Origins of the Modern States," in *The Development of the Modern State*, edited by Heinz Lubasz (New York, Macmillan, 1965), p. 19. For contemporary examples, see Robert H. Jackson and Carl G. Rosberg, "Personal Rule: Theory and Practice in Africa," *Comparative Politics* 16 (1984), pp. 421-442.

7 Ezra Suleiman, *Elites in French Society: The Politics of Survival* (Princeton, Princeton University Press, 1978), p. 20.

8 The present distinctions between subtypes of transcendentalism and instrumentalism also draw upon Hayward and Berki, *State and Society*.

9 Bertrand Badie and Pierre Birnbaum, *The Sociology of the State*, translated by Arthur Goldhammer (Chicago, University of Chicago Press, 1983), p. 137.

Among other things, the fact that France and Germany, as compared to England, had greater problems in maintaining their political democracy lends credence to this argument.

2 The Turkish Experience

It would be instructive to study the Turkish experience of transition to democracy as Turkey also has a state tradition, but this tradition was structured on patrimonial rather than on different versions of feudal roots. It would thus be expected that in Turkey the trials and tribulations of democracy would be more severe and each political crisis more traumatic than in countries such as France and Germany where historically the estates constituted a countervailing power to the kings, and, therefore, the kings, on the whole, were never given a free rein to the same extent as the patrimonial sultans were.[10]

Therefore it was not surprising that the initial opening up in mid-1940s of the Turkish political system led neither to a confrontation among different socioeconomic groups, nor to a conflict between central authority and powerful local forces which could exert influence on the state of affairs at the center, but it evinced a configuration comprising, on the one hand, the state elites who posed as guardians of Atatürkism as they themselves interpreted it, and, on the other hand, a not well-organized periphery. The upshot was a vicious circle: the state elites were sensitive to the crisis of integration and were therefore intolerant toward the periphery, whilst the periphery, mostly smothered, and therefore overly defiant whenever it could afford to be, was prone to add fuel to and reinforce the prejudices of the state elites. The political culture of both has been forged in such a milieu, which has in turn exacerbated the perceived crises of integration and legitimacy. The latter crisis was a spin-off from the former.[11]

On three different occasions (1960, 1971, and 1980) the crises in question led to military intervention. In the wake of each, particularly in 1960 and 1980, resort was made to "mixed" constitutions, for carving an arena for the state as against "politics." The idea of a mixed constitution which

---

[10] I take up the absence of an estate tradition in Ottoman-Turkish political life in my, "Center and Periphery in the Ottoman Empire with Special Reference to the Nineteenth Century," *International Political Science Review* 1 (1980), pp. 81–105. The patrimonial aspects of the system are discussed in Şerif Mardin, "Power, Civil Society and Culture in the Ottoman Empire," *Comparative Studies in Society and History* 11 (1969), pp. 258–281.

[11] Here and at places below concerning some characteristics and development of Ottoman-Turkish political life I heavily draw upon my *The State Tradition in Turkey* (Walkington, England, Eothen Press, 1985).

goes back to the Roman usages - i.e., a government was "republican" if it contained "monarchic," "aristocratic," and "democratic" elements - was embodied in the first attempt to institutionalize a polity that would operate sensibly. Montesquieu wished popular sovereignty to be equally present in the legislature, the executive, and the judiciary. All three in their "discordant concord" constitute the life of the state: "These three powers are forced to move but still move in concert."[12] Thus, de Tocqueville wished democracy to remain within the limits of a *liberté, modérée, et régulière.*

Concerned that left alone the political regime may drift toward extreme instrumentalism, following both the 1960 and 1980 military interventions, the state wished to *regulate* democracy in Turkey. As I have indicated elsewhere,[13] the 1961 Constitution did not allow sole emphasis to be placed on the "national will." Not unlike the "republican synthesis" of the French Third Republic, or the "constitutional dualism" of the Bismarckian Reich, the 1961 Constitution legitimized the de facto political influence of the bureaucratic intelligentsia. Article 4 stipulated that the "nation shall exercise its sovereignty through the authorized agencies as prescribed by the principles laid down in the Constitution." The 1924 Constitution had simply stated that the nation would exercise its sovereignty through the Grand National Assembly. During the single-party years (1920-1945), Atatürk's charisma had provided the necessary prop for the transcendentalist state. In the absence of such a premise the transcendentalism in the multi-party regime had to rest on a legal base. Thus emerged the 1961 Constitution which stacked the civil bureaucratic elite against the representatives of the nation. At the time the makers of the coup also had faith in the Republican People's Party led by İsmet İnönü, who, after Atatürk's death, valiantly continued to defend the state. In the absence of a civil-society-as-public[14] that would have exercised a moderating influence, this was the solution devised at the time for checking tendencies in the Turkish polity toward extreme instrumentalism.

---

12 Alexander Passerin d'Entréves, *The Notion of the State: An Introduction to Political Theory* (Oxford, Clarendon Press, 1967), p.121. The idea of a mixed constitution goes back all the way to the Glossators; the idea was later picked up by Thomas Aquinas. See Otto Gierke, *Political Theories of the Middle Ages,* transl. by Frederic William (Maitland, Boston, Beacon Press, 1959), pp.43-45.

13 "Recent Instability in Turkish Politics: End of a Monocentrist Polity?", *International Journal of Turkish Studies* 1 (1979-1980), pp.102-113.

14 In coining this phrase I benefited from Gianfranco Poggi's concept of the bourgeoisie-as-public by which he refers to members of civil society who are able to transcend their private concerns and who would elaborate a public opinion on matters of general interest (*The Development of the Modern State: A Sociological Introduction,* London, Hutchinson, 1978, p.82). Civil-society-as-public should be taken as the polar opposite of Hegelian civil

Furthermore, according to Article 153 of the Constitution, no provision of the Constitution was to be interpreted to nullify certain specific laws which were passed during the Atatürk era. The clear intention was to maintain Atatürkian thought as a political manifesto, and to put an end legally to the supremacy of parliament. The Constitution did not simply stipulate that the Turkish state was a republic; it also elaborated the characteristics of the regime. Article 2 of the Constitution stated that the Turkish Republic was "a national, democratic, secular, and social state under the rule of law, based on human rights, and the fundamental principles set forth in the Preamble." The Preamble in question specifically mentioned "the reforms of Atatürk" as the core of the fundamental principles in question. The Turkish state elite of the early 1960s have thus propagated a juridical concept of the state, placing greater faith in the rule of law (read, *Rechsstaat,* or *l'état de droit*) than in the rule of parliament (or moderate transcendentalism).

The post-1961 Constitution period in Turkey soon faced a deadlock. The political parties could not develop a Turkish version of *Parteinstaat,* which was implied by the Constitution. The state elite for their part were not ready to give a breathing spell to the political elite. As a result, for reasons too long to be treated here, three significant developments took place: (1) fragmentation of the bureaucratic intelligentsia; (2) politicization of the civil bureaucracy; and (3) "defection" of the Republican People's Party to the periphery. In the process, the polity was gradually polarized, showing unmistakable signs of debilitating pluralism, or extreme instrumentalism.

The 1980 military intervention took place in the wake of these developments. Under the mixed Constitution of 1982, it is the military and not the civil bureaucratic elite or any other civilian institution, which is the ultimate guardian of the state, More immediately, however, the office of the President, not unlike in the situation after 1923, is the locus of the state.[15] Article 105 of the 1982 Constitution stipulates that no appeal shall be made to any legal authority including the Constitutional Court against the decisions and orders signed by the President of the Republic at his discretion.

---

society, i.e., "a sphere of universal egoism" (Shlomo Avineri, *Hegel's Theory of the Modern State,* Cambridge, Cambridge University Press, 1972, p. 142.)

[15] Within the theoretical framework at hand there is no need to identify, after Hegel, the "absolute class," i.e., the civil bureaucracy, with the state. On this point see my, "The State and Public Bureaucracies: A Comparative and Historical Perspective," *Comparative Studies in Society and History* 27 (1985), pp. 86-110, and Richard Kraus and Reeve D. Vanneman, "Bureaucrats versus the State in Capitalist and Societal Countries," in *Ibid.*, pp. 111-122.

The present state-civil society cleavage differs in another fundamental respect from the earlier one. The new state elite, unlike the post-Atatürk intellectual-bureaucratic elite, take Atatürkian thought not as a political manifesto. When they intervened the military adopted the monetarist economic policy that the Justice Party had developed prior to the intervention, and recruited the primary architect of that policy, Turgut Özal, as Assistant to the Prime Minister responsible for economic affairs. Later, President Kenan Evren also allowed Turgut Özal and his party to participate in the elections, and, when Özal won the majority of the votes in the general elections of November 6, 1983, President Evren allowed him to form the government.

The present state elite, again in contrast to the post-Atatürk intellectual-bureaucratic elite, do not presume that they are an inherently superior group in sole possession of the truth. Atatürkian thought is now only a justification for the state elite's taking upon themselves the responsibility of ensuring that the general interest is not given short shrift. Defining the general interest, however, is not viewed as an all-embracing task. As already noted, the drawing-up of economic policy is left to the political elite. If the political elite's policies coincide with the demands and interests of some sectors of society, they are not *ipso facto* rejected. The Atatürkian thought is not regarded as a source for all public policies. It is taken as a *technique* and not as a *manifesto* concerning public policies. It serves as a justification for rejecting radical ideologies of both the left and the right.

The basic functions of the new sovereign state in Turkey seem to be twofold. The first function is that of safeguarding the indivisible integrity of the nation. The state will see to it that,

> None of the rights and freedoms in the Constitution shall be exercised with the aim of ... destroying fundamental rights and freedoms, of placing the government of the state under the control of an individual or a group of people, or establishing the hegemony of one social class over the others, or creating discrimination on the basis of language, race, religion, or sect, or of establishing by any other means a system of government based on these concepts and ideas. (Constitution, Art. 14)

It is obvious that the new state elite do not consider themselves responsible for only law and order, but also for external security of the country and the socialization of the young. The new state elite also expect that when necessary the political elite should be able to transcend their narrow interests. There should be emphasis on responsibility as well as representativeness. Politics should be engaged in in accordance with some gentlemanly rules. The political parties should take as their framework a functional (economic) rather than a cultural cleavage, and the polity should not be overly politicized and polarized.

Second, the new state elite are intent upon developing a new pattern of normative ethics. In a recent book by the chief of the general staff, entitled *Atatürkism: Book Three* (1983) heretofore little-mentioned quotations from Atatürk are found not only on the state and the principles of Atatürkism, but also on such topics as toleration, division of labor, and the like. The general thrust of the new normative ethics is best expressed in the responsibility attributed to parents for the raising of their children. Children should be brought up so that they are able to express their opinions freely, while respecting those of other persons. However, parents should also ensure that their children become genuinely interested in matters concerning the "nation" and "civics."

It seems that the first function attributed to the new normative ethics is to create a new kind of Turk who in the political system is to have the role of "citizen," and not that of "subject." For participation and tolerance towards others' opinions are two features of the new system of ethics. The second function is that of building into the system those spontaneous restraints that elsewhere make less necessary the need for a sovereign and autonomous state. Thus, there is emphasis on solidarity around the idea of "motherland."

The normative ethics that the new state elite are intent on developing are, of course, indispensable for a moderately instrumental polity. In this sense, the approach of the new state elite resembles the original "Kemalism" of Atatürk rather than the "Atatürkism" of the post-Atatürk intellectual-bureaucratic elite. Embodied in the former was an inherent belief in the capacity of the people "to catch up and even surpass the contemporary civilization"; built into the latter was an elitism which could not conceive the development of instrumentalism in the Turkish polity; such an attitude was an upshot of an incurable disdain toward the people.

Whether those spontaneous constraints indispensable for a moderately instrumental polity can be injected into the system through a positivistic approach, that is, through education, rather than through multiple confrontations of civil societal groups, is, of course, open to question. What is significant, however, is that whereas earlier democracy in Turkey was no more than tutelary, now that no comprehensive political manifesto is clamped upon the Turkish polity by the new state elite, at least in certain spheres, particularly in the economic one, there is scope for genuine democracy.

There is, of course, also the hope that within the extent to which such a democracy is practised, the spontaneous constraints in question may gradually develop, preparing the ground for the emergence of a greater degree of democracy. The new state elite are optimistic that such a development may take place if only the various actors in the Turkish polity would operate with due regard to the norms and arrangements implied by the mixed Constitution of 1982, and further elaborated by the President on various occasions.

Basically leaving aside the crucial question already mentioned of whether ground can be laid to achieve a greater scope for "politics" rather than "state action" under such controlled conditions, and without necessarily passing a value judgement on the merits and virtues of the current arrangements, the present volume, purports to address itself to the question of to what extent has post-November 6, 1983 politics in Turkey evolved in line with what may be called the transient and partially transcendental regime that the post-1980 state elite have in mind.

Chapter 2
Political Modernization, the State, and Democracy: Approaches to the Study of Politics in Turkey

C. H. Dodd

1 Introduction

Since in order to study anything we must be equipped with some notions of what it is important to look for, all scholarship is in a fundamental sense value-laden, though this does not of course mean that impartiality in the conduct of research is impossible within the framework chosen. The ways in which Turkish politics are observed must depend, then, on the values of the observer and the values of the society for which he or she is writing. Whilst this is the case for scholars it is even more so for journalists. Any perusal of the press in Britain (and a number of other countries, no doubt) will show, for instance, that since 1980, human and political rights in Turkey have been the most discussed aspect of recent Turkish politics. Working on a broader canvas, academic students of Turkey have tended to concentrate on questions posed by liberal and democratic experience, political development/modernization theory, Marxist and neo-Marxist theory, and most recently by the revival of "state" theory. The actual political experience of third-world states has also sometimes been brought into the reckoning and the sociological aspects of politics have not been neglected by some writers. The object of this chapter is to comment upon some of these broad approaches to the study of Turkish politics, with the notable exception of the Marxists and neo-Marxists, and to suggest that analysis of Turkish democracy needs to be more refined than it usually has been, certainly among less academic writers.

2 Political Modernization

Political modernization may be described as a general process of change in the political sphere, closely related to other areas of society, which is conceived to comprise (a) expansion and centralization of governmental powers and the differentiation and specialization (and subsequent re-integration) of political functions and structures; (b) increased popular participation in politics (with inputs mainly controlled through articulating and aggregating structures); (c) increased popular identification with the political system; (d) the secularization of politics; and (e) a good measure of sub-system autonomy.[1] Within this framework the need for strong and adaptable political structures has been insisted upon, these structures and institutions operating in the public interest, not just in the interests of the individuals who form them. "The existence of political institutions (such as the Presidency or Central Committee) capable of giving substance to public interests distinguishes politically developed societies from undeveloped ones."[2] In this development the creation of mutual trust among public authorities and between them and the citizens has been insisted upon; so too has the creation of legal systems guaranteeing equality of legal redress to all citizens, including, to some extent, redress against the government. Among these characteristics of a developed political system there has been discussion of which might be developed first.[3] State-building (embracing secularization, the creation of political institutions and bureaucracy) has often occurred first (as, notably, in the development of the modern European state) but nation-building, and even universal participation, could also be developed first, and this has occurred in some cases. Clearly there are some internal contradictions in the political modernization or development syndrome - state-building may require the suppression of political participation in ethnically or otherwise divided societies. Also there is no guarantee that the expansion of political participation to produce a common will necessarily provides support for what political institutions may perceive to constitute the general interest. And there are well-nigh insuperable problems in deciding how to define the boundary between politics and society in a way to ensure that the latter has autonomy. However, in outline the system is clear enough.[4]

---

[1] See C. H. Dodd, *Political Development* (London, Macmillan, 1972), p. 15.

[2] Samuel P. Huntington, *Political Order in Changing Societies* (New Haven and London, Yale University Press, 1968), p. 28.

[3] An interesting discussion is in Dankwart A. Rustow, *A World of Nations: Problems of Modernization* (Washington D. C., the Brookings Institute, 1967), pp. 120–132.

[4] The problem of boundary maintenance, and other problems, are analysed critically in the important article by S. E. Finer, "Almond's Concept of the Political System: A Textual Critique," *Government and Opposition* 5 (1970), pp. 3–21.

The way the Ottoman Empire modernized in the nineteenth century was primarily by first developing the bureaucracy at the expense of the military and religious centres of power. The Janissaries were destroyed in 1826, and during the course of the century the religious institution was subjected to constant attacks on its wealth and privileges. Nevertheless, there were also some quite important developments in the extension of political and legal rights to individuals and in the creation of participatory institutions (like the short-lived parliament of 1876, later revived after the Young Turk Revolution). Modern legal systems of western provenance also began to be created during the nineteenth century and were largely completed by Mustafa Kemal Atatürk. Nation-building came late in the development process after failures to create an Ottoman state based on the participation of all groups constituting the Ottoman Empire.[5]

In short, until 1945 the Ottoman Empire and modern Turkey placed major emphasis on the creation of a modernizing authoritarian regime; liberal-democratic processes were not, or could not be, encouraged though formal liberal and democratic institutions were established. This was not in accordance with the general thrust of political modernization theory. For it cannot be gainsaid that political modernization theory does incline political development towards modern liberal democracy and it tends to gloss over some of the real difficulties lying in the way of such an end result. The models of liberal democracy underlying political development theory are not explicit; save in a few cases, the equation of political development and liberal democracy was not admitted by its advocates. However, as Lucian Pye has written,

> Certainly implicit in the view of many people is the assumption that the only form of political development worthy of the name is the building of democracies. Indeed there are those who would make explicit this connection and suggest that political development can have meaning only in terms of some form of ideology, whether democracy, communism, or totalitarianism.[6]

More precisely, the notion that a developed system would possess subsystem autonomy was enough to exclude a totalitarian outcome, whilst active participation and self-identification with the regime exclude authoritarian systems. The structural and functional approach operated at a level of generality which could certainly be used to analyse greatly differing political systems, even if the stance was biased. However, whilst this breadth certainly allowed analysis of a wide range of political systems to be un-

[5] See Dodd, *Political Development*, pp. 37 ff., for an application of D. Apter's theory of instrumental and consummatory change to the political modernization of the Ottoman Empire. See also Metin Heper, *The State Tradition in Turkey* (Walkington, England, Eothen Press, 1985), especially Chapter II.

[6] Lucian W. Pye, *Aspects of Political Development* (Boston, Little, Brown, 1966), p. 40.

dertaken, it was also unfortunately at the expense of ignoring questions about politics which have always been thought important to most students of the subject. For instance, one writer has argued that economic development did not depend on any particular type of bureaucracy and certainly not on the "westernization" of public bureaucracy.[7] This may well be true but unfortunately it directs attention away from the vital importance of the *nature* of public bureaucracy. For the quality of political life the dilemma of political development/modernization theory was that if it was specific, and therefore operational, it was imbued with the values of liberal democracy (in the American form principally, though with some British overtones) or it was so general as to miss posing many of the questions about politics which we know instinctively to be important.

Although it was mainly directed towards political problems in the developing world, political development/ modernization theory has not affected the conceptualization of politics by those who have studied the third world as much as might have been expected. Nor has the study of Turkish politics been undertaken to any extent in political development theory terms. One scholar has recently claimed that their "Anglo-Saxon" background has led some scholars astray in their interpretation of Turkish politics.[8] However, this does not seem to arise from their concern with modernization theory but from their being used normally to operating within liberal and democratic norms. In fact, the principal influence of political modernization/development theory may have been a negative one in the third world in general, and in Turkey in particular, in that it has not generally prompted thinking and research into the actual problems of third world politics, some of which might still have suggestive echoes for Turkey. For instance the state in the third world is not generally the "all-powerful monolith"[9] which the virtual collapse of political parties might suggest. It has also been observed that

> Where the state provides a source of power and wealth entirely disproportionate to that available from any other organized force within society the quest for state power takes on a pathological dimension.[10]

Is there not an element of this in Turkey before 1980? In third-world states the political structure is often permeated by society and unless a state-minded military steps in, it will disintegrate into an extractive type of

---

[7] Joseph La Palombara, "Bureaucracy and Political Development: Notes, Queries and Dilemmas" in *Bureaucracy and Political Development*, edited by J. La Palombara (Princeton, Princeton University Press, 1963).

[8] Heper, *The State Tradition in Turkey*, p. 87.

[9] Christopher Clapham, *Third World Politics. An Introduction* (London, Croom Helm, 1985), p. 40.

[10] *Ibid.*

regime. In such circumstances bureaucratic stability becomes impossible. So does the maintenance of shared values between society and state and, consequently, of legitimacy. What takes the place of a state - which must depend on shared values and accepted structures of law and administration - is often a neo-patrimonialism which displaces legal-rational authority. This neo-patrimonialism (which emphasizes paternal-like, familial and group loyalties among persons of unequal status) finds ample opportunity to suffuse the institutions of the modern state. It leads to corruption in administrative institutions, to the inability to delegate administrative authority, to rapid mobilization of political support by powerful persons and to clientilism. Powerful men within the state apparatus have ample opportunity to gather under their wing loyal supporters who need the benefits they can provide, whether these entail material advantages, like jobs or contracts, legal or physical protection, or other forms of intercession. That these factors are also to some degree operative in Turkey has been attested to in the writings of Turkish scholars, but owes little or nothing to political development theory as such.[11]

3 The Revival of the State

In recent years the notion of the state has revived in popularity in political science. This may well be due to a reduction of American influence in the subject, the re-emergence of a self-confident continental European scholarship in politics, and to the abiding concern with the fortunes of states in the third world - especially as so few of them have fulfilled earlier expectations of becoming nation-states, and in some cases seem hardly to constitute states at all, riven as they are by factions and feuds.[12] If these states do not appear to have much "stateness" this is also being alleged, if to a lesser degree and for different reasons, of Britain and the United States, and countries following their example, and said to be in the "Anglo-Saxon" tradition.

The French authors of a recent popular book claim, for instance, that "the state in England is a rather backward one, without intending to give

[11] In the writings notably of Şerif Mardin and Metin Heper, and to cite a particular study, in *Political Participation in Turkey: Historical Background and Present Problems*, edited by Engin D. Akarlı with Gabriel Ben-Dor (Istanbul, Boğaziçi University Publications, 1975).

[12] Recent literature on the state includes Bertrand Badie and Pierre Birnbaum, *The Sociology of the State*, translated by A. Goldhammer (Chicago and London, University of Chicago Press, 1983); Gianfranco Poggi, *The Development of the Modern State* (London, Hutchinson, 1978); Richard Scase (ed.), *The State in Western Europe* (London, Croom Helm, 1980); Kenneth Dyson, *The State Tradition in Western Europe* (Oxford, M. Robertson, 1980).

an evolutionary connotation to the term 'backward'."[13] (Any other connotation would probably sound worse.) In this analysis France becomes the very model of the state

if the state is defined as a system of permanently institutionalized roles which has the exclusive right to the legitimate use of force ... and if that system is insitutionalized in the form of a political and administrative machine run by civil servants on an impersonal basis according to meritocratic criteria.[14]

This virtually amounts to the large claim that the purely *political* organization does not count for much and that the state is essentially an administrative state. The analysis of American and British democracy rests on a sharp distinction being made between state on the one hand and civil society on the other, a distinction which curiously neglects the autonomy of the political organization in between; it assumes that political institutions are instruments of society. So it can be asserted that "Britain is ruled not by a state but by a social class, an 'establishment' in association with the middle classes and the local gentry"[15] (a class not much heard of in fact in Britain now, or for some time).

As for the United States, this would appear to be an even clearer case of government by a civil society, or, rather, by the economic elites which have arisen in that liberal society. On this analysis these principles "served to strengthen a certain individualistic bias and to legitimate inequality of condition among the citizens, since such inequality was seen as resulting from an ostensible equality of opportunity."[16] The conclusion is "that legitimate power was, therefore, wielded not by a state, but rather by the elite groups that organized American society."[17] It will be observed that this analysis carries certain Marxist overtones, emphasizing as it does the major political influence of economic and social elite groups, but this is not necessarily inherent in the view that in some political systems the state is merely instrumental. For the demands from society to which the state may be said to respond instrumentally may be various in provenance; they may well derive from organized groups of various sorts – from labour, for instance or from the professions. However, on this view, a British and American type of liberal-democratic system is less "stateful" than that of

---

[13] Badie and Birnbaum, *The Sociology of the State*, p. 123. This view, it seems, is derived from Tom Nairn, "The Twilight of the British State," *The New Left Review* 101-102 (1977), pp. 3-61 and Keith Thomas, "United Kingdom" in *Crisis of Political Development in Europe and the United States*, edited by Raymond Grew (Princeton, Princeton University Press, 1978), pp. 41-97.

[14] *The Sociology of the State*, p. 105.

[15] *Ibid.*, p. 123.

[16] *Ibid.*, pp. 126-127.

[17] *Ibid.*, p. 127.

France or West Germany, say. A quite contrary view could be developed to assert, however, (a) that Britain and the United States are in fact liberal and democratic states with the state represented in the political and legal institutions to a much greater extent than is allowed for in the Badie and Birnbaum analysis; (b) that the role of political institutions in the continental European states is underplayed; and (c) that the use of the term state for a political system which emphasizes features of bureaucratic leadership, idealized or not, is open to question and that such states would be better described as *authoritarian types* of states.[18] This is not to deny that considerable differences exist among Western liberal democracies. Moreover, given the quite extensive French influence in the Ottoman development of modern political institutions, to see Turkish politics within the continental European tradition may well be promising.[19]

In fact, Professor Heper's timely reminder of the importance of the "state" in Ottoman and Turkish political history prompts some comparisons with continental liberal and democratic states. It is almost certainly the case that discussion of Turkish liberal democracy has been guided too much by reference to and contrast with, American and British styles of liberal democracy and that a more promising way forward in Turkish political studies is through comparative continental European studies, though with some concentration on Southern European states where, as in Turkey, a greater degree of neo-patrimonialism in politics is likely to be encountered.

4 Liberal Democracy

4.1 European Patterns

The basic characteristics of the liberal-democratic state may be said to be (a) the guarantee of a range of political freedoms, notably freedom of expression, freedom of association or assembly; (b) the existence of representative political institutions which make major political decisions according to majority rule (but with regard for minorities); (c) an executive

[18] For a critique of the Badie and Birnbaum analysis see C. H. Dodd, "State and Bureaucracy: The Anglo-U.S. Case Reviewed," in *The State and Public Bureaucracies. A Comparative Perspective,* edited by Metin Heper (New York · Westport, Connecticut · London, Greenwood Press, 1987), pp. 159–173.

[19] As revealed, now, in Heper's *The State Tradition in Turkey.* For a less questionable classification of states see Bernand Crick, *Basic Forms of Government* (London, Macmillan, 1976).

accountable to elected institutions or to the electorate; (d) a judiciary with considerable, if not complete, freedom from political influence. Such a system is also normally seen to benefit from the inputs, and checks and balances, provided by a pluralist society, and indeed in the United States the input from groups in society generally exceeds that provided by strictly political or administrative institutions. The executive, or government, may be more or less powerful, depending on the number and type of checks and balances which exist. The values underlying these arrangements reflect those of society at large and, as history has shown, are therefore vigorously defended in times of crisis. The liberal and democratic state is not the instrument of society, but, rather, society politically organized. Like any other state it obtains general compliance with its laws and decisions, relying, if necessary, on force.

Easy enough though it is to state the principles of liberal democracy, it is difficult to find any two liberal and democratic states that do not differ profoundly - particularly in the emphasis accorded to different features of the model. One major reason for this is that liberal democracy tends to raise a host of problems - more, often, than it solves. For instance, do the interests of all amount to the public interest? Are the interests of all, anyway, represented or really distorted by electoral and other devices to ascertain public opinion and interests? Will the majority not be tempted to suppress the minority and thus destroy one of the basic principles of the liberal and democratic state? Should the government (and/or its administrative arm) give some lead to society, or merely respond to pressures? All these and other matters tend to be decided differently by states regarding themselves as liberal-democratic in essence, and probably rightly so. To take the case of the French Fifth Republic, it is one view, as we have seen, that the "state" is all-powerful, meaning by this the bureaucracy and, perhaps, the President.

Many students of French politics would deny this claim, however. They point out that the founders of the French Fifth Republic were intent to check administrative power, that administrative actions have often lacked internal logic and coherence, that the power of bureaucracy is greatly weakened by its internal divisions (often political), by its incapacity actually to carry out its tasks, and that in sum "the principal diplomatic, defence, constitutional, and economic decisions have been made by politicians, not by civil servants."[20] It is also argued that whilst parliament now has reduced powers it remains a major focus for political debate and is one of the major areas of recruitment of the political elite. Nor is the President in practice so omnipotent as the Constitution would suggest - his

[20] Vincent Wright, *The Government and Politics of France,* 2nd edn. (London, Hutchinson, 1983), p. 126.

very election depends on party coalitions. It is all in fact a rather more untidy liberal and democratic reality than it seems, though it cannot be denied that in the French Fifth Republic rather authoritarian administrative promotion of what is centrally conceived to be the public interest does occur more than in other liberal and democratic states.

In West Germany by contrast it is the political parties which seem to play a larger role in this regard, showing a quite unusual capacity to reconcile their particular interests for the general advantage. And in this system politicians dominate the bureaucracy "to ensure that the bureaucracy does not remain aloof from society."[21] The state, whilst allowing political freedoms to civil servants generally, faces the difficulty, consequently, of having to exclude from the bureaucracy those of extremist (anti-liberal and anti-democratic) views, and also of having to exclude parties which seek to impair or abolish the free democratic order, or endanger the existence of the Federal Republic. Clearly the parties have a special status in the Federal Republic, a special responsibility to participate in forming the "will of the people"; with the educational task this implies leadership in many areas of the system. The "party-state" has been seen by some to represent a move away from democracy, but this development perhaps underlines the points (a) that liberal democracies have to be states if they are to defend and sustain the principles on which they are based, and (b) that distinctions between civil society, on the one hand, and the state, on the other, are difficult to make (as, in another context, political development theory discovered).

4.2 Turkish Democracy

There are clearly different emphases in different liberal-democratic states and their individual modes of operation are by no means easy to grasp. The principles according to which they operate are quite straightforward, however, and if they are under threat they have to be defended. In the process of their own defence liberal-democratic states are then often accused of being authoritarian, as with McCarthyism in the United States. The chief critics in such cases usually turn out to be those of liberal and democratic beliefs in other states which do not face the particular problem in question. But certainly a liberal and democratic state under attack is inclined to over-react, though it may be safer to do this than to under-react, since if this suggests a lack of confidence (in a disturbed environment) it will usually encourage opponents.

---

[21] Gordon Smith, *Democracy in Western Germany*, 2nd edn. (London, Heinemann, 1982), p. 70.

The Turkish Constitution of 1982 provides a fair enough plan for the creation of a liberal and democratic state. The President has certainly been accorded rather greater than normal powers in a system in which he does not have the added legitimacy of popular election (as in France). These powers are primarily the right to appoint the Chief of the General Staff, and to prepare the agenda for and preside over the National Security Council (and over the Council of Ministers, too). The Chief of the General Staff (head of the armed forces) is, however, formally responsible to the Prime Minister (whatever the present position may be in practice). The major powers of appointment enjoyed by the President are indeed considerable, for he also appoints members to the Constitutional Court, the Council of State, the Supreme Council of Judges and the High Court of Appeal. (He also appoints the Chief Prosecutor nominated by this Court.) It will be interesting to examine how far the President actually makes these decisions, but clearly the potential for influence is there. So it is, too, in the President's powers of appointment to the State Supervisory Commission and the High Board of Education. By contrast to his powers of appointment the President's emergency powers are not at all great and there is no separate sphere of presidential legislative authority. Nor does the election of the President to office by the Grand National Assembly impose any significant restrictions on who may be elected – a factor which may greatly modify the present presidential role of impartial arbiter.[22]

The major limiting provisions in the Constitution are on the rights of individuals, but there are restrictions on publications which threaten the external security and integrity of the state or which are judged to incite crime, uprising, or rebellion. Nor may associations which are not political parties engage in politics; nor may civil servants. Whilst strikes are not banned, unless they have political ends, they are strictly regulated – as, too, are demonstrations. Like every other constitution the 1982 Constitution is concerned to prevent a recurrence of the immediate past. The West German Basic Law of 1949 showed a similar pre-occupation. The overall aim is to discipline politics, as shown by the rule that political parties are neither to engage in co-operation with associations, unions and other bodies, nor to receive material aid from them. Yet this is more important for small sectional parties than for those which hope to broaden their appeal. Before 1980 it seems that Ecevit was careful not to become too closely connected with DISK (the left wing trade union) for fear of reducing the general appeal of the Republican People's Party. It is, however, anyway difficult to police the processes of politics. De Gaulle proclaimed

[22] See C. H. Dodd *The Crisis of Turkish Democracy* (Walkington, England, Eothen Press, 1983), pp. 60–79.

the need to discipline pressure groups, seeking instead to emphasize the state interest above their particularistic concerns. Yet the Fifth Republic has only been patchily successful; actual governmental relations with groups range "from domination to subservience, from collusion and complicity to baleful and begrudged recogniton, and even outright hostility."[23]

There can be little doubt that Turkey has an adequate enough framework for liberal democracy, but a number of crucial problems exist. One is the extent to which the system can tolerate two-party adversarial politics given that coalition politics involving anti-systemic minor political parties (now unlikely to arise anyway) has clearly proved unviable for Turkey by the experience of the 1970s. The two major parties in the past have not been ideologically much divided, but personal animosities have arisen and neo-patrimonial attitudes have not been helpful. (They maintain party cohesion, but they spread party influence into other parts of society, including the bureaucracy in the wrong ways, since they undermine legal-rational norms of behaviour and increase social antagonisms.) If the two major parties likely to emerge seek to expand by pulling in votes from the centre, an ideological dimension to their rivalry will be avoided. That some eighty per cent of the electorate in the late 1970s voted either People's Party or Justice Party suggests a large moderate centre to which to appeal, but it would be rash to assume of the Turkish electorate (as of most) that they vote for the two major parties on the grounds of their moderate policies, especially in those areas as in the East, where patron-client relations are strong and voting is more a community than a private act, or where pragmatic and material interests are important.[24] If a damaging adversarial style of politics develops it must clearly be prevented from swamping other institutions - notably the bureaucracy, and of course, the military. For the bureaucracy to take the lead and claim to act on behalf of the state is not going to be easy because, as we have seen, the Constitution, unlike that of the Fifth Republic, allows no independent legitimacy to the Executive and grants it no legislative powers. Such a constitutional development would anyway have been very dangerous for liberal democracy in Turkey where the political culture is much less hostile to the state than in France. It could easily lead to the emergence of an authoritarian, if idealist, state. Turkey clearly needs a coherent and centralized bureaucracy but one fortified in its higher reaches, at least, with a sound political education appropriate to a liberal-democratic state. How such might be acquired, and how it might be extended by precept, example and practice to wider ranges of society, is another large question

---

[23] Wright, *The Government and Politics of France*, p. 254.

[24] See Walter Weiker, *The Modernization of Turkey* (New York and London, Holmes and Meier, 1981), pp. 143-150.

which cannot be discussed here. Its importance is without question, for as it has been justly said, "In the Chronicles of time, some have indeed died for love, and many more have died for their faith; but incomparably the greatest number of those who have died violent deaths, are those who have died for politics."[25]

[25] S. E. Finer, *Comparative Government* (London, Allen Lane, 1970), p. 589.

Chapter 3
Freedom in an Ottoman Perspective

Şerif Mardin

'İlgasıyla ehl-i İslâmın kuvve-i asabiyesine zaaf geldi'. Cevdet Paşa on the end of the Janissary corps

1 Introduction

Namık Kemal, the Turkish writer and leader of the first constitutionalist movement in Turkey, was born in 1840. By 1868 he was writing some of the most impassioned prose on liberty that the nineteenth century has seen. There is something mysterious in this ability to swim in what appears as an alien current originating outside the mainstream of Ottoman culture. Part of Kemal's libertarian stance is traceable to the influence of ideas which originated in Western Europe and trickled to Istanbul in the 1850s and 1860s. But today, this seems to be an insufficient explanation of his affinity for a form of Western European liberalism. I believe I can offer an explanation of this attitude whose roots go further back than the nineteenth century and which relies on a less simplistic causal chain while showing extreme complexity. This chapter should therefore be considered an exercise in exploration, a first "flounder" in a wide area which remains to be mapped.

My explanation is based on two views concerning the concepts of political "freedom/liberty." The first is that an essentialist understanding of freedom must be abandoned and instead freedom must be seen as an historical emergent. Two basic components are involved in this historical process. The first is what may be called a longing for a "seamless" society. Such a longing seems to be a constantly recurring phenomenon which reappears in various epochs and in many different societies. For example, it clearly marks the modern Muslim fundamentalists' search for a *nizam-i*

İslamî (Islamic order). Victor Turner has described this dimension of social relations, which becomes an aspect of political relations, as follows:

Field experience and general reading in the arts and humanities convinced me that 'social' is not identical with the 'social-structural'. There are other modalities of social relationships ... communitas is a relationship between concrete, historical, idiosyncratic individuals. These individuals are not segmentalized into roles and statuses but confront one another, rather in the manner of Martin Buber's 'I and Thou'. Along with this direct, immediate and total confrontation of human identities, there tends to go a model of society as a homogeneous and unstructured communitas ...[1]

The general thrust of this dimension of society is the same as that of millenarism. In the Muslim context, Marshall Hodgson speaks of the Muslim's search for the "seamless" society in the fifteenth century as follows:

In a sense ... [Shiism] accepted the Sûfî political notion of a universal mystical hierarchy over, against and above the military powers (i.e., the state) but it rejected the political outcome of the Sunnî synthesis of the Earlier Middle Period, as not, in practice, satisfying the demand of populist egalitarian, justice, which the Muslim conscience demanded ... This ... Shiism, commonly devoted to a *bâtinî*, 'inward' and esoteric doctrine often carried elements of a gnostic type approach to understanding the cosmos and human beings in it: in a cosmos where truth and good were veiled, the elite soul could escape misery and falsehood by esoteric knowledge of the secret ultimate reality.[2]

Hodgson's "esoteric knowledge" was the foundation of a traditional Muslim concept of freedom. Its political consequences lie in two directions: first in the saliency of the concept of a soul which searches for esoteric knowledge and considers the community of saints (saints both in heaven and on earth called *aktâb* in the traditional wording) as components of the ideal society. This soul resists all attempts to deflect it or capture it, and its greatest resistance is to the official sphere. Second, some of those who search for esotoric knowledge have ultimately attempted to establish the Kingdom of God on earth. It is no coincidence that in modern times the most systematic advocates of an integral *nizam-i İslamî* all have a *sufi* past. Traces of this idea are to be found in Ottoman culture. In Western Europe the history of freedom demonstrates a similar link between millenariagnostic aspirations and the emergence of one of the meanings of "freedom." The second dimension of the concept of freedom as a historical emergent lies in the necessity of having to view the substantive content of "freedom" as resulting from historical confrontations between social groups. Four types of confrontation appear to have determined the meaning of freedom.

---

[1] Victor Turner, *The Ritual Process: Structure and anti-Structure* (Chicago, Aldine, 1969).
[2] Marshall Hodgson, *The Venture of Islam*, vol. II (Chicago, Univ. of Chicago Press, 1977).

(1) The Western Christian, pre-medieval, idea of a "moral economy," that is, an ideal model of a society where man's selfishness is controlled by the higher laws of God which provide for the common good of society and which also protect the community of interests from interferences on the part of autocrats.

(2) The conceptions concerning freedom which emerged from the struggles between Church and Empire: Innocent IV (1239-1245) and Frederick II are landmarks which will clarify my approach.

(3) The conception concerning freedom which emerged from the struggles between Western feudals and the monarchy: Magna Carta and its interpretation by later publicists are our benchmarks.

(4) The idea of freedom which emerged from the conflict between the bourgeoisie and various forms of what it considered to be absolutism.

It seems to me that what is ordinarily attempted to be conveyed by the concept of political freedom consists of a mix of ideas having emerged from these different strata. An interesting aspect of the civilization of Islamic societies is that the first three of these strata have what could be termed Islamic "parallels." By contrast, the stamp left on Western society by feudal conflicts and by the struggles of the bourgeoisie has no Islamic equivalents. Thus, when Muslims state that they, too, have a tradition of "freedom," this assertion is partly - but only partly - correct. They are incorrect as a crucial shift occurs with Magna Carta: the collective purpose seen in early Christian ideas disappears and is replaced by matters relating to the "control of the purse," what Muslim publicists usually see as self-seeking egoism.

A second step away from the collectivist definition of freedom is taken at the stage at which the bourgeoisie imposes its views: individualism is now necessarily linked with political freedom. Both of these steps are missing in Islamic societies and the concepts of freedom relating to them are those which are systematically berated by modern Muslims. The Muslim parallels of the earlier Western strata are: (a) a similar millenarian conception, as indicated in Marshall Hodgson's interpretation above; (b) a very similar concept of the "moral economy"; and, (c) the role of the *ulema* as a religious order questioning the legitimacy of political rule. This role is less marked than that of the Church and seldom fulfilled, but potentially ready for use. It has left an important mark on the modern Islamic revival through theories of such theologians as ibn-Taimiyya.[3]

In the Ottoman Empire, too, one may identify these strata. In the case of Namık Kemal, for instance, we know that mysticism was one of the sources which had fashioned his idea of freedom. Elsewhere, I have attempted to underline the importance of this dimension of Ottoman cul-

[3] Fazlur Rahman, *Islam* (Garden City, N.Y., Doubleday, 1968), p. 89; first published in 1966.

ture, the longing for a "seamless" society.[4] I believe it is an area that needs to be researched because it seems to be a component of the modern Turkish attitude towards freedom which lies deep beneath the surface of more modern utterances. Elsewhere, I also tried to show that within the boundaries set by the *shari'a* (boundaries which were defended by the *ulema*), we encounter an area which may well be characterized as the Ottoman equivalent of "civil society".[5] But what is even more interesting is that a concept of a tacit social contract may be found in the background of what to this date have been described as "mere" uprisings with no systemic moral underpinning. This is the issue I wish to take up here. It will also allow me to make a major point: that while the alliances between the social classes which were involved in the defence of the Ottoman social contract changed radically with time, the place of the military in its enforcement did not.

2 The Ottoman "Tacit" Contract

In May 1876 a group of Ottoman pashas dethroned Sultan Abdülaziz, who had been reigning since 1861, thus bringing to an end a period of uncertainty and disorientation in Ottoman domestic and foreign politics. The pashas were intent on giving a stable administration to the Ottoman Empire, and from their intervention emerged the first Ottoman constitution of 1876. The unceremonious dismissal of the Sultan was no isolated event; it was clearly a link in a chain of uprisings against unpopular monarchs which had a long history in the Ottoman context. A key date in the modernization of Turkey, therefore, 1876, brings to mind a central aspect in the long span of Ottoman history, namely, the legitimacy that underpinned the Ottoman political system, and the forces of institutionalized protest that can also be discerned in it.

To be sure, the rebellions observed throughout Ottoman history are a mixed bag of Janissary uprisings, attempts by notables to increase their power, and palace intrigues engineered by ambitious princes or by their mothers. But we have to make a distinction between anarchy and what could be more properly named "popular rebellions." There exist a sufficient number of cases of Ottoman rebellions with a justification and of uprisings with what appears to be a tacit recourse to a theory of legitimate

4 Şerif Mardin "A Note on the Transformation of Religious Symbols in Turkey," *Turcica* 16 (1984), pp. 115 and 127.

5 Şerif Mardin "Le Concept de Société Civil en Tant Qu'elements d'Approche de la Société Turque," *Les Temps Modernes* 39 (1984), pp. 53-65.

revolt for us to take up this thread in Ottoman history and to give it the consideration which no one has accorded it to date. One must bear in mind that in retrospect, the history of Western European democracy from its origins onwards also looks like a series of unrelated episodes of violence and intrigue.

The dynamic of the Ottoman popular rebellions, which clearly shows the self-justifying stance I have mentioned, retained its central characteristic over centuries although its operating mode changed with time. The military, in the Turkish case the Janissaries, and later, the generals, had a role to play in maintaining this Ottoman political equilibrium. However, "popular opinion" was the other term of the equation; it is the substance of what I term a popular rebellion.

It is only by reference to the force of such a long-enduring pattern of legitimation for popular movements - both in the stability of this legitimation and in the transformation of the pattern - that we can understand the relative facility with which modern Turkish democracy has developed. For, indeed, there does exist an enduring populist, egalitarian, democratic strain in Turkish history which shows greater institutionalization than in other Middle Eastern countries and which has enabled this country to emerge from a series of soul-searching tests with pride. The obstinacy with which all parts of the Turkish population have continued to define politics as an area which belongs to them is only one aspect of the content of this democracy. The extent to which popular demands for democracy have been heard and have forced rulers to tread with circumspection is the other side of the coin.

It is, after all, remarkable that the series of military interventions which Turkey has experienced since 1876 has not as yet resulted in the formation of an enduring military regime. This pattern of the pendulum swinging back to civilian regimes is a subtle, latent force in Turkish society, but persons who remember accounts of the humility with which Sultans gave themselves up to representatives of rebellions organized in the bazaar will have an inkling of the way the same system operated in traditional times. In our times these "collective representations" still have some important residues. Clearly, it is a historical pattern which is worth studying in greater detail. A preliminary view of such a study would state that Ottoman history as we know it is Ottoman history written by Ottoman officials or by persons who have used the chronicles written by Ottoman officials, and that the history of Ottoman society is, obviously, more than what its officials thought about it. Thus, what officials see as "anarchy" turns out to have justifications which they fail to mention. To understand Ottoman society, we should also try to recapture what may be called the mechanism of "Ottoman civil society," a phrase which I hesitate to use because of its connotations.

To find out how these mechanisms worked, we can start with a description of the Ottoman *ancien regime,* the society and the state which preceded the inception of the Westernizing reforms begun in 1839 by the proclamation of the charter known as the Hatt-i Hümayun of Gülhane. At its nadir the Ottoman state consisted of a center which succeeded in organizing a rich mosaic of religious groups, tribal units, ethnic elements, and prosperous (or not so prosperous) cities into an integrated network. Ottoman officials were proud of this synthesis which had eluded the Islamic Empires which had preceded the Ottomans. It is by this pride as much as by the Muslim nature of the central machinery that the Ottoman state should be characterized. This characteristic pride in the state was justified by the sophistication of the system of education which consisted of two well-differentiated streams: the system of religious education and the system which led to the Palace School, and from this on to military and administrative careers. One might note in this connection that in classical Ottoman political theory the state and religion were described as twins, but, of these, the *state* was undoubtedly the more equal of the two. It was also justified by the judicial system, the system of military mobilization integrated with a fiscal system, a standing army composed of foot soldiers and a cavalry, a system of records and accounting, and a decentralized system of relations with non-Muslims.

One of the most interesting aspects of this political arrangement was the attitude which was adopted towards provincial notables and tribal leaders. This attitude accepted the local influence of these leaders as a fact of life, a datum, but, whenever possible, tried to dilute it with officials who were appointed from the center. The system of so-called military fiefs had allowed such control by the center over the periphery at the time of the expansion of the Empire. But even when the so-called *timar* (fief) system declined, and the formerly docile *Sipahis* (cavalry) or their successors began to arrogate to themselves unheard of privileges and responsibilities, control by officials at the center was not negligible.

In short, Ottoman officials had only suspicion and scorn for any privilege which was obtained by powers which were not integrated with the machinery of the state. They constantly rescinded or abolished privileges obtained when the state was weak. It is significant that the highest tide in the power of Ottoman notables, the provincial grandees who, with their own militia, forced themselves into the Ottoman capital in 1808, lasted only a decade. In the most general sense, the Ottoman state never allowed the growth of the corporate bodies similar to those which existed in the West, such as estates of the realm, provinces, chartered cities and companies, universities, and bodies of magistrates. One piece of the Western European social structure was thus missing in the Ottoman State. Montesquieu stated that it was the absence of such "intermediary bodies" which characterized so-called Oriental despotism. But Montesquieu was one more person who saw the operation of foreign political systems in terms of the units of his own political system and, thus, noticed which of them were missing in foreign lands. This, of course, may be a useful preliminary comparison, but it is no way to understand how a foreign system is internally structured, and certainly, it offers no way of recapturing the essential social spring of the Ottoman Empire.

Let us start with the Sultan. The Sultan was the capstone of the machinery of the state and his relation to officials was patriarchal-patrimonial. For the Sultan, the Ottoman realm was a huge *oikos,* a family establishment over which he ruled by divine right. But, this was only one side of the picture, for, in retrospect, we can see that the Sultan's legitimation did not derive from his person but from the symbolic force of the dynasty. Individual Sultans were quite vulnerable, and, in many instances, they were unseated by discontented groups. However, these groups were careful to preserve the dynasty itself.

In the perspective provided by Turkish and Western historians, the rebellions which I take up here appear to be no more than insurrections planned and organized by palace camarillas or by ambitious mothers who wanted to place their sons on the throne of Osman. But a second reading of such events can give us a different view of their function and reveal what may be called the moral economy of Ottoman society, a concept that there existed socioeconomic arrangements in Ottoman society which provided a protective shield over Ottoman subjects, and which had to be respected. This view of society contained the idea of a tacit contract of the Sultan with his subjects, a contract which he was obliged to observe if he was to keep his throne.

The idea of a tacit social contract as one which may be applied to the Middle East is a key contribution to the study of Middle Eastern societies by Edmund Burke III. To understand it we shall have to backtrack to a feature of Ottoman society which took its inspiration from an Islamic concept. Basic to this view was the notion taken from a Quranic verse that the entire community was entrusted with ordering the good and prohibiting evil. As indicated by the vocabulary, this is primarily a religious obligation. "Evil" is defined as not observing the norms set by Islam but, since the Islamic community was by definition also a political community, the principle of the "pursuit" of the good was valid in the political sphere as well. A practical extension of the "principle of the pursuit of the good" may be seen in the concern for *hisba,* good order. Responsible for this was the *muhtasib,* an Islamic institution which also exists in the Ottoman Empire in the form of the office of the *İhtisap Ağası.*

An official appointed by the police and responsible for trades and local commerce, under the supervision of the *qadı,* existed in towns of any size. At first known merely as 'head of the *suq*' ... he was given the more religious title of *muhtasib*, that is to say the officer responsible for the *hisba*, i.e., the duty of promoting good and repressing evil by concerning himself in theory with all questions of public moral, the behavior of non-Muslims and women and the rules of professional ethics.[6]

The arguments one finds proffered during Ottoman popular insurrections by the rebels are arguments which underline that such duties as pertained to the *muhtasib* revert to the Muslim community when the obligation to command the good has not been carried out by the state.

This is only a clue to an understanding of the tacit contract between ruler and people. A more important argument which reinforces this clue is the set pattern which Ottoman popular rebellions followed. The earliest stage of such a rebellion was gossip, talk about the misdeeds of the ruler and officials. This campaign was amplified at one stage by allusions to a general state of social decay in sermons given in mosques. Sometimes warnings could take a very direct form. In the year that preceded the rebellion of Patrona in 1730, hails of stones were thrown against the walls of the Palace for two days without the culprits being apprehended. A third stage of the rebellion was the co-optation of the armed forces. It is here that the Janissaries came in. A usual way of expanding the supporters of the rebellion was to agitate in the bazaar. This agitation might be carried out by Janissaries or by men of religion. Often theology students joined in. In all these stages there were reasons proffered for the outbreak and the reasons could be summarized as claims that the ruling power had failed to keep its promises.

What is remarkable is that when the rebellion exceeded its self-appointed goal of re-establishing the contract, when it took the form of one-sided demands by Janissaries or rebellious leaders, the "civilian population" of bazaar merchants and men of religion started a counter-move to stabilize the system and counter the excesses. This was the case when Istanbul was invaded by rioting soldiers from the provinces in the first years of the reign of Murat IV (1624-1640) or during the so-called Patrona rebellion (1730), or in the events that preceded the extermination of the Janissaries in 1826.

What made the organization of the rebellions possible was that the Janissaries were not confined to their barracks - as in modern times - but mingled with the "bazaar" population, of which they were a part. Notice, then, that rebellion had two dimensions, one military and the other civilian, and that the two were supposed to work in tandem.

---

[6] Claude Cahen, "Economy, Society and Institutions," in *The Cambridge History of Islam*, vol. 213, *Islamic Society and Civilization*, edited by P. M. Holt et al. (Cambridge, Cambridge University Press, 1977), p. 529.

In fact, truly "popular rebellions" as described here, seem to have peaked as an increasing number of Janissaries took up professions in the bazaar as "fruitsellers, grocers, and bakers" in the graphic language of Koca Sekbanbaşı, the author of one of the most interesting reform proposals of the early nineteenth century.[7]

After the elimination of the Janissaries in 1826, popular rebellion had no basis of power left with which to promote its demands. The Westernization reforms begun in 1839 produced a new army which was much more directly at the command of the governmental center, much better disciplined and constrained within the framework of a new type of military life which did not allow the military to mix with civilians. Yet it is remarkable that the old Ottoman tradition of protest and rebellion soon emerged in a new form. This is the so-called Kuleli "event" of 1859, a conspiracy against the government, which resulted in its authors being condemned to various sentences. It is usually considered an adumbration of the demand for representative government of Namık Kemal and his friends, who were collectively known as the Young Ottomans. Its structure is extremely interesting for our purposes. One of the two leaders of the Kuleli "event" turns out to be a Doctor of Islamic Law, a member of the so-called *ulema*. Interestingly enough, this person did not take part in this movement, which sought a more liberal political regime, not because he was won over to the ideas of the Enlightenment, but, on the contrary, because he was a fundamentalist Muslim, a member of the Nakşibendi order, who believed that the *traditional* Ottoman liberties had been infringed by the westernizers who had initiated the Tanzimat reforms.

The situation now becomes somewhat confused, because the second leader of the same movement of 1859 was a Polish exile who had become an Ottoman pasha, and who, for his part, was intending to promote the European ideas of 1848. What we see here is the gradual meeting of a traditional Ottoman view of liberty and popular legitimation and a newer view with different roots.

This alliance of Doctors of Islamic Law and persons representing nineteenth century liberalism continued when a younger generation of Ottoman Turks took over the leadership of the constitutionalist movement in the 1860s. These men, the Young Ottomans, who began to propagate their ideas around 1865, had a leadership which consisted, on the one hand, of young bureaucrats trained in the translation bureau of the Ministry of Foreign Affairs, that is, secular officials oriented toward the West, and, on the other, of a journalist-cleric, Ali Suavi, and some sympathetic *ulema*. Members of the military as such were only a small minority in the move-

---

[7] *Koca Sekbanbaşı Risalesi*, edited by Abdullah Uçman (Istanbul, Tercüman Binbir Temel Eser, n.d.), p.32.

ment, but it is remarkable that the contribution of the most distinguished of these military men, Hüseyin Vasfi Paşa, was not to publish inflammatory articles on liberty, but to provide a plan to ram and sink the *caique* of the Sultan. When he *did* publish, he published the most radical of Young Ottoman sheets in Geneva, propagating the ideas of the French Commune. It would also be a military junta which would finally cut the Gordian knot.

The pattern, then is one which continues the Ottoman tradition. Civilians complain, (now through articles in newspapers), clerics lend legitimacy to their protests and spread discontent through Friday sermons in mosques, and the military provide the force necessary to topple the regime. Indeed, we know that Kemal was aware of the mechanism for enforcing the Ottoman tacit contract. In one of his articles in *Hürriyet* he stated:

> It was the sight of thousands of Janissary bodies rotting in the Golden Horn which have made our people unable to speak their mind since the *Vak'a-i Hayriye,* for the Janissaries provided a countervailing force to the oppression of officials.[8]

In one respect, however, a rift was to appear in what until then had been an alliance of the better-off traders and craft leaders, scholars of Islamic Law, and the military. In the 1860s the Young Ottomans quickly discovered that Ali Suavi, the firebrand Islamic agitator who had worked so closely with them and who published their first ideological journal, the *Muhbir,* had, in fact, ideas that differed considerably from theirs. Both the Young Ottoman leader Namık Kemal and Ali Suavi believed that the *shari'a* provided the philosophical foundation for an Ottoman constitution and for parliamentary government. But, therefore, their ideas were completely at odds. Namık Kemal believed in a modified form of universal suffrage. Ali Suavi did not, and was shocked to find that in Europe "butchers" were given the vote. Namık Kemal believed in "chambers" filled with representatives of the peoples. Ali Suavi's picture of democracy was that of the Sultan sitting under an oak tree and receiving petitions from his subjects. In short, the basis of legitimacy on which the older alliance was built was beginning to erode. The divergence of views between Kemal and Suavi was not due to differences as to the role that Islam would play in the constitutional system, but to different ways of looking at society.

Despite their superficial agreement regarding the *shari'a,* Namık Kemal and Ali Suavi differed at a deeper level. Both were for adopting Western technology to strengthen the Ottoman Empire, but Kemal used a new set

[8] Namık Kemal, "Usul-u Meşveret Hakkında Mektuplar," *Hürriyet,* 14 September 1968, p. 6.

of concepts to understand social relations. Ali Suavi saw the *shari'a* as bringing with it a set of practices, values, and settings of a familiar kind (the image of the Sultan sitting under an oak tree shows this quite clearly), which he accepted with what might be described as a certain philosophical "innocence." For Namık Kemal, a new structure of political relations had become desirable and the *shari'a* was, if you wish, "used" by him to provide the philosophical underpinning of the political scheme he was proposing.

Namık Kemal's attitude may be described as one which is characteristic in the rise of a new class, which, in relation to the Western world, has, in the widest sense, been named the "knowledge class." This class may be seen as the group deriving its legitimacy from its *preferred* access to a certain type of knowledge. Together with this knowledge there came a method which attempted to find a dynamic of society behind the façade of the social order as described by the received ideology. To the extent that Namık Kemal saw a higher natural law "behind" the *shari'a* he was adopting this stance. For Ali Suavi the true model was the golden age of the Ottoman state. In the 1890s it was the persons best educated under the Hamidian system, the military, who began to see themselves as constituting the "knowledge class." Thus, the Young Turk conspiracy against Abdülhamid II. Also, as a result of a new development in the 1890s, the entire meaning of the old tacit contract of society changed. What had to be pursued was no longer the religious ideal of the good, but the secular ideal of the preservation of society through science. Atatürk subsequently inherited this view of legitimation. At this point, a second rift occurred: the ideals of the bazaar became diametrically opposed to the ideals of the second generation of dissenters, the Young Turks. The same early alliance between a secular intelligentsia - now formed in military schools - and *ulema,* which had occurred in the 1860s emerged with even greater force in the 1890s. If we look at the Ottoman tradition of legitimate protest in the perspective of Young Ottoman and Young Turk protests, we therefore see that it marks the beginning of a transformation of a tradition which henceforth assumes increasing importance. Kemalist Turkey was founded on this type of legitimation, and entrusted power to those who "knew."

Of one thing we can be sure: the institution of a tacit social contract between ruler and ruled had such a continuous history in the Ottoman Empire that its mark was indelible and that the invisible political ink of this contract marked the attitudes - and also the political aptitudes - of both leaders and followers in the Turkey of the twentieth century.

Two nineteenth-century examples of how these latent values already functioned should be mentioned here. Cevdet Paşa recounts how he first became aware of an aspect of social relations which he identified with "public opinion." In 1870 at the burial of the Grand Vizier Âli Paşa, whom the masses knew as "Godless," no one had uttered a word when the traditional call for the release of the sins of the deceased had been requested from the audience. Cevdet Paşa was thunderstruck by the unexpected way in which the people of Istanbul "voted with their silence." While the tradition found a means of expressing itself among the lower classes, it also had an expression at the Sultanic level. Tahsin Paşa, Sultan Abdülhamid's first secretary, tells us that the Sultan had confided to him that, at one time, he had the urge to slap the Ambassador of Great Britain because of his impertinence and that he had refrained from this because he had realized that he was an official. The word he used, *memur,* usually has humbler connotations. The Sultan assured Tahsin Paşa that in dealing with a *memur,* the Sultan could not take such liberties.

Because of the inability of the Doctors of Islamic Law to adjust to new concepts of society, the history of Turkish liberty became increasingly a function of secular intellectuals. This is unfortunate, because it obscures the long historical experience of the Turkish masses with "pre-" or "para-democratic" institutions. It is only with the perspective from this experience that we can follow the later emergence of multiparty politics. It should be underlined once more that folk experience had been centered around a *collectivistic understanding of freedom* - not around a freedom concerned with the defense of individual rights, but one concerned with keeping the right sort of society functioning.

Much has been said about the origins of Mustafa Kemal's ideas concerning the gradual establishment of a democracy in Turkey. What did the man who would lead Turkey as Kemal Atatürk read? Where did he get his ideas? How did a general become so clearly involved in sophisticated political speculations?

In answer to these questions, it may be said that he read Montesquieu or Rousseau - which is true - or that he had the opportunity to read a well-informed Turkish or foreign press, or that he had the best education an Ottoman could have, which is also true. But the most valid way of looking at what the French would call his *engagement* on behalf of democracy and for a system of real participation in public affairs, would seem to be the Ottoman tradition of social contract. True, this tradition was vague and diffuse. True, it had been modified through time. But it was a living, pulsating, resonant element in the daily life of the Turks. Together with ideas about modern democratic institutions, it was a powerful, structuring element of Turkish society.

What we see in Atatürk is not so much a *theory* of politics as an ease in addressing the people, an ability to develop arguments supportive of democracy, and a faith in democratic processes which is truly unique. That Kemalism should have had both individualistic *and* collectivistic aspects is not difficult to explain. Individualism came from reading about the West and living in a world increasingly penetrated by it; collectivism was the Ottoman inheritance.

Multi-party democracy brought another one of these traditional structuring streams into play: the one that went back to the collaboration between popular forces and *ulema*. Just as in the case of Atatürk we cannot explain his sophistication regarding a system of popular participation and of civil liberties without bringing in the Ottoman background, so too, we cannot understand the crystallization of multi-party democracy in Turkey after 1946 without invoking a tradition in which the people felt legitimated in their demands for political participation and in the defence of their "civil liberties."

A sign that the provincial population in Turkey was remarkably advanced in terms of political organization appeared already during the Turkish War of Independence, when, at the start of the movement, spontaneous committee structures appeared throughout Anatolia to organize resistance against the foreign occupation - in many cases led by local *ulema*. It is from this same base that modern party organization seems to have taken its force much later. Whatever we may think about one or other change in the political constellation that appears in Turkey, it is on these divergent but at the same time confluent streams that we can start to make our analysis of the problem of freedom and its future in Turkey.

Part II
Political Structure

Chapter 4
The Status of the President of the Republic under the Turkish Constitution of 1982: Presidentialism or Parliamentarism?

Ergun Özbudun

One of the most important differences between the Constitution of 1961 and 1982 concerns the status and powers of the President of the Republic. On the one hand, the 1982 Constitution, like its predecessor, sought to ensure the political impartiality of the President: it kept him politically irresponsible and maintained the office of the Presidency as the "representative of the Turkish Republic and the unity of the Turkish nation" (Article 104). On the other hand, the Constitution transformed the Presidency from a largely symbolic and ceremonial office, as it was under the 1961 Constitution, into an active and powerful one, with important political and appointive functions. It did not go, however, to the extreme of adopting a presidential system. The system of government remained essentially parliamentary, in the sense that the executive branch maintained a dual structure with a President politically not responsible, with a Council of Ministers politically responsible, to the legislature - with the latter the distinguishing mark of a parliamentary system was retained. Thus, it can be argued that the 1982 Constitution created a "mixed" or "hybrid" system of government, perhaps along the lines of the French Constitution of 1958.

The President of the Republic is elected for a term of seven years by the Turkish Grand National Assembly from among its own members. To be eligible, the candidate must be at least 40 years of age and have received higher, that is, university-level, education. In contrast to the Constitution of 1961, a group of deputies not less than one-fifth of the full membership of the Grand National Assembly may nominate a person for President from outside the Assembly. The President is not eligible for re-election for a second term. The President-elect, if a member of a political party, must resign from his party, and his membership in the Assembly is terminated upon his election (Article 101).

The President is elected by a two-thirds majority of the full membership of the Assembly. If this majority cannot be obtained on the first two ballots, an absolute majority of the full membership will suffice on the third ballot. If the third ballot does not produce such a majority, a fourth ballot will be held between the two candidates who received the highest number of votes on the third ballot. And if the fourth ballot does not produce an absolute majority of the full membership, the Assembly will dissolve automatically and new general elections will be held immediately (Article 102). This procedure for the selection of the President is essentially similar to that in the 1961 Constitution, with the exception of the provisions on the fourth ballot and the automatic dissolution of the Assembly, which are intended to prevent a deadlock as was witnessed in 1980.

The provisions summarized above are designed to ensure the impartiality of the President of the Republic by severing his ties with his political party, terminating his membership in the Assembly, establishing the principle of no re-election, and requiring a more than simple majority for his election. The difference in the terms of office of the President (seven years) and of the Assembly (five years) also helps to accomplish the same objective. The possibility that the President may have to work with Assemblies composed of different party majorities, may increase the electoral chances of an independent figure or at least a moderate party member being acceptable to other major parties.

As a cardinal principle of the parliamentary system of government, the President is not, as a rule, authorized to act alone in executive matters. All presidential decrees must be countersigned by the Prime Minister and the ministers concerned, who will bear political responsibility for such decrees (Article 105). The President is not politically responsible for his actions connected with his office. Since it is one of the fundamental rules of public law that authority and responsibility must go hand in hand, the absence of political responsibility of the President and the constitutional requirement that all presidential decrees must be signed by the Prime Minister and the ministers concerned, mean that the executive function is, in reality, exercised by the politically responsible component of the executive branch.

The President's freedom from responsibility is also extended to criminal matters connected with his office. Here, too, the responsibility is assumed by the Prime Minister and the ministers concerned. The President can be held criminally responsible only for high treason *(vatan hainliği),* in which case he may be impeached by a vote of at least three-fourth of the full membership of the Assembly on the proposal of at least one-third of the membership. Upon impeachment, the President is tried by the Constitutional Court (Article 105, 148).

The Constitution of 1982 differs from its predecessors chiefly in the scope of the presidential powers, which it expanded substantially. The Constitution gives a long list of such powers and classified them as those pertaining to legislative, executive, and judicial functions (Article 104). Among his powers related to legislative functions are: delivering, if he deems it necessary, the inaugural address at the beginning of each legislative year; summoning the Grand National Assembly into session again when he deems it necessary; promulgating laws; returning laws to the Assembly for reconsideration; submitting proposed constitutional amendments to popular referenda; appealing to the Constitutional Court for the annulment of laws, law-amending ordinances, and the Standing Orders of the Assembly on grounds of unconstitutionality; and dissolving the Assembly and calling for new elections.

The President's powers pertaining to the executive function are as follows: appointing the Prime Minister and accepting his resignation; appointing or dismissing other ministers as proposed by the Prime Minister; presiding over the meetings of the Council of Ministers whenever he deems it necessary; accrediting Turkish diplomatic representatives to foreign states and receiving the diplomatic representatives of foreign states; ratifying and promulgating international treaties; representing the office of the Commander-in-Chief of the Turkish Armed Forces on behalf of the Grand National Assembly; mobilizing the armed forces; appointing the Chief of the General Staff; calling the meeting of the National Security Council and presiding over it; proclaiming martial law or a state of emergency in collaboration with the Council of Ministers; signing governmental decrees; pardoning the sentences of certain individuals on account of illness, disability, or old age; appointing the chairman and members of the State Supervisory Council and instructing it to carry out investigations and inspections; appointing the members of the Board of Higher Education; and appointing university rectors.

Finally, the President's powers pertaining to the judicial function are: appointing the members of the Constitutional Court, one-fourth of the members of the Council of State (the highest administrative court), the Chief Prosecutor of the Court of Cassation and his deputy, the members of the Military Court of Cassation, the members of the High Military Administrative Court, and the members of the Supreme Council of Judges and Prosecutors.

Impressive though this list is, some of these powers are more formal than substantive in the sense that the President may exercise them only upon the proposal or prior action by another body. Many require the participation of the Prime Minister and the ministers concerned who thus assume political responsibility for those actions. In some others, the President may act independently, without seeking the concurrence of the Prime Minister and the ministers concerned. The latter category of presidential acts are excluded from judicial review, including that of the Constitutional Court (Article 105).

While these changes represent a considerable increase in the powers of the Presidency, a closer examination suggests that the Turkish President is not nearly as powerful as his French counterpart. The main differences between the French and the Turkish Constitutions with regard to the status and powers of the President can be summarized as follows:

(1) A parliamentary system of government is characterized, among other things, by the dualistic structure of its executive, which is composed of two distinct elements. One is the politically irresponsible and chiefly symbolic head of state; the other is the politically active and responsible Prime Minister and the Council of Ministers. This picture contrasts sharply with the monistic executive of the presidential system where the President is the sole source of the executive power. Although both the French and Turkish Constitutions retained the dualistic executive, the Turkish Constitution did so much more markedly than the French one. In France, the President of the Republic normally presides over the Council of Ministers (Article 9) while the Turkish President does so only "when he deems it necessary" (Article 104), a prerogative which President Evren has so far very rarely exercised. The difference involves more than a legal nuance. In the French case, the President actively takes part in the decision-making by the Council of Ministers. In the Turkish case, however, the exceptionality of the procedure means that the President's participation in the Council of Ministers is more formal and symbolic than real, designed to underline the solemnity of certain exceptional occasions.

(2) Under the much discussed Article 16 of the French Constitution, when the institutions of the Republic, the independence of the nation, the integrity of its territory, or the fulfillment of its international commitments are threatened in a grave and immediate manner, and when the regular functioning of the constitutional governmental authorities is interrupted, the President of the Republic shall take the measures commanded by these circumstances, after official consultation with the Premier, the Presidents of the Assemblies and the Constitutional Council. He shall inform the nation of these measures in a message. These measures must be prompted by the desire to ensure to the constitutional governmental authorities, in the shortest possible time, the means of fulfilling their assigned functions. The Constitutional Council shall be consulted with regard to such measures. Parliament shall meet by right. The National Assembly may not be dissolved during the exercise of emergency powers. It thus appears that the French President is constitutionally empowered to

act alone in cases of emergency. He alone determines whether the conditions stipulated by the Constitution have in fact materialized and whether they pose a threat "grave and immediate" enough to justify the proclamation of a state of emergency. Furthermore, he alone determines the measures to be taken to cope with the emergency. The Constitution imposed practically no limitation upon the emergency powers of the President except stating that "the National Assembly may not be dissolved during the exercise of emergency powers by the President."

In contrast, the Turkish President plays a much more limited role in cases of emergency. Martial law or a state of emergency can be declared not by the President of the Republic acting alone, but by the Council of Ministers meeting under the chairmanship of the President. Furthermore, such proclamations have to be submitted immediately to the Grand National Assembly for approval. Thus, an area which in France is left to the exclusive jurisdiction of the President is regulated in Turkey through a division of powers among the President, the Council of Ministers, and the Assembly. Similarly, while the French Constitution leaves the nature of the emergency measures almost entirely up to the discretion of the President, the Turkish Constitution requires that such measures be regulated by law. A novelty of the 1982 Constitution is that during martial law or state of emergency it allows the Council of Ministers meeting under the chairmanship of the President to issue law-amending ordinances that are not subject to the judicial review of constitutionality by the Constitutional Court. These emergency ordinances, however, have to be submitted for approval to the Grand National Assembly on the same day as they are published in the Official Gazette. Thus, it is clear that the President is not authorized to act alone in cases of emergency but his emergency powers are shared with the Council of Ministers and the Grand National Assembly.

(3) As has been pointed out, in a classical parliamentary system all acts of the head of state (be it a monarch or a president) must be countersigned by the Prime Minister and the ministers concerned, who thus assume political responsibility for such acts. Both the French and the Turkish Constitutions maintained, as a rule, the principle of counter-signature. Both, however, departed to some extent from it by creating a certain category of presidential acts which do not require the signatures of the Prime Minister and the appropriate ministers. In other words, under both Constitutions there is a certain area where the President can act alone. The French Constitution, however, is much more specific about it. Under Article 19, the acts of the President of the Republic, other than those provided for under Articles 8 (first paragraph), 11, 12, 16, 18, 54, 56, and 61, shall be countersigned by the Premier and, should circumstances so require, by the appropriate ministers. These acts are the following: (a) to ap-

point the Prime Minister and to accept his resignation; (b) to submit to a referendum certain bills enumerated in the Constitution; (c) to dissolve the National Assembly; (d) to proclaim a state of emergency and to enact emergency measures; (e) to send messages to the two Assemblies of Parliament; (f) to refer a law or an international treaty to the Constitutional Council for review of constitutionality; (g) to appoint three of the nine members of the Constitutional Council, as well as its President.

In contrast, the Turkish Constitution did not enumerate the occasions on which the President is authorized to act alone. The Constitution simply states (Article 105) that all Presidential acts, except those which according to the Constitution and other laws can be enacted by the President himself without the counter-signatures of the Prime Minister and the minister concerned, shall be countersigned by the Prime Minister and the appropriate minister. In no instance, however, does the Constitution explicitly specify that the President may act without such counter-signature. In some cases, it is clear that the President can act only in collaboration with the Prime Minister and the ministers concerned. For example, although the appointment of the Chief of the General Staff is enumerated among the powers of the President (Article 104), Article 117 states that the Chief of the General Staff is appointed by the President "upon the nomination of the Council of Ministers." Similarly, while the President is constitutionally empowered to accredit Turkish diplomatic representatives to foreign states and to receive foreign diplomatic representatives to Turkey, there is no question that such power is purely formal and that the President needs the counter-signatures of the Prime Minister and the Council of Ministers for such appointments. The same is true for the ratification and promulgation of international treaties. In other cases, although the text of the Constitution is not clear one way or another, the constitutional custom requires that the presidential decree be countersigned by the Prime Minister and the appropriate minister. Such is the case in granting pardon to individuals on account of old age, illness, or disability. In still other instances, where the appointive powers of the President are involved, the President acts alone according to the current practice, but his discretionary powers are limited in that he has to make his appointments from among the candidates nominated by another body. This is the case for a majority of the judges of the Constitutional Court, members of the Supreme Council of Judges and Public Prosecutors, judges of the Military Court of Cassation and of the Supreme Military Administrative Court.

In most of the remaining cases, it is generally agreed that the President is empowered to act alone. Thus, he is entitled to summon the Grand National Assembly during recess, to return laws to the Assembly for reconsideration, to submit constitutional amendments to referendum, to appeal to the Constitutional Court for the annulment of laws, law-amending ordinances and the Standing Orders of the Assembly on grounds of unconstitutionality; to dissolve the Assembly in cases specified by the Constitution, to appoint the Prime Minister and to accept his resignation, to appoint the members and the chairman of the State Supervisory Council, etc. Although this is an impressive list, a closer look suggests that these powers do not really constitute a major departure from the counter-signature rule of the parliamentary government system. The principle of counter-signature involves executive matters. The instances in which the Turkish President can act alone, however, do not as a rule pertain to the executive function, but they involve matters pertaining to his relations with the legislature and the judiciary. To put it differently, they derive not from his capacity as the chief executive, but from his capacity as head of state. As such, they do not conflict with the principles of counter-signature. In executive matters, the President has still to act only in collaboration with the Prime Minister and the appropriate ministers.

The much criticized provision of the Turkish Constitution to the effect that the decrees enacted by the President acting alone are not subject to judicial review (Article 105) should be understood in this same light. Since these acts are not normally in the executive field, the absence of judicial review cannot be considered as a breach of the cardinal principle of the "rule of law." The rule of law requires that all *executive* acts should be subject to judicial review from the point of legality. In most Western democracies, on the other hand, the non-executive acts of the head of state which may involve his relations with the legislative or the judicial authorities are left outside the scope of judicial review. Such acts have been variously termed as "acts of state" (in England), "political questions" (in the United States), and *actes du gouvernement* in France.

(4) Perhaps the most important difference between the French and the Turkish Presidents concerns the method of their election. The Turkish Constitution requires that the President be elected by the Grand National Assembly.[1] As already noted, General Evren was elected President by popular vote only by way of a provisional article of the Constitution. The French Constitution, on the other hand, followed a somewhat reverse route. Under the original 1958 Constitution, the President was to be elected by a special electoral college comprising the members of Parliament, of the General Councils and of the Assemblies of the Overseas Territories, as well as the elected representatives of the municipal councils as specified by the Constitution (Article 6). All in all, the electoral college com-

[1] This provision will go into effect in 1989 when the next President will be elected; the present President Kenan Evren assumed that title by the adoption by referendum of the 1982 Constitution. At the time, Evren was Chairman of the National Security Council and Head of State.

prised over 80,000 members. The purpose of the introduction of this method was to reinforce the authority of the President. In actual fact, however, the President could not be expected to derive much prestige from an election dominated by rural notables, more than half of whom came from villages with less than 1,500 inhabitants. To put it differently, the electoral college did not faithfully represent French public opinion; it represented a minority of the country and, what is more, its least developed and most archaic minority. "The Government which was dependent on the National Assembly which in turn was elected by direct universal suffrage remained closer to democratic legitimacy."[2] It was predicted that, after General de Gaulle, the French constitutional system would evolve toward a classical parliamentary system where the Council of Ministers is the active and effective component of the executive and the powers of the head of state are, in fact, exercised only in co-operation with the government.

The constitutional amendment of 1962 radically altered the situation. The amendment abolished the electoral college system and stipulated that "the President of the Republic shall be elected for seven years by direct universal suffrage." Now, the President is the only official elected by direct universal suffrage of the entire country. In this sense, he enjoys a democratic legitimacy much more direct than that of the Prime Minister and the government. The latter do not depend directly on popular vote, but do so only indirectly through the confidence conferred upon them by the National Assembly, itself elected by the people. Thus, the constitutional reform of 1962 put the President on an equal footing, as far as democratic legitimacy is concerned, with the National Assembly, and above the government. Thereby, it introduced an element of presidentialism into the previous essentially parliamentary system, transforming it into a genuine mixed regime, half-parliamentary, half-presidential. It can now be argued that even the nominal powers of the President have become real powers.[3]

In the Turkish case, a reverse development can be predicted, assuming that constitutional institutions will be allowed to function normally, i.e., in the way they were designed by the Constitution. The present authority and influence of President Evren is due to two exceptional circumstances. One is that he is the leader of the 1980 military intervention and, in this sense, the chief architect of the 1982 Constitution. The other is that he is popularly elected by direct universal suffrage, on the basis of the provisional article of the Constitution mentioned above, by an immense major-

---

[2] Maurice Duverger, *Institutions politiques et droit constitutionnel,* vol. 2, *Le Système politique français* (Paris, P. U. F., 1976), p. 239.
[3] *Ibid.*, pp. 246–248.

ity (92 percent). The fact that his election was combined with the constitutional referendum does not detract from his claim to democratic legitimacy. Most observers would agree that the popularity of General Evren was a principal factor in the extraordinarily high "yes" votes for the Constitution, rather than the other way around. The next President of Turkey will, however, be elected not by direct popular vote, but by the Grand National Assembly. Thus, Turkey will enter into a period similar to that in France prior to the constitutional amendment of 1962. The government, which constantly has to maintain the confidence of the Assembly, will be seen as a more direct emanation of democratic legitimacy. Furthermore, a President who is elected by the Assembly is likely to be more attentive to the desires of the parliamentary majority and of the government which should be politically identical with that majority even if he is not constitutionally eligible for re-election since he will be an emanation of the will of parliament, and not of a popular mandate. In all likelihood, the President himself will be a member of the majority party, marking the beginning of a reverse process. In contrast to what happened in France after 1962, the powers of the President will tend to become nominal powers. The Prime Minister will once again become the effective head of the executive, and the system will evolve from a modified or weakened parliamentarism (some French authors call their system *parlementarisme atténué*) into a more traditional form of parliamentarism.

Chapter 5
The 1983 Parliament in Turkey: Changes and Continuites

Ersin Kalaycıoğlu

1 Introduction

The viability of a political system, such as the legislative system, implies that it develops a capacity to cope both with the influences of its environment, and with the internal conflicts and strains, without any disruptions in its performance.[1] When a legislative system possesses such a capability to successfully cope with its environment, and simultaneously, with internal stress, it can be defined as an institutionalized legislative system.

Among other things, as a legislative system institutionalizes, its rules, customs, and traditions begin to be revered, vigilantly preserved, and carefully adhered to by the incumbent deputies. The senior members may be expected to oversee their implementation and to encourage the new members to learn and internalize them. In other words, the more institutionalized a legislative system is, the more established are the binding rules of legislative conduct.[2] This is significant, because co-existence of groups of deputies with different interests and opinions becomes less of a problem when rules of legislative conduct are established and adhered to by the deputies in question.[3]

---

[1] Nelson W. Polsby, "The Institutionalization of the U.S. House of Representatives" *American Political Science Review* 62 (1986), pp. 144-168. More generally see, David Easton, *A Systems Analysis of Political Life* (New York, John Wiley, 1965).

[2] Weston H. Agor, for instance, cites various examples of how such norms and rules contribute to the integration of a legislative body: "Senate: The Integrative Role in Chile's Political Development," in *Comparative Legislative Systems: A Reader in Theory and Research*, edited by Herbert Hirsch and M. Donald Hancock (New York, Free Press, 1971), pp. 249-260.

[3] Nelson Polsby, "The Institutionalization," p. 145.

Also, an institutionalized legislative system tends to be more capable of adapting to the changes in its environment. As the need for adoption of new functions, infusion of new elite groups into the legislative system, the appendage of some new structure, and/or more emphasis on some specific function arises, an institutionalized legislative system enjoys a greater chance to make the necessary adjustments.[4]

The existence or non-existence of a set of rules, values, and norms that successfully regulate legislative behavior, and the overall impact of such rules on the legislative system are critical factors for the present analysis. Especially for those legislatures having more than one party to function without paralysis or serious handicap, it is needed to inculcate, in the minds of their legislators, what some political scientists, such as Giovanni Sartori, call a belief in the merits of cultural pluralism.[5] No community can sustain a context of peaceful exchange of ideas or meaningful debate on conflicting interests, if and when parties to a conflict view each other only in terms of "friend versus foe" or "evil versus good." Without the recognition of the legitimate existence of a "dissenting minority" by parties to a political conflict or competition, every such conflict would tend toward degeneration into some form of war.[6] The emergence of a consensus on "the rules of the game" should be expected to lead to a decrease in the frequency of unruly behavior. Unruly behavior would then become an oblivious form of political interaction as rule-abiding behavior becomes the "norm" for incumbent legislators.

In this context, I would like to suggest that long periods of tenure of legislators are critical. Especially, Nelson W. Polsby's analysis of the institutionalization process of the U.S. Congress has demonstrated that the emergence of peaceful interactions among Congressmen was preceded by an extensive period (about a century) of decreasing turnover of seats in the Congress.[7] A long period of "being together" tends to help the group to develop and shape a set of rules and norms that bind the behavior of legislators in their actions and interactions.[8]

---

[4] Gerhard Loewenberg, *Modern Parliaments: Change or Decline?* (Chicago, Aldine, Atherton, 1971), chap. 1; Alfred Grosser, "The Evolution of the European Parliaments," in *European Politics: A Reader*, edited by Mattei Dogan and Richard Rose (London, Macmillan, 1971), pp. 453 ff. Both give excellent examples of how the institutionalized legislative systems developed their capabilities to adapt to their volatile environments.

[5] Giovanni Sartori, *Parties and Party Systems: A Framework for Analysis*, vol. I (Cambridge, Cambridge University Press, 1976), pp. 14–15.

[6] Frederick W. Frey, "Patterns of Elite Politics in Turkey," in *Political Elites in the Middle East*, edited by George Lenczowski (Washington D.C, American Enterprise Institute, 1975), pp. 65–67; Sartori, *Parties and Party Systems*, pp. 196–197.

[7] Nelson W. Polsby, "The Institutionalization," pp. 148–149.

[8] See for instance, Robert Axelrod, "The Emergence of Cooperation among Egoists," *American Political Science Review* 75 (1981), pp. 306–318.

The present argument singles out lengthy periods of tenure as the most critical source of legislative institutionalization, and thus implies that any development that leads to a major perturbation vis-à-vis the lengthy tenure of legislators will have far-reaching consequences. If and to the extent that newcomers are inexperienced in legislative politics their socialization into legislative roles and their adoption of the established norms of legislative conduct are likely to be quite improbable during a single term or two. The senior members of the legislature in question having either been ousted from office or overwhelmed by the influx of new legislators can have very little or no influence at all on most of the newcomers. Consequently, the established norms of legislative conduct will start to erode and begin to be "forgotten."

It is not so difficult to envision, under such circumstances, the sprouting of legislative behavior guided solely by the re-election motive of individual legislators or only by the realization of the goal of the political parties within the legislature, but unconstrained by the binding norms of legislative conduct. The final outcome of such a process is recurring and frequent displays of unruly legislative behavior.

In the present chapter the major characteristics of the 1983 parliament in Turkey will be examined, in view of the preceding theoretical considerations. First to be taken up is legislative change in Turkey, during the multi-party era, since 1946. Second, an attempt will be made to analyse the institutionalization crisis of the Turkish Grand National Assembly, with special reference to unruly legislative behavior. Third, the configuration of political attitudes within the current parliament which is most likely to be influenced by legislative change in Turkey, will be examined. Finally, in view of the findings on the above-mentioned features of the Turkish Grand National Assembly (TGNA), the discussion will be focused on the current legislative-executive relationships in Turkey.

2 The Turnover of Seats in the Turkish Grand National Assembly

It has been 40 years since Turkey began to practice multi-party politics, in 1946. Within this period there have been frequent turnovers of seats in the TGNA. In 1950 a major realignment of the electorate catapulted the Democrat Party (DP), the major opposition party between 1946–1950, into power. In 1960 a military coup brought the DP rule to an abrupt end and new elections took place in 1961, which led to coalition governments under the leadership of the Republican People's Party (RPP), the ruling party between 1923 and 1950 and the leading opposition party between

1950 and 1960. As a result, there occurred an influx of new parties and deputies to the lower chamber of the TGNA.[9] The 1965 general elections altered the composition of the lower chamber of the TGNA once more, as the new governing party, namely the Justice Party (JP), captured the majority of the seats in the Assembly. In 1971 a new military intervention led to a two-year interim period of rule by supraparliamentary cabinets. With the general elections of 1973 another major realignment of the electorate began to occur,[10] which aided the RPP in obtaining the plurality of the seats in the lower chamber of the TGNA.

The 1977 general elections did not change the distribution of seats in the TGNA among the leading political parties in any major way. Following the last military intervention in 1980, the existing political parties were initially banned from activity and were, later on, legally terminated. The activities of the TGNA were also suspended in 1980 and were only re-instituted after the preparation and adoption of a new constitution in 1982 and with the general elections that were held in November 1983.

The old parties that had been terminated, as well as the new parties that adopted the names, symbols, or slogans of the old parties were kept out of the November 1983 elections. Hence, another major turnover of legislators occurred in the TGNA in 1983.

In sum, in 1950, 1965, and 1973 through the realignment of the electorate, and in 1961 and 1983 through the implementation of new laws regulating electoral and party politics (which were promulgated by the intervening military regimes), the TGNA witnessed major turnovers of deputies serving in its lower chamber (see Table 1).

Even though Turkey goes back to multi-party politics with the TGNA playing a central role after each interruption, frequent disruptions in the activities of the TGNA should be expected to engender far-reaching consequences on the legislative system.

---

[9] Actually the real change occurred during the next elections, in 1965. In 1961 the DP was outlawed and completely eradicated from the arena of Turkish politics. It was unclear as to what extent the Justice Party, which was then formed, adopted the DP's heritage, and consequently the RPP showed a better performance in the 1961 elections than it had during the 1950s. By 1965 it was evident that the JP clearly stood in the DP's place and captured the majority of seats in the lower chamber of the TGNA. Incidentally, the new Constitution of 1961 had appended a Senate to the lower chamber *(Meclis)*. The Senate is not included in my following analysis. The 1982 Constitution jettisoned the Senate, and now the TGNA has only one chamber, namely the *Millet Meclisi*.

[10] See Ergun Özbudun and Frank Tachau, "Social Change and Electoral Behavior in Turkey: Toward a 'Critical Realignment'?" *International Journal of Middle East Studies* 6 (1975), pp. 478ff.

Table 1 The previous parliamentary experience of the Deputies of the Turkish Grand National Assembly (lower chamber) (1920–1983)

Proportion of those Deputies with previous parliamentary experience (in proportion to the number of seats in the lower chamber of the TGNA)

Year	(%)	Year	(%)
1920	23	1954	49
1923	37	1957	47[a]
1927	63	1961	16
1931	71	1965	50
1935	66	1969	47
1939	68	1973	43
1943	67	1977	53
1946	59	1983	15[b]
1950	19	–	09[c]

Sources: Frederick W. Frey, *The Turkish Political Elite,* (Cambridge, Mass., M.I.T. Press, 1965), p.164; Frank Tachau, with Mary-Jo D. Good, "The Anatomy of Political and Social Change: Turkish Parties, Parliaments, and Elections," *Comparative Politics* 5 (1973), Table 1, p.555; Kâzım Öztürk, *TBMM Albümü: 1920–1973,* (Ankara, Önder Matbaası, 1973), passim.

[a] My calculation on the basis of information presented by Kâzım Öztürk, *TBMM Albümü*

[b] Includes all the deputies who served in all of the national level parliamentary bodies, including the 1961 Constituent Assembly and the 1981 Consultative Assembly, in the pre-1983 period

[c] Only includes those deputies who served in either chambers of the pre-1980 "multi-party" parliaments, and the "Senators for Life," who happened to be the ex-members of the 1960 military junta; those who served in the above-mentioned 1961 and 1981 assemblies are excluded from this figure

3 Unruly Legislative Behavior in the TGNA

As examples of unruly legislative behavior, in this chapter an attempt has been made to single out those actions of the deputies of the TGNA that have been in violation of such norms as are expected to guide their role behavior, especially during the floor debates, and also that behavior that undermines the due process of legislation or even communication among the members of different political parties in the TGNA.

It was possible to identify nine different types of unruly behavior conducted by the deputies of the TGNA. Listed according to increasing degree of offense, these are: protests, insults, exchange of insults, threats of assault, throwing of objects, (such as ashtrays or attaché cases), pushing and shoving, assaults, physical fights, and finally attacks with a deadly weapon, such as a revolver. The category of protests refers to such behavior as shouting, clamping on the desks by a whole group of Deputies to an extent that the voice of a Deputy or the Speaker addressing the Assembly could not be heard. Brief (i.e., 15-30 minutes long), or even lengthy (i.e., a day or two long), recesses often followed the above-mentioned forms of behavior.

Individual insults directed by a Deputy to a single opponent or a group of opponents and those insults that are exchanged between two Deputies or two groups of Deputies have been separately considered under two categories. The first type has been referred to as insults and the second as exchange of insults. The latter type of behavior was often observed to precipitate further actions, hence it constituted a more intense form of unruly legislative behavior than the former.

By threat of assault is meant that situation where a Deputy, or a group of Deputies, threatens or tries to physically attack an opponent or a group of opponent deputies, but either stops short of an actual attack or is stopped by fellow Deputies. Throwing an object to an opponent or pushing or shoving an opponent deputy are quite obvious categories that require no further explication. The category of assault refers to those cases where a Deputy attacks another, but the individual who is attacked fails to respond in kind. On the other hand, physical fights refer to those cases where the Deputy, who is physically attacked by another, responds in kind, and at least, a first fight erupts. Finally, the category of attack with a deadly weapon is quite self-explanatory.

Figure 1,[11] illustrates the overall trend of unruly legislative behavior. It simply presents the number of occurrences of any and all of the above-mentioned types of unruly behavior between 1946 and 1985, without making any reference to their severity.[12]

An examination of Fig. 1 would show that every period following an in-

[11] The data presented in Fig. 1 consist of incidents of unruly legislative behavior conducted by the deputies of the lower chamber of the TGNA. Similar data for the Senate are not included in the following analysis.

[12] The source of all computations presented in Fig. 1 is the press coverage of the incidents of unruly legislative behavior on the front pages of the major daily newspapers, namely *Cumhuriyet, Vatan,* and *Milliyet*. The entire period of 1946 through 1985, except for the regular recesses or periodic interruptions of the TGNA, was completely searched and no sampling technique was used in the compilation of the data. The daily *Cumhuriyet* was used for the entire period of 1946 through 1985. *Vatan* was used for the period between 1946 and 1950, and *Milliyet* was used for the period between 1960 and 1985. Incidents of unruly legislative acts were first located on the front pages of one of the above-mentioned daily papers and further cross-checked in either of the two other above-mentioned newspapers. On some dubious cases, the minutes of the lower chamber of the TGNA were also cross-checked.

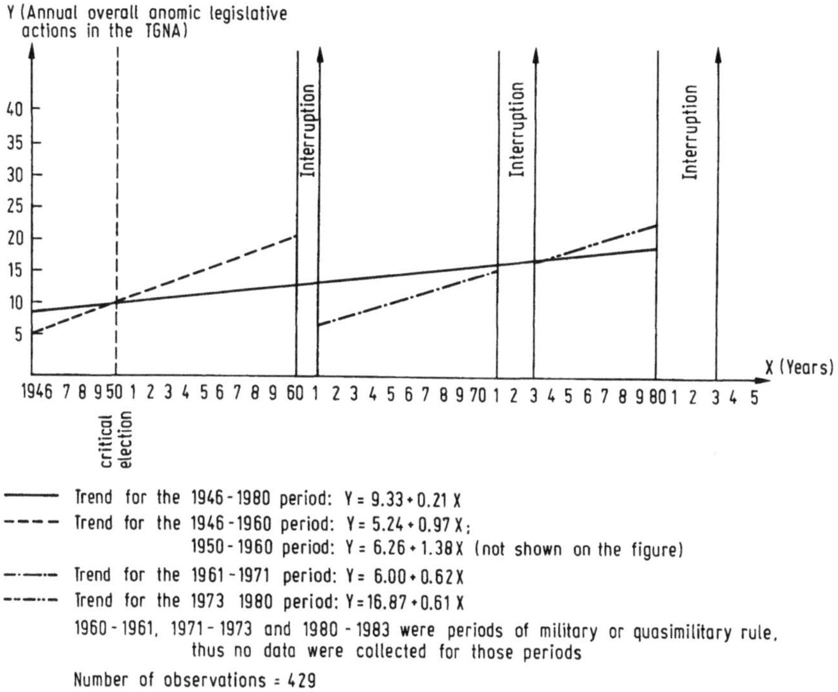

Figure 1 Trends of anomic legislative behavior in the TGNA

termission has a "cool" start. A very few cases of unruly behaviors occur in the TGNA in the first year or the first few years beginning each such period. Gradually, the frequency of the above-mentioned incidents increases over the years, resulting in a trend with a positive slope. Occasionally, tension in the TGNA leads to a period of complete paralysis or stalemate, which in turn prompts a sharp drop in the number of occurrences of unruly behavior in the TGNA, due to a sudden halt in the "due process" of legislation.

When the 1983 parliament is placed into the above-mentioned pattern, we observe that it also experienced a "cool" period between November 1983 and June 1985. In June 1985 unruly behavior began during the debates on the new "Police Law." Not a day passed without such an act being conducted by the deputies of either the governing Motherland Party or the opposition Populist Party during these debates. It seems as if the "cool" period of the 1983 parliament has come to an end. It should not be surprising to witness a greater number and varied forms of unruly behavior in the TGNA from now until the end of the term of the 1983 parliament.

4 Unruly Legislative Behavior and Political Attitudes

In a legislative system where no binding norms of legislative conduct exist, legislators are either likely to be motivated to behave under the guidance of their political attitudes shaped earlier, or to follow the directions of their political party or leader, so as to boost their chances for re-election.

4.1 Attitudes toward Political Opposition

Many students of Turkish politics tend to argue that, especially due to historical or cultural factors, Turkish political elites lack tolerance toward political opposition. Some even contend that their perception of the world in "friend-versus-foe" terms tends to introduce a slant into the Turkish political system toward transforming every conflict into some form of battle.[13] Hence, the pre-legislative experiences of the Turkish MPs should be expected to inculcate a feeling of lack of tolerance toward political opposition in them.

My recent survey did not yield any signs of widespread lack of tolerance among the deputies of the 1983 parliament in Turkey.[14] However, a

[13] Frederick W. Frey, "Patterns of Elite Politics," pp.65-67; Şerif Mardin, "Opposition and Control in Turkey," *Government and Opposition* 3 (1965), pp.375-387; George Harris, "The Causes of the 1960 Revolution in Turkey," *Middle East Journal* 24 (1970), pp.439ff.

[14] This data set consists of 125 interviews conducted with the members of the TGNA. I could reach 379 members out of the full 399. (The chamber has 400 seats, but one seat had been vacant before I started my survey research.) Eight deputies did not agree to be interviewed, and a total 371 deputies were presented with written questionnaires and were requested to fill them out. Between the last week of September and the first week of November 1984 I was able to collect 125 questionnaires filled out, of the 371 distributed. To measure tolerance or lack of tolerance toward political opposition I constructed a unidimensional, additive scale of the reactions that the deputies of my sample gave to nine statements. The statements in the questionnaire were as follows:

- The continuing allegations about the election results by a political party that has lost an election and thus has just become an opposition party hampers the performance of democracy.
- To succumb to the insistence of the political opposition on some political and economic issues and to give concessions is an expression of incompetence.
- It is not sufficient for an opposition party to become a governing party by means of getting the required number of votes, but it is also necessary for it to prove that it will defend the society and the state.
- In democracies, opposition does not enter a debate on the fundamental issues with the governing party, but usually observes the latter's policies and makes criticisms about their implementation.
- We should prefer to have a single political party to ensure unity and solidarity, rather than having a larger number of parties in order to ensure that differing views and opinions can be expressed.

comparison of these results with my earlier findings about the distribution of similar attitudes among the masses, the local notables, and the national elite pool in Turkey of the 1970s,[15] suggests that the deputies of the current TGNA express less tolerance toward political opposition than any of the above-enumerated groups.

In view of the above-mentioned findings, it can be concluded that the institutional crisis that the TGNA experiences is only partly accountable for the lack of tolerance toward political opposition. It is possible that the recruitment process sifts through those members of the national elite who are less tolerant toward political opposition to become deputies of the TGNA. As I have noted elsewhere, another likely source of expression of lack of tolerance toward political opposition is the re-election motive of the deputies.[16] Being a party-man, visibility or press coverage and the con-

- Opposition parties unfairly criticize the government.
- The policies that are propagated by the opposition are often different from the policies of the government, yet they include choices which are as healthy as those of the policies of the government.
- Opposition parties endanger democracy.

The missing data are coded as zero, hence, when I summed up the nine scale values to form my scale of tolerance toward political opposition, those who registered no information were kept in the sample but their missing responses were sifted out by being coded as zero.

The resulting scale ran between 1 and 13. The arithmetic mean, skewness, and kurtosis of the scale values are presented in the following Table in comparison with scales which tap the same attitudes and have the same range of scale scores for the masses, local notables, and the national elite groups in Turkey during the 1970s. The latter findings are derived from a study I conducted earlier with the help of data collected by İlter Turan through a survey carried out in Turkey under the auspices of the University of Iowa in 1974: see my "Elite Political Culture and Regime Stability: The Case of Turkey," a paper presented at the Conference on the Centennial of Mosca's Theory of the Ruling Class, University of Northern Illinois, DeKalb, Illinois, September 7-9, 1981, pp. 7-12).

	Masses	Local notables	National elites	MPs (1984)
Mean	8.0	10.6	10.8	7.1
Skewness	−0.6	−1.6	−2.3	−0.04
Kurtosis	−0.7	3.7	8.7	−0.4

[15] I discovered that a higher percentage of the deputies serving in the current TGNA obtained a scale score that indicated less tolerance toward political opposition than either of the three other samples I had used in my earlier study mentioned above. About one-half of the deputies who were interviewed showed some feeling of lack of tolerance toward political opposition. This does not indicate that lack of tolerance toward political opposition is very widespread among the deputies of the TGNA, but interestingly enough, the deputies of the TGNA show less tolerance toward political opposition than the national elite groups, the local notables, and the masses.

[16] Ersin Kalaycıoğlu, "Elites, Political Culture and the Political Regime in Turkey," a paper

sequent public notice that an MP receives can be easily manipulated to build an image that the MP in question is vigorously working to protect the interests of his constituents and/or to defend the country against some evil, such as "communism." Thus, both being involved in unruly legislative behavior and being intolerant toward political opposition may contribute to, rather than undermine the political career of a deputy of the TGNA.

Finally, it must be pointed out that my findings may only be true for the 1983 parliament in Turkey. The deputies of the Motherland Party may have answered the questions with reference to the two opposition parties in the parliament that lacked political clout in 1984. The deputies of the opposition parties may have registered their frustrations with the Motherland Party in the parliament, on the one hand, and with extra-parliamentary opposition, on the other. So far as the 1983 parliament is concerned it can be maintained that the majority of the deputies may be considered quite tolerant of political opposition. However, a higher proportion of the deputies, in comparison to the local notables and the national elites, show less tolerance toward political opposition.[17]

4.2 Party Loyalty

The overwhelming emphasis that the Turkish political elites pay to the group with which they are affiliated often attracts attention.[18] It is even argued that "the capacity to subordinate the self to the group can be unfortunate if carried to an extreme, as seems to occur frequently in contemporary Turkey. An extreme commitment to hierarchy and discipline can lead to rigidity and institutional excess.[19] Such a well-established attitude in the political culture of the country should be expected to find some manifestations among the members of the political parties. Consequently, we should also be able to find some traces of such an attitude of subordination to a political party exhibited by the deputies of the TGNA. In order to tap the attitudes of the deputies of the TGNA toward their political parties, I posed them four questions and constructed an additive and unidimensional scale of party loyalty.[20]

---

presented at the annual meeting of the Middle Eastern Studies Association of Northern America, San Francisco, California, November 28 to December 1, 1984, pp. 18ff.

17 See the Table in note 14, above.

18 Frederick W. Frey, "Patterns of Elite Politics," pp. 67-68.

19 *Ibid*, p. 67.

20 To measure party loyalty of the deputies in question I posed four questions, through which I requested the interviewees to "totally accept," "accept," "reject," or "totally reject" the views aired in the statements contained by the questions. The above-mentioned statements were:

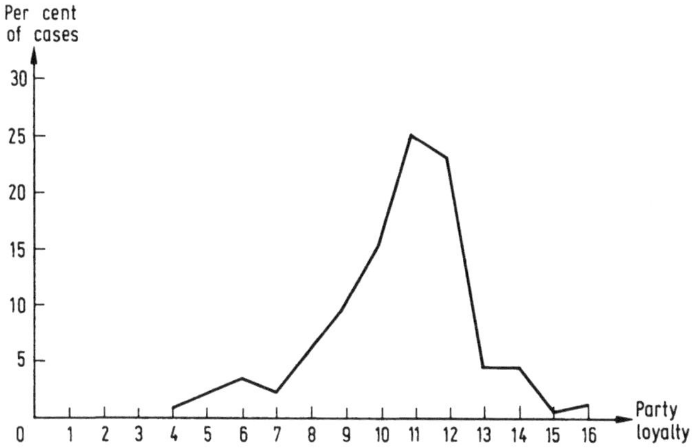

		N	%
Lowest	4	1	0.9
	5	0	0.0
	6	4	3.4
	7	3	2.4
	8	7	5.8
	9	12	9.9
	10	19	15.7
	11	31	25.4
	12	29	23.8
	13	6	5.0
	14	6	5.0
	15	1	0.9
Highest	16	2	1.8
Total		121	100.0
Missing		4	

Skewness = -1.47
Kurtosis = -5.03
Mean = 10.6
Median = 10.9
Mode = 11.0

Reliability = 0.55 (Unstandardized)
Cronbach's Alpha = 0.51 (Standardized)

Figure 2 Distribution of value of party loyalty among the deputies of the TGNA (1984)

• Political party membership is a supreme duty beyond and above every personal need or desire.
• In order for the state to be governed and for his party to come to power, a party member ought to devote his life to his party.
• It is incumbent upon a party member to be loyal to the decisions of his party, even if it contradicts his own thoughts and convictions.
• In order to prove that his party's orientations and views are the best, a party member should consider making any possible type of sacrifice one can think of.
The missing values are processed as I treated them in the construction of the scale of tolerance toward political opposition, see note 14, above. I constructed an additive, unidimensional scale of party loyalty that ran between the lowest score of 4 and the highest score of 16, exactly in the same way as I constructed the scale of tolerance toward political opposition, see note 14, above.

My findings, (see Fig. 2), help me demonstrate that loyalty to political party is not intensely felt among the deputies of the 1983 parliament. Scale scores are concentrated in the middle, and they may again be signifying a changing attitude among the deputies of the TGNA. However, the distribution of the scale values may also be reflecting the fact that the parties in question are newly founded and that they are not therefore well established; party discipline was not yet very much felt by the deputies in 1984. The deputy-party relationship might have been too fragile in 1984. My findings may indicate the "warming up" of the deputy-party link in the TGNA. Only future research will demonstrate which of the above-mentioned explanations of Fig. 2 is valid.

5 Political Career Patterns and Professionalization

High turnover rates of seats in the TGNA, through their undermining influence on the establishment of binding norms of legislative conduct and also through the emergence of unruly legislative behaviors, tend to inhibit the professionalization of deputyship of the TGNA.

By professionalization is meant the development of the role of deputyship into a pattern of actions and a constellation of expectations that are learned or adopted after a lengthy period of service in a legislature, preceded by a period of apprenticeship in a party organization or in the local political machinery, which help one to develop the above-mentioned expectations. Thus, when the role of deputyship is professionalized, being an MP encompasses a certain career that is pursued as an end in itself and enables one to earn one's living. It is then no longer the performing of tasks that a person with a non-political profession would carry out only for four to five years and never again, quite like the mandatory military service in Turkey, or such as an extension of one's non-political career or hobbies.

The 1983 parliament in Turkey has the highest rate of "newcomers" as incumbent deputies of the TGNA, ever since and including the very first parliament of 1920 (see Table 1). In this context it is appropriate to consider further the pre-legislative political attitudes and affiliations of the deputies of the current TGNA.

My findings indicate that only about 15 per cent of the deputies of the current TGNA developed any interest in politics early in life. About one-fourth of the members seem to be very "latecomers" into politics. Twenty-four per cent of the interviewees responded that their interest in politics developed no earlier than 1983. About one-third of the respondents indicated that their concern with politics developed after they reached middle age. Only 29 per cent of the respondents maintained that they started to develop an interest in politics during their youth.

Incidentally, about one-half of the deputies who were interviewed noted that they had never been a member of a socio-political association (*dernek* or *kuruluş*) or of a political party. Only about 32 per cent of the interviewees pointed out that they had lengthy periods of affiliation with a political party, that is, six years or more. Of those deputies who noted that they had some previous party affiliation, 67 per cent also reported that they had held some administrative posts in the political party organization. If that can be taken as an estimate, about one-third of the deputies in the current TGNA had some experience with party politics and administration prior to their election in 1983. Yet, about 35 per cent of the deputies interviewed reported that they had never been involved in any election campaign before that of the November 1983 elections. Finally, few deputies consider following a legislative career all their lives. About 10 per cent of the interviewees reported that they did not intend to run for re-election. Another 35 per cent argued that they had nothing to lose in politics and could go back to their previous jobs or find new ones and continue their lives without any remorse, if they lost in the next elections.

In conclusion, it can be argued that the majority of the deputies of the current TGNA were catapulted into their legislative roles without any first-hand, prior experience with party politics and without having a lengthy apprenticeship period. Only a relatively small proportion of about one-quarter or less of the deputies may be referred to as professional political actors.[21] Even though it is not reflected in the quantitative analysis, most of those included in the category of "professional political actors" had never held any administrative or political posts at the national-level branches of a political organization, such as a political party. Consequently, almost all of the above-mentioned group of professional political actors had some previous political experience only at the local level, before they were elected to the TGNA.

These findings point to the fact that the 1983 parliament in Turkey hosts an overwhelming proportion of "non-professional" political actors. Hence, most of the current deputies are in the process of learning and practising the role of being a legislator at the same time. Certain criteria such as seniority or merit for promotion or recruitment into intra-legislative positions cannot be consistently applied in the TGNA, since the former is in such dearth, and the latter has almost no basis of being judged.

---

[21] During the interviews some deputies expressed their resentment that in one of the questions the term professional politician was employed to designate them. They argued that they did not consider themselves "professional politicians." One deputy refused to be interviewed on the grounds that he was not a "politician."

Except for such ceremonial occasions as the selection of a speaker for the plenary session of a new parliament, no established criterion can be applied with consistency over long periods of time (such as more than a decade) to such processes as the recruitment of new incumbents to intra-legislative positions. For example, the speakers of the lower chamber of the TGNA are hardly selected on the basis of the application of the same and/or a set of specific criteria, nor do they get to serve for periods of time long enough to transform the position of speaker into one that is sought after or one that marks the zenith of a legislative career. The role of speaker does not require extensive prior experience with legislative politics in the TGNA. It does not always mean that the speaker of the TGNA is a deputy, who has almost reached the end of his career and is thus rewarded by the parliament for his services to the institution. Only a single speaker of the TGNA has died on the job, and a few speakers served for long periods of time prior to their election as speakers (see Table 2).

Table 2 Professionalization of the role of speaker

	Length of parliamentary experience prior to election as Speaker (years)	Length of service as Speaker	Lapse of time between the end of each Speaker's term and his death (years)[a]
Arithmetic Mean	12.9	4 years 4 months	14
Minimum	0.0	11 months	3
Maximum	28.0	11 years 5 months	20

Source: Kâzım Öztürk, *TBMM Albümü 1920–1973,* (Ankara, Önder Matbaası, 1973), pp. XXXIII–LIII; and *TBMM Albümü 1984,* Dönem XVII, (Ankara, TBMM Basımevi, 1984), pp. XXIX–XXI

[a] Only those Speakers who died are included in the calculation

In short, it is difficult to argue that the job of being a deputy in the TGNA is highly professionalized. Gaining the status of deputy in the TGNA is also relatively easy, when compared with gaining a similar status in the U.S. Congress, the French National Assembly, the British Parliament, or the Finnish Ediskunta. Under these circumstances, one is inclined to conclude that the professionalisation of the role of deputyship in the TGNA is still in the process of being established.

6 Executive-Legislative Relations

The findings of this study suggest that the current TGNA is still continuing with its institutionalization process. Furthermore, the political parties that it hosts are quite new formations in Turkish politics. The deputies of the TGNA are mostly "non-professional" political actors, who are in the parliament for the first time in their lives. Lack of institutionalization of the TGNA and of the parties within it has not much helped to make the legislature less vulnerable to the encroachments of the executive branch.

The 1982 Constitution has already given additional powers to the executive branch of the government over the legislative. Some of the earlier advantages of the executive, such as its rule by decree, were also bolstered by the new Constitution.[22] Coincidentally, the Motherland Party government has not been hesitant in making liberal use of governmental decrees in implementing the measures that re-shaped the Turkish economy. Except for a few drafts on rather subtle political issues, such as the responsibilities and duties of the police, amnesty for political and other criminals, and the higher education law, over which even the deputies of the Motherland Party were divided, the proposals of the cabinet were acted upon by the Assembly without any problems. What the opposition, notably the Populist Party, could do was to have recourse to the Constitutional Court to rescind about a dozen laws, but they met with little success. Intra-legislative interaction between the government and the opposition parties has been overwhelmingly dominated by the former. Motherland Party, which so far has faced no problems in drawing up the parliamentary time-table, the agenda, and limiting the allocation of time to oral questioning. The government has thus successfully steered every issue that the Motherland Party leaders did not wish to tackle, away from parliamentary debate. Furthermore, the government has so far been able to push every piece of legislation through the committees and the floor of the TGNA. Committees are dominated by the deputies of the Motherland Party. Even though slight modifications were made in the drafts of bills submitted to the committees, the overall content of legislation enacted by the 1983 parliament has been in keeping with what the government had initially intended or designed.

A novelty in the relationship of the legislature with the executive branch is the placement of some Motherland Party deputies as staff members in some ministries. Even though the legality of this practice is debated, it continues and it is not yet clear whether it will be continued in future. It must also be pointed out that no systematic inquiry into this practice has so far been conducted. In other words, it is not yet clear

[22] Articles 119-122.

whether this practice is designed to aid, and actually helps, the deputies to perform better constituency service, or to help the deputies to become better equipped with the information necessary to keep track of the performance of various ministries. More time and systematic research are needed to make a better assessment of this new practice.

Nevertheless, the 1983 parliament has, so far, served mostly as a stage for airing complaints about the actions of the bureaucracy and of the government. It has also started to show in 1984 and in 1985 that it can have more influence in controlling the government, by way of reshaping or stopping the government-sponsored legislation. The former occurred with the debate of the Police Bill of June 1985, and the latter occurred with the administrative reform bill that aimed at instituting regional governors with extraordinary powers over the provincial ones. Yet, these are only a few exceptions. Most bills were legislated without any noteworthy confrontation between the ruling and opposition parties, or even without much debate. Again, observers have to wait until the end of the term of the current parliament to make a full appraisal of the emerging executive-legislative relationship, which has been in a state of flux since 1983.

In conclusion, it can be said that the TGNA has still a long and arduous process of institutionalization ahead of it that is to unfold before our eyes in the years to come. The process of the establishment of binding norms of legislative conduct and compatible customs, as other historical cases would attest, is quite gradual. Patience with the internal dynamics of the legislative system is often a very frustrating experience for the citizens, as well as for the elites of the less developed countries, who yearn for rapid economic and political development. Without a lengthy period of experience (i.e., half a century or more) and with low rates of turnover of seats in the lower chamber of the TGNA, it would be quite surprising to run across evidence of an institutionalized setting in the Turkish legislative system.

Part III
Political Processes and Political Actors

Chapter 6
Political Parties and the Party System in Post-1983 Turkey

İlter Turan

1 Introduction

After its assumption of political power on 12 September 1980, the National Security Council, comprising the junta members, suspended all political activity in Turkey. Approximately a year later, it abolished all political parties which existed at the time of its intervention. From the beginning, the Council emphasized the temporary nature of its rule, and promised the restoration of competitive politics after public peace and governmental effectiveness had been restored.

During its tenure of office, the National Security Council, in co-operation with the Consultative Assembly which it had proceeded to establish, engaged in a restructuring of the Turkish political system and its institutions. The aim was to create a new framework which, the decision-makers hoped, would prevent the emergence of those features of Turkish politics which had led to the breakdown of governance through a competitive political process during the pre-1980 period.

The present chapter will examine the restructuring of the party system in Turkey during and after the 1980–1983 military intervention.

2 The Pre-1980 Period

It would be appropriate to begin by examining the characteristics of Turkish political parties and the party system before the military intervention of 1980. Such an analysis appears to be necessary since, in their efforts to restructure Turkish party life, the military leaders were responding to what they perceived to be the problematical aspects of party politics.

3 Characteristics of Turkish Political Parties

During the period in question, Turkish political parties were national institutions organized along the same lines as the administrative division of the country into provinces and sub-provinces. They were intended to operate as hierarchically linked and internally democratic organizations in which a sub-provincial convention of elected delegates would elect those who would represent them at provincial meetings. The provincial conventions, in turn, would choose representatives to attend the national meetings in which the national leadership of the party would be elected and the national policy of the party determined. This organizational model based on grassroots democracy, however, failed to produce political parties with strong traditions of internal democracy - because other conditions needed for its successful operation were lacking.

Local party organizations were generally loose structures, membership records were not well kept, dues were not regularly collected. Rather, they were dominated by a group of activists who tried to perpetuate their domination by utilizing two instruments which were available to them. First, they served as gatekeepers for access to national leaders or officers of the party, members of parliament, and if the party was in power, to ministers or even the prime minister. Second, they were in a position to determine who would attend the sub-provincial and the provincial conventions, and who would serve as delegates in the provincial primaries in which the candidates to be placed on the ticket for the national elections were chosen.[1]

The powers of the local party leaders vis-à-vis the rank and file tended, on many occasions, to destabilize local party politics. Because it was often difficult to affect or change the behavior of local party leaders through

[1] For a more detailed description of the organizational characteristics of Turkish political parties, and the implications of these characteristics on the Turkish political processes, see Sabri Sayarı, "Aspects of Party Organisation in Turkey," *Middle East Journal* 30 (1976), pp. 187-199. See also, Dankwart A. Rustow, "The Development of Parties in Turkey," in *Political Parties and Political Development*, edited by Joseph LaPalombara and Myron Weiner (Princeton, Princeton University Press, 1966), pp. 107-133; Arif T. Payaslıoğlu, "Political Parties and Political Leadership: Turkey," in *Political Modernization in Japan and Turkey*, edited by Robert E. Ward and Dankwart Rustow (Princeton, Princeton University Press, 1964), pp. 411-433.

democratic procedures, intra-party opposition took the form of factional rebellions, threats to leave the party, or actual departures.

Intra-party politics at the national level resembled in many ways local party politics. Once a leader established himself in power, he tended to stay in that position regardless of his political performance. Not assured of success by using the ordinary intra-party procedures, elements not satisfied with party leadership formed factions within the parliamentary party to challenge the leadership; upon failure, they left their party.

The instability of political parties at the local, national, and parliamentary level owing to the ineffective operation of intra-party democracy, was compounded by two other factors. First, political parties functioned primarily as clientelistic networks through which benefits deriving from being in government would be distributed. Opposition parties, in this context, were only rival clientelistic networks eager to come into power. To the extent that public resources were limited and the demands made on them by various networks were sometimes conflicting, it was not possible for government parties to meet all of them. Those among party members and groups who felt that they were not accorded adequate attention or benefits, would not hesitate to rebel or leave their party. Similar pressures operated on opposition parties because some of their deputies might be lured by the government parties with promises of sufficient rewards.

Second, during the 1961-1980 period Turkey experienced a significant process of social transformation characterized by rapid urbanization, industrialization, and the expansion of the market economy. Cleavages of both a functional and a non-functional nature multiplied. Increasing societal differentiation complicated the job of political parties in aggregating interests. New parties with divergent ideologies came into being to capture the preferences of disaffected constituencies.

In their rhetoric, the new parties appeared to be more like parties of ideology than like parties of brokerage. But any cohesion which ideology might have provided had to be supplemented by concrete benefits which could best be secured by being in government. Thus, the very pressures which had led to the breakdown of old intra-party coalitions and to the emergence of new parties, operated on new parties, too, rendering it difficult for them to retain their cohesion. Expressed differently, the organizational characteristics of the new parties resembled in many ways those of the old parties; and hence, they were plagued by problems similar to those experienced by the long-established parties.

The groups which established new parties and those who supported them expected, among other things, to become integrated into clientelistic networks through which they could enjoy public patronage. True, as said earlier, the old established parties possessed clientelistic networks, but they were not comprised exclusively of them. In addition to catering to specific constituencies, they appealed to broad categories of people who were sympathetic to their ideologies, ideas, policies, and/or leaders. Furthermore, the clientelistic networks which the major parties such as the Republican People's Party and the Justice Party possessed were highly sophisticated and broadly based, bringing together leaders of occupational groups, labor, business, and other organized interests.

The new parties did not possess as extensive a body of sympathizers as the old parties. Hence, their reliance on the distribution of patronage was greater than the major, established parties in achieving internal cohesion and ensuring further growth. The new parties pursued a strategy of developing new networks under their control. And when in power (as coalition partners), they utilized public resources to promote further their proliferation. On the other hand, to control the centrifugal tendencies generated by the presence of rival groups of clientele, they buttressed the carrot of patronage with the stick of highly disciplinarian leadership and emphasis on ideology.[2]

4 Characteristics of the Party System

The characteristics of Turkish political parties had implications for the operation of the party system. Particularly as the two-party system of the 1960s gave way to a multi-party system during the 1970s, the insecurity of party activists and their leaders, owing to the instability of parties as organizations, intensified. In order to hold their ranks and constituents together, each party tried to maximize the ideological distance between itself and the others, particularly those which it saw as its major rivals. It was hoped that such a strategy would make it psychologically costly to members and supporters to change their preferences. As the supporters of one party began to view those of the others as the enemy, the cohesion of each party would be maximized.

In practical terms, this strategy led the two major parties of the center, the Republican People's Party and the Justice Party, to shift their orientation further to the left and to the right, respectively, in order to make sure

---

[2] For a more elaborate discussion of small parties and their characteristics, cf. Ilter Turan, "Turkey: the Reshaping of Domestic and External Politics," *Middle East Annual* 2 (1983), pp. 152-156. Also see, Ergun Özbudun, "Political Parties and Elections," in *Südosteuropa Handbuch, vol. 4, Türkei*, edited by Klaus-Detlev Grothusen (Göttingen, Vandenhoeck and Ruprecht, 1985), pp. 269-272. About patron-client relationships in Turkey with reference to political parties, cf. Sabri Sayarı, "Some Notes on the Beginning of Mass Political Participation in Turkey," in *Political Participation in Turkey: Historical Background and Present Problems*, edited by Engin D. Akarlı with Gabriel Ben-Dor (Istanbul, Boğaziçi University Publications, 1975), pp. 121-133.

that they would not lose electoral support from their followers which their small rivals were targeting. The result was the gradual erosion of the center, and the polarization of the party system.

The relations between political parties grew to be increasingly hostile. However, the dispersal of the vote among several parties preventing a parliamentary majority by a single party necessitated coalition governments. It proved a different matter, however, to form coalition governments; in some cases it took an inordinately long time. Once a government was formed, it was plagued by internal differences and constant centrifugal pressures. Coalition partners tried simultaneously both to retain their separate identity by maximizing the ideological distance between themselves and their partners in the eyes of their constituents and to stay in a coalition so as to allocate as much public resources as possible to their clients, since catering to their needs and interests constituted a necessary means of keeping their party loyalty. Coalition governments in which the partners were mainly interested in diverting public allocations to their own constituents so that they could grow at the expense of their partners, hardly proved a suitable environment for political action. Governments became paralyzed and immobilized. They could not initiate major new policies to cope with the economic and political problems the country was facing.

In order to maximize their support, each party attempted to enlarge its own clientelistic networks. To this end, some parties worked to create new associations under their domination. To cite an example, two new national federations of labor were created, one by the National Salvation Party and the other by the Nationalist Action Party. Each of these unions had official backing from these parties when they shared power in coalition governments so that these two parties might both possess their own instruments for establishing linkages with labor.

Many occupational, professional and other voluntary associations which, in the past, had only been marginally interested in political activity, also become arenas in which militants of rival parties competed for domination of the organization. Thus, political polarization was complemented by the growing politicization of every aspect of public life.

The intense competition between political parties exacerbated a tendency which had become increasingly manifest after the transition to civilian politics following the military intervention of 1960. The mood of political liberalization which the military leadership of that time had helped create gave way to the emergence of political movements which had not been allowed in the political spectrum before. In the 1960s, the most prominent among these had been the Socialist Labor Party of Turkey, and later the religious-conservative National Order Party. Both had been closed down during the indirect military intervention of 1971. After 1973, new parties and other political organizations representing a variety of ideological orientations of the far left and the far right proliferated. While popular amongst some workers, students and intellectuals, and adept in organizing strikes, marches, and demonstrations, the organizations of the far left were overridden with factions and quarrels among them, and they did not demonstrate notable electoral success. The National Salvation Party marked by its pro-religion views and the Nationalist Action Party, pursuing an intensely nationalistic line with racist overtones, were successful at the polls, enabling them to participate in coalition governments.

These parties and movements harbored orientations and pursued behaviors which ran contrary to the central values on which the Turkish Republic was established. These values included secularism, a non-racial conceptualization of nation and nationality, the non-recognition of religious affiliation and ethnicity as a proper basis for representation, together with the rejection of the idea of class struggle. Facing challenges from right and left, the Justice Party and the Republican People's Party, moved to co-opt the sympathizers of these parties and movements. Slowly, the center disappeared. In this process, however, ethnicity and religion had been rendered political, and an explosive situation obtained as demonstrated by communal riots and fighting as well as increasing terrorism which characterized the period preceding the 1980 intervention.

5 Restructuring of the Party System

The military leadership which assumed political power in September 1980 identified the political parties, their leaders, and the party system as major contributors to the domestic strife, incessant terrorism, eroding public authority, and growing chaos which prevailed in Turkey prior to their intervention. Therefore, setting up a new basis for the establishment and functioning of political parties and the party system became one of their major concerns.

5.1 Legal Restructuring

The major policy tools available to the military leadership in the structuring of political parties and the party system were legal in nature. In devising the new Constitution and electoral laws, party problems received much attention. As had also been the case after the 1960–1961 intervention, a new law specifically dealing with political parties was enacted. A prominent characteristic of these laws is that they are highly detailed, containing similar provisions, often repetitive in nature, reflecting the excessive concern of the leadership that the pre-1980 politics not be restored.

Before taking up the new arrangements, it may be useful to summarize those aspects which have remained the same. Articles 68 and 69 of the new Constitution, continuing the tradition of that of 1961, define the rules by which political parties may be established, operated, scrutinized by public authority, and closed down. Political parties are described as indispensable institutions of a democratic political life. They may be established without prior consent of the government. However, if they violate the Constitution or the laws, they may be closed down by the Constitutional Court through due process.

The principles which will guide the functioning of parties are indicated both in the Constitution and the Political Parties Law (PPL). A set of provisions direct political parties to subscribe to and abide by the central values of the Republic. Article 14 of the Constitution sets the limits on the exercise of fundamental freedoms. They may not be used to challenge the national unity and the territorial integrity of the Republic, to abrogate the fundamental freedoms themselves, to establish the rule of a person or a group, to have one social class establish domination over others, to promote divisions based on language, race, religion or sect, or to advocate a regime based on such divisions. These general provisions are summarized once again in Article 68 pertaining to political parties:

> The by-laws and programs of political parties may not be in conflict with the principles of national unity and the territorial integrity of the state, human rights, national sovereignty, and the democratic and the secular character of the Republic.

Furthermore, "No parties advocating domination of society by a group and the establishment of a dictatorship may be founded."

Articles 5 and 78-90 of the Political Parties Law elaborate further the limits on the political goals which may be pursued by parties. These provisions, taken together, define the scope of ideologies that may be espoused by political parties. Communist parties and parties oriented toward ethnic separatism, religious distinctions and racial differences are not allowed to exist in the party system. Although the current restrictions are more comprehensive and detailed than earlier laws, they have been present in the pre-1980 Constitution and laws, and do not constitute a major deviation from earlier practice.

The new elements in the legal framework pertaining to political parties and the party system appear to be directed toward the achievement of three goals: preventing excessive politicization of citizens and groups, keeping political parties internally more democratic, and rendering both political parties and the party system more stable.

The new laws aspire to prevent the excessive politicization of citizens and groups through the penetration of political parties into the associational life of the country. This is done in several ways. The Constitution bans political parties from establishing auxiliary branches for youth, women, and other groups (Article 68). Similarly, the founding of extra-party organizations such as clubs, associations, labor unions, co-operatives, foundations, occupational and professional associations by political parties, as well as developing political ties and various modes of political co-operation with such existing organizations are banned. Parties are also barred from receiving aid or financial support from such organizations and associations (Article 69). Other articles of the Constitution prohibit voluntary associations (Articles 33 and 34) and labor unions (Articles 52 and 54) from pursuing political goals, engaging in "political activities," developing links with political parties, co-operating or co-ordinating their activities with them, receiving aid from or giving aid to them. In the Political Parties Law, these restrictions are repeated and rendered more explicit (Articles 66, 91, and 92). More broadly, voluntary associations are meant to be non-political and limit their activities to those directly connected with the purposes for which they have been established.

Although the intentions of these provisions are understandable, they may be highly problematical in the operation of a democratic political process. In other democracies, political parties have hardly constituted a sufficient mechanism for the articulation and the aggregation of interests. There is, in each society, a highly sophisticated and complex network of voluntary associations which are regularly or intermittently linked with political parties to serve the interests of specific constituencies. This was also the case in the faltering democracy of the pre-1980 period in Turkey. The laws at that time, while banning voluntary associations from making financial contributions to political parties, were not so specific as to how voluntary associations might or might not establish informal linkages with political parties and vice versa. The new laws charge political parties with the articulation of all interests, which assumes a level of organizational capability which the current Turkish political parties do not possess, and it is a moot point whether any political party within a democratic system could possess such capabilities. Under the current restrictions many interests may simply fail to be represented, resulting in frustrations in many segments of society.

The laws, as noted earlier, do not permit political parties to receive financial contributions from voluntary associations, and the latter are barred from making such contributions. Initially, the Political Parties Law made parties reliant exclusively on individual contributions on which there was a limit of TL 1 million (currently 5 million) per person per annum (Article 66). A change was effected in 1984, restoring the pre-1980 practice of annual government grants to political parties which meet certain qualifications. Although this change has served to reduce the financial plight of the larger parties, the current system, following the precedent of the pre-1980 practice, still opens the way to citizens with better means to acquire an undue influence in the political process. Small contributions from large numbers of citizens without the assistance of other voluntary associations have not proven in the past to be an effective way of securing financial support for political parties.

It is not difficult to see that the ban on associations to engage in political activity and to keep their distance from political parties will necessitate judgements on what is "political" and what constitutes a "political linkage" between political parties and voluntary associations. The laws do not provide specific guidelines on this point. One might be justified in expressing the fear that government parties would tend to be more benevolent in their judgements of those groups whose activities they happen to approve of or benefit from, but to act more stringently in their interpretations of "political" and "political linkages" of those groups whose activities they may find problematical or undesirable. Such a contingency would serve to undermine the democratic political process by opening the way to the polarization of Turkish politics again, intensifying the desire of the opposition to come into power no matter what, and the desire of majority parties to retain their power at any cost.

As for the measures intended to render political parties and the party system more stable, the Law on the Election of Deputies (LED) contains two provisions to limit the number of parties which qualify for parliamentary representation. Article 33 allows representation only to those parties which have obtained 10 per cent of the valid votes cast in national or by-elections. Article 34 introduces a further cut-off provision at the electoral district level by stipulating that a candidate may not get elected unless the candidate or the candidate's party has received a number of votes which exceed the number obtained by dividing the total number of valid votes cast by the number of deputies to be elected from that district. An amendment passed in 1987 stipulates that in those constituencies where six deputies are returned to parliament the total number of valid votes cast should be divided by five and not by six.

Discrimination in favor of larger and nationally organized parties is also evident in the requirement that a political party needs to have been organized and to have held its provincial convention in at least half (later two thirds) of Turkey's provinces six months prior to the elections in which it intends to participate (PPL, Article 36; LED, Article 45).

One may wonder whether these provisions are not too stringent so as to constitute a source of instability in the future by denying sizeable groups access to parliamentary representation, and thus pave the way to their emphasizing extra-parliamentary forms of political activity.

At the level of parliamentary parties, the Constitution has attempted to deal with another source of instability: party changing by deputies in the

National Assembly. Article 84 of the Constitution makes it possible for a parliamentary majority to terminate the membership of a deputy who has changed his or her party or who has accepted ministerial appointment in a cabinet not supported by his or her party. Such a deputy is also denied the privilege of being designated a candidate by the central organs of a party in the national elections following the change of party. This measure is a clear response to party changing by deputies which made and unmade governments during the electoral period immediately preceding the military intervention of 1980. A more careful and longer-term analysis of party changing, however, reveals that party changing has contributed to the achievement of political stability by facilitating party realignments in the legislature during the previous transitions from military to competitive politics.[3] During 1983–1987, this article appeared to breathe artificial life into parliamentary parties which had lost their electoral bases, and to stand in the way of a realignment of deputies by moving to parties which appeared to have a stronger popular backing. Eventually, the provision became inoperational. No one was willing to enforce it and deputies and parties found ways of getting around it.

Finally, the new legal framework attempts to render intra-party democracy more operational. First, Article 69 of the Constitution notes that intra-party activities and decisions cannot run counter to the principles of democracy. This provision is repeated in more detail in the Political Parties Law (Article 93). In addition, several techniques have been used in the laws to enhance the functioning of political parties in an internally democratic fashion. To begin with, the selection process of party leadership at all levels, through elections which take place during the biennial conventions has been placed under the scrutiny of the judiciary (PPL Articles 20 and 21). The presence of the judiciary in party conventions is intended to render the intra-party electoral process more regular and open so as to deny an advantageous position to the incumbent leadership in the running of elections.

Second, limits are imposed on the length of service of leaders. The national president of a political party can serve for no longer than six consecutive terms of two years modified later to five terms of three years (PPL Article 15). Provincial and sub-provincial leaders, on the other hand, can also serve for five consecutive terms (PPL Articles 19–20). In this way, a circulation of leaders is assured.

Third, membership lists are placed under the supervision of the sub-provincial election committees which are comprised of judges, other high-ranking civil servants and representatives of political parties. These com-

---

[3] İlter Turan, "Changing Horses in Midstream: Party Changers in the Turkish National Assembly," *Legislative Studies Quarterly* 10 (1985), pp. 21–34.

mittees are responsible for reviewing the lists every six months (PPL Article 42) which, it is hoped, will encourage proper record keeping and prevent irregularities.

Finally, the new law has opened primary elections to be conducted under the supervision of sub-provincial election committees to all registered members of political parties (PPL Article 42). In the past only delegates elected at sub-provincial party conventions (in practice, often designated by the incumbent sub-provincial party leadership) had been allowed to participate in the primary elections. The broadening of the base of participation in the nomination process will reduce the influence local party leaders previously enjoyed, and make the intra-party electoral process more democratic.

The legal framework described in the foregoing pages was completed with the ratification of the Constitution by a popular referendum in 1982, the enactment of the Political Parties Law and the Law on the General Rules of Elections and Electoral Registers in April 1983, and the Law on the Election of Deputies in June 1983. It was within this framework that new parties were established and a transition to competitive politics was made.

6 New Parties and the Party System

The National Security Council assumed an active role in the shaping of the emergent party system. In doing this, the military leadership appears to have been guided by a consideration to prevent the pre-1980 parties from emerging under new names and engaging in the kind of activities they had engaged in during the last years of their existence. They were also particularly concerned with preventing the new parties from engaging in a confrontation with the military.

A provisional article of the new Constitution (Provisional Article 4) banned the leaders of the government and the major opposition party in the legislature at the time of its dissolution from being involved in party politics for a period of 10 years beginning with the day of the ratification of the Constitution. Similarly, deputies and senators belonging to such parties were disallowed any political party activity for five years. The same restrictions appeared in the Provisional Article 1 of the Political Parties Law. The ban in question was lifted in 1987.

The Political Parties Law contained other provisions to serve the same purpose. Article 95 stipulated that the founders, the national president, the members at all levels of the executive and disciplinary committees as well as the members of the parliamentary groups of all parties which had been abolished by the military government could not serve as founders, executives or other officers of a new party. No new party could be established if the majority of its members belonged to a party which had been banned. This restriction, too, was discontinued in 1987.

Article 96 specified that new parties could not use the names and symbols of parties which had been abolished on October 16, 1981. Furthermore, new parties were prohibited from claiming that they constituted the continuation of the pre-1981 political parties. Finally, Article 97 barred political parties from criticizing or opposing the decisions and policies which had been pursued by the National Security Council.

To give themselves some control over the kind of parties which would emerge during the transition to competitive politics, the National Security Council was empowered by a provisional article in the Political Parties Law (Provisional Article 4) to review, and if it deemed appropriate, disqualify founders of political parties until the results of the first national elections were made public. Although this review would not stand in the way of the founding of political parties as such, since parties would fail to meet some of the requirements of electoral laws until the founding members reached a certain number, the military leadership was in a position to deny a number of parties the opportunity to compete in the first national elections, and to support a set of parties which they favored.

Concomitant with or shortly after the ban on political activity was repealed on May 16, 1983, several new parties made their appearance on the Turkish political scene. Two of these, the Nationalist Democracy Party and the Populist Party, were formed with the encouragement of the military leadership. They were expected to represent the center-right and the center-left, respectively. They were meant to constitute the key elements of the new party system. A third party, the Motherland Party, was established under the leadership of Turgut Özal, who had been in charge of formulating and implementing the economic stabilization program and austerity measures demanded by the IMF first as undersecretary in the Justice Party government during the period immediately preceding the military intervention and then as deputy prime minister for nearly two years under the military regime. A fourth party, the Great Turkey Party, was led by a retired general, Ali Fethi Esener. Later, two other parties, the Social Democracy Party led by Erdal İnönü, the son of the famous statesman, and the Welfare Party, comprised of not well-known personalities but thought to be oriented toward the defunct National Salvation Party, also entered the political arena. Several other small parties were also established.

The military leadership was ambivalent toward the parties other than the ones they chose to support to begin with. The Great Turkey Party in particular, was identified by the public as the continuation of the Justice

Party. Its leaders did not discourage such associations, but rather cultivated them. Before the party had an opportunity to develop into a full-fledged organization, the National Security Council decided to show its determination not to allow a return to pre-1980 politics, and issued an order closing down the Great Turkey Party on May 31, 1983.

The closing of the Great Turkey Party brought to the limelight a new party, the True Path Party. The founders included a number of personalities who had served as Justice Party deputies and ministers in earlier periods. Not as aggressive in its attempts to establish connections with the past in the short run, this party survived, but without being able to participate in the 1983 elections because an insufficient number of founding members had met the approval of the National Security Council prior to the deadline for taking part in the national elections.

The Social Democracy Party, intending to fill the void which it believed existed in the center left rather than trying to constitute a continuation of the defunct Republican People's Party, also survived, but was not able to participate in the 1983 elections.

The Motherland Party was allowed to take part in the elections, if not enthusiastically. Özal proved to be a capable politician, and led his party to victory in November 1983.

As new parties were being established and a new party system was beginning to take shape, the National Security Council continued its efforts to introduce a new ecology for political life in Turkey. In addition to deciding which political parties might be able to compete in the oncoming elections, the Council empowered itself on June 12, 1983 to veto the candidates the parties put up. Before the elections of November 6, 1983 took place, 392 candidates from the Motherland Party, 398 candidates from the Nationalist Democracy Party, and 389 candidates from the Populist Party had been vetoed.

All through the autumn, parties which had qualified to participate in the elections campaigned vigorously. President Evren took many opportunities to interject the viewpoints of the National Security Council into the debate, suggesting that the military leadership desired to create a new party system, comprised of new parties and personalities. Right before the elections, he expressed an open preference that the Nationalist Democracy Party be favored by the electorate despite indications from opinion polls that this party in fact enjoyed the least favor with the electorate.

7 Post-Election Party Politics

7.1 Aftermath of November 6, 1983

The national elections which were held on November 6, 1983, confirmed the predictions of the opinion polls which ironically, had been banned by the government as a means to influence the outcome. The Motherland Party captured 45.1 per cent of the vote and 211 seats; the Populist Party 30.5 per cent of the vote and 117 seats; the Nationalist Democracy Party 23.3 per cent of the vote and 71 seats. Thus, the desire of the military leadership that there be a majority government was realized, although the particular party which had achieved the parliamentary majority may not have been their first choice.

The results of the elections have not been carefully analysed so far. A brief study conducted by a Turkish weekly, using the ratio of wage earners to the general working population as an indicator of the level of economic development of the provinces, shows that the Motherland Party fared best in the economically more developed and the sociologically more differentiated provinces. The Populist Party also had its best showing in similar provinces. The Nationalist Democracy Party, on the other hand, exceeded its national average in provinces where the percentage of the population engaged in agriculture was highest for the nation.[4] Keeping in mind that the Motherland Party and the Populist Party had emphasized social and economic concerns in their campaigns, whereas the Nationalist Democracy Party had dwelt upon questions of law and order and governmental authority, it may be cautiously inferred from the election results that economic questions were found to be more relevant in the economically more developed regions of the country, while themes of law and order proved appealing in those regions which had been economically and sociologically least transformed.

Having achieved a comfortable parliamentary majority, the Motherland Party formed the government. The first state of the transition to competitive politics had thus been completed.

7.2 Local Elections of March 25, 1984

The military intervention had brought to a halt not only national but also local electoral politics. New elections for mayors, city councils, and provincial councils were held on March 25, 1984.

Although local elections are not always taken as indicators of how parties might fare in national elections, in the Turkish experience, their out-

---

[4] *Yankı* 659 (1983), p. 18.

come, especially at the aggregate level, has not deviated substantially from those at the national level. But the particular elections in question assumed added importance because those parties which had not been allowed to participate in the first national elections had completed the formalities to qualify for taking part in the local elections. The electorate would now have a chance to choose among six parties, three of which (the True Path Party, the Social Democracy Party, and the Welfare Party) had been denied access to the national elections. The local elections would show how the officially sanctioned parties would fare in a more competitive environment.

The results showed that the Motherland Party had been accepted as a credible political organization by the electorate, having received 41.5 per cent of the vote in the provincial council elections. The Social Democracy Party received 23.4 per cent, the True Path Party 13.2 per cent, the Populist Party 8.8 per cent, the Nationalist Democracy Party 7.1 per cent, and the Welfare Party 4.4 per cent of the vote.

The outcome of the elections produced an enigma for the two parliamentary opposition parties since they appeared to have lost the electoral bases which they had briefly enjoyed in the less competitive environment of the 1983 national elections. New national elections seemed untimely since the country had only recently gone through two election experiences. Nor could they be justified by the argument that the government party no longer enjoyed majority support. Thus, a peculiarity of the politics of transition had become manifest: an electorally credible government party, and two parliamentary opposition parties without significant electoral bases in society.

8 The Transformation of the Post-1983 Party System

The outcome of the local elections led to internal debates among the losers with regard to how they should plan their future, a development which worked to undermine the cohesion of parliamentary parties. Both in the Populist Party and the Nationalist Democracy Party, factions emerged challenging the ability of the leaders to lead the parties. There followed a debate on the possibility of uniting with extra-parliamentary parties through a temporary Constitutional amendment so as to allow for once the changing of party affiliations by suspending the limitations of Article 84 which were intended to discourage such moves. Not convinced of their party's leader to provide effective leadership, a number of deputies left the Nationalist Democracy Party to become independents.

In July 1984, both the Populist Party and the Nationalist Democracy Party held their national conventions. In both instances, the party leaders were replaced by their secretaries-general, Aydın Güven Gürkan and Ülkü Söylemezoğlu, respectively. This change opened the way to attempts to forge closer links with extra-parliamentary parties. The initial leaders, Necdet Calp of the Populist Party and General Turgut Sunalp of the Nationalist Democracy Party, had been identified too closely with the policies of the military leadership in the latter's efforts to create a new set of parties and a new party system. This had made it personally difficult for them to admit defeat and, in effect, to end the political life of the parties which they had been instrumental in creating.

On the center left, Gürkan launched a move to unify the Social Democrats. Initially, he consulted Rahşan Ecevit, the wife of the former prime minister and the leader of the defunct Republican People's Party, who had announced her plans to establish a new party. Mrs. Ecevit was not sympathetic to the idea of integrating her yet unborn political party with that of the Populists. Gürkan then turned to İnönü of the Social Democracy Party who proved much more amenable to the idea of a merger.

The two leaders initiated a long and cumbersome process of negotiations to effect a merger. Although neither party had a long past, apparently sufficient time had lapsed to generate organizational and personal interests to render the negotiations a delicate balancing act.

In order to insure that the merger would not be construed as party changing, it was agreed that the Populist Party would hold an extraordinary convention to change its name to Social Democratic Populist Party. Next, the Social Democracy Party would hold a convention and vote to unite with the new Social Democratic Populist Party. Finally, the new party would hold an extraordinary convention and elect its national officers complying with an agreement on how positions would be distributed between the leadership cadres of the two former parties. İnönü agreed to Gürkan's serving as the president of the new party. In turn Gürkan agreed to hold the next convention in six months time – well before the next regular convention. The Social Democratic Populist Party came into being as the result of a merger which was realized in November 1985. At its next convention, Mr. İnönü assumed the party's leadership, an office which he continues to hold today.

The founding of the Social Democratic Populist Party set a pattern which was soon to be emulated by others, though not precisely in the same manner. For example, in December 1985, the Democratic Left Party of Mrs. Ecevit was established, after numerous announcements that the party was about to be formed. A group of deputies of the Populist Party, who decided to remain independent when their party merged with the Social Democracy Party, joined the new party. After the ban of former political leaders was repealed through a constitutional amendment approved by a public referendum in September 1987, Mr. Ecevit, the leader of the pre-1980 Republican People's Party, assumed the leadership of the Democratic Left Party.

On the center right, the True Path Party also worked to find a formula whereby it could acquire parliamentary representation. The opportunity presented itself when the Nationalist Democracy Party leadership decided to dissolve their party. The intention was to make it possible for deputies to become independents so that they could move to the Motherland Party without "technically" changing parties. Some independents did indeed join the Motherland Party, but many also moved to the True Path Party. The president of the True Path Party, Mr. Hüsamettin Cindoruk, explicitly identified himself as a caretaker until Mr. Süleyman Demirel of the pre-1980 Justice Party could return to political life as the party's leader. This became possible after the repeal of the constitutional ban on the political rights of the pre-1980 party leaders.

Two other parties of the pre-1980 period were also resurrected under different names. Neither of them, however, was represented in the 1983-1987 legislature. The first, which has already been mentioned, was the Welfare Party, a conservative religious party whose chairmanship was eventually assumed by Mr. Necmettin Erbakan, the leader of the former National Salvation Party. The second was the ultra-nationalist, Nationalist Work Party, successor to the pre-1980 Nationalist Action Party. The leader of the latter, Mr. Alpaslan Türkeş, became the president of the former upon the repeal of the ban on his political activities.

Prior to the elections of 29 November 1987, the Turkish party system looked considerably different from that which had been devised by the military leadership. Two of the three parties which the military leaders had allowed to compete in the 1983 elections had ceased to exist. The Motherland Party was the only product of the system which seemed to have made an established place for itself. It claimed that it was a new party and did not pretend to have inherited the legacy of any of the pre-1980 parties. On the other hand, all three parties, which had acquired parliamentary representation by means briefly described above, related themselves, in one way or another, to the past. The Social Democrats identified with the Republican People's Party; the Democratic Left Party appeared to be a personalistic party relying on the charisma of the former leader of the Republican People's Party; and the True Path Party claimed to be the reincarnation of the Justice Party. Yet each of these parties included new members and came up with new ideas such that none could rightly be called a replica of one of the pre-1980 parties.

It is with this background that the 1987 elections took place in November. Because six parties competed in these elections, the cut-off provisions, which had not been consequential in the 1983 elections contested by only three parties, played a crucial role. The Motherland Party, the Social Democratic Populist Party, and the True Path Party, getting 36.3, 24.7 and 19.3 per cent of the vote, respectively, gained parliamentary representation. The others, namely, the Democratic Left, the Welfare, and the Nationalist Work parties, getting 8.6, 7.1 and 2.1 per cent of the vote, respectively, were excluded from parliamentary representation. Whether these small parties will be able to continue to exist under a legal system which favors big parties is a question time will answer.

As part of their search for a means to establish long-term political stability in Turkey, the military leadership of the 1980–1983 period set out to create a new party system, attempting to make a clean break with the past. New parties were formed with new cadres, representing a different ideological spectrum, and substantial changes were made in the electoral system through new legislation. What has emerged after five years is a synthesis of the old and the new.

The party system continues its evolution. The 1987 elections were the first totally open elections in which all parties tried their luck. What we may expect now is a process of consolidation in which the losers and the winners may attempt to forge new coalitions so that none will be kept out of the legislature on account of not having been able to garner more than ten per cent of the national vote in future elections.

Chapter 7
The 1983 General Elections in Turkey: Continuity or Change in Voting Patterns*

Üstün Ergüder and Richard I. Hofferbert

1 Introduction

Following over three years of military government, in November 1983, an election was held for a Turkish national parliament. Under a new constitution, approved by referendum in 1982, the election produced a civilian government headed by Prime Minister Turgut Özal, based on a parliamentary majority for his Motherland Party. The Constitution and the rules under which the November election was conducted represented a deliberate attempt on the part of the military directorate, headed by General Kenan Evren, to remold the electoral and partisan structure of Turkish political life. The question confronted in this study is: To what extent do the results of the 1983 elections suggest that the effort succeeded in remolding the Turkish polity in such a way as to enhance the chances for a viable democratic order?

Throughout the three years of military rule, and reaching a crescendo in the election campaign of November, 1983, the military's major spokesmen put principal blame for economic and civil deterioration of the 1970s generally on the political party system and specifically on the political leaders who had been in place since the (military inspired) Constitution of 1961. In addition to the restoration of civil order, the major instrument of political reform was to be a rewriting of electoral and parties' laws. This statutory activity was supplemented by tight control over participation in the first National Assembly elections under the new Constitution.

---

* The authors are grateful to the Westview Press for permission to use this material here, a slightly different version of which first appeared in *Elections in the Middle East: Implications of Recent Trends* (Colorado, 1986) edited by Linda Layne.

Implicit in the military government's strategy, and explicit in much of its rhetoric, was a specific theory of the cause of Turkey's problems and a set of solutions to attack these causes. In that theory, party organizations and leadership behavior loomed large. Briefly, it states that not only intense but also non-consensual party competition, especially in the late 1970s, had led to parliamentary and governmental immobility. That immobility, in turn, had important consequences, threatening the state and its perceived distinctive, traditional role as the anchor of Turkish society.[1] Immobility also detailed the contemporary function of the state as a modernizing agent. Long Ottoman history has provided the military leaders with an instinctive assessment that, whenever the center (the state) is not able to exert its authority in order to perform its traditional functions, centrifugal tendencies have shaken an empire characterized by a complex social mosaic of ethnic and religious groups.

The "transcendental" conception of the state,[2] as binding and virtually defining Turkish society, was under many threats in the 1970s, including:

- The lack of parliamentary majorities
- Ever-changing coalition governments vulnerable to the threats and demands of ideological extremes
- Excessive use of patronage by clientelistic parties, some of which were experiencing a share of governmental power for the first time
- Inability to lead or legislate to deal with increasing economic woes and violence[3]

The immediate culprits, in the eyes of the military, were, on the one hand, a set of institutions that seemed to have failed to fulfill their promise, and, on the other hand, a set of politicians who had failed to provide leadership. The pluralist aspects of the 1961 Constitution, the parties, and the electoral system were the institutional villains. The politicians to blame included virtually everyone who had occupied a highly visible party role in the 1970s.

The thesis of this chapter is that, even though the manifest goal of the military government between 1980 and 1983 may have been to restrain the

---

[1] Şerif Mardin, "Opposition and Control in Turkey," *Government and Opposition* 1 (1966), pp. 375-387.

[2] For the development of this concept see Metin Heper, *The State Tradition in Turkey* (Walkington, England, Eothen Press, 1985). On the relationship of state and society, see Şerif Mardin, "Power, Civil Society and Culture in the Ottoman Empire," *Comparative Studies in Society and History* 11 (1969), pp. 258-281; and Şerif Mardin, "Center-Periphery in the Ottoman Empire: A Key to Turkish Politics?" *Daedalus* 102 (1973), pp. 169-190.

[3] For a discussion of the problems of Turkish democracy at the time, see Kemal H. Karpat, "Turkish Democracy at Impasse: Ideology, Party Politics and the Third Military Intervention," *International Journal of Turkish Studies* 2 (1981), pp. 1-43.

pluralist thrust of recent Turkish politics, the unintended consequence may have been to align the party system along a more modern dimension. The reforms may have set a framework conducive to the consensual conflict management characteristic of Western democracies.

The military leaders conceived and implemented three important measures directly related to reshaping Turkish politics. First, they submitted a new constitution for popular approval. It was approved by an overwhelming majority (92 per cent) of the population in the referendum of 1982. Second, the Turkish Political Parties Law and the Electoral Law were each overhauled. Third, for the parliamentary election of November 1983, the military directorate screened all potential parties, banning all but three from actual competition. The directorate also proscribed participation and even public discussion of politics by a specific list of party politicians who had been prominent in pre-1980 Turkish goverment and politics.

The 1982 Constitution seems to be a reaction to its 1961 predecessor. The new document, with some overtones of presidentialism,* emphasizes governmental authority as against legislative unruliness, the latter being a trait of the 1960s. The new document emphasizes executive power especially in dealing with socio-economic problems by enabling the legislature to authorize the executive to issue decrees having the force of law. Only fundamental, individual, and political rights (states of emergency and martial law excepted) are immune from executive decrees. These may turn out to be extensive powers when one of the parties controls the majority in the Turkish Grand National Assembly (TGNA).

The electoral law was rewritten to make it more likely that instead of the unstable coalition governments (like that of the 1970s) one-party majority governments will be returned to the TGNA. The broad contours of proportional representation (d'Hondt) was preserved, but political parties with less than 10 percent of the national vote were excluded from seat allocation under the new law. Futhermore, parties with less than the average[4] necessary for seat allocation in an electoral district were also excluded from seat allocation in that district. The major metropolitan electoral districts like Istanbul, Izmir, Adana, and Ankara were divided into smaller and less populous districts, further reducing the tendency of a proportional system to reward minor parties and to fragment the party system.[5]

---

* For a contrary view see Özbudun's chapter in this volume (Editors' note).

[4] Calculated by dividing the total number of votes cast in that district by the number of seats to be allocated in the same electoral district. This was amended in 1987; now in those constituencies where six deputies are elected the average is found by dividing the total number of valid votes cast by five and not by six.

[5] For a discussion of the new electoral law, see Ersin Kalaycıoğlu, "The Turkish Political

Aside from the immediate impact on specific persons involved or excluded from the elections of 1983, are there likely to be any detectable long-term systemic effects of these practices and reforms on Turkish political life? An examination of the conditions prior to 1983 is a prerequisite for answering this question.

2 Maladies of the Party System

2.1 Volatility

Our central objective is to test the impact of the party reforms implemented in the elections of 1983. To do that, we must, of course, have a measure of the prior form. One answer is that there simply had not been much form. The dominant feature of the Turkish political landscape between 1950 and 1980, but especially in rising magnitude through the 1960s and 1970s, was volatility in the bases of party support.

Mogens N. Pedersen[6] has developed for European elections between 1948 and 1977 an index of political volatility, based on individual parties' performance in successive elections.[7]

The scoring procedure essentially indicates the ability to predict party fortunes in one election from their performance in the preceding contest.

System in Transition: Multi-Party Politics in the 1980s," *Political Perspectives: Current Turkish Thought* (Istanbul) 56 (Fall 1985), pp. 17-18. For the effect of constituency size on proportional representation, see Duncan Black, *The Theory of Committees and Elections* (Cambridge, Cambridge University Press, 1971), p. 76 and D. W. Rae, *The Political Consequences of Electoral Laws* (London, Yale University Press, 1967), p. 30.

[6] See Mogens N. Pedersen, "The Dynamics of European Party Systems: Changing Patterns of Electoral Volatility," *European Journal of Political Research* 7 (1979), pp. 1-26.

[7] Referring to W. Ascher and S. Tarrow, "The Stability of Communist Electorates: Evidence from a Longitudinal Analysis of French and Italian Aggregate Data," *American Journal of Political Science* 19 (1975), pp. 480-481, Pedersen defines electoral volatility as "... the net change within the electoral party system resulting from individual vote transfers," (p. 3). Pedersen measures electoral volatility by aggregating the changes in the percentages of votes obtained by each party from one election to the next. If we let:

$$P_{i,t} = \text{per cent vote obtained by party } i \text{ at election } t$$

then the change (^) in the strength of party *i* will be measured by:

$$\hat{}P_{i,t} = P_{i,t} - P_{i,t-1}.$$

The total net change *(TNC_t)* in the party system is measured by (sign differences not considered):

$$TNC_t = \text{Sum}_{i-t} [\hat{}P_{i,t}]$$

The higher the score, the lower the predictability. The western European scores average 8.1, with a range of 16.8 for France to 3.7 for Austria over the period. Between 1950 and 1979, by comparison, Turkey's national volatility score averaged 19.3. Clearly, there is less "structure" in such a state of volatility.

Turkey's is, of course, a very recent experiment in democracy in a country that is, by any commonly accepted index, considerably less economically developed than any of the European examples included in Pedersen's analysis. Had comparable data been available for other LDCs, even for those at a level relatively similar to that of Turkey, it is probable that Turkey's performance in the past generation and a half would not have appeared so relatively unstructured.

Accelerating in the late 1960s and through the 1970s, Turkey was going through a fundamental redefinition of the cleavages of political competition. While having not yet solved the National Revolution, as it would be termed by Lipset and Rokkan,[8] Turkey was fully in the throes of the Industrial Revolution. In fact, in the 1950s, Turkish politics briefly came rather close to having one dominant dimension of a nearly two-party competition between the DP and RPP. That dimension was principally defined by the conflict between center and periphery, with undeniable overtones of more modern economic conflicts.

2.2 Fragmentation and Polarization

Volatility is but one manifestation of the "Bermuda Triangle" through which Turkish democracy struggled in the 1970s. Linked to volatility were fragmentation and polarization, especially among the governing elites.

Two major developments have been identified to explain increased instability. First, the Turkish parliamentary system changed from a "predominant party system"[9] to a hybrid between "moderate" and "polarized pluralism".[10] Second, there was a change in patterns of party support,

---

Cautioning the reader "... that the net gains from winning parties numerically are equal to the net losses of the parties that were defeated in the election ...," Pedersen, finally, uses the following formula "... as slightly easier to calculate and to interpret ..." to measure votality *(V)*:

$$V_{(t)} = \tfrac{1}{2} \times TNC_t, \text{ where } 0 < \text{or} = V_t < \text{or} = 100.$$

[8] Seymour M. Lipset and Stein Rokkan "Cleavage Structure, Party Systems and Voter Alignments: An Introduction," in *Party Systems and Voter Alignments: Cross-National Perspectives*, edited by Lipset and Rokkan (New York, Free Press, 1966), pp. 1–65.

[9] Giovanni Sartori, *Parties and Party Systems (Cambridge, Cambridge University Press, 1977), passim.*

[10] For similar conclusions on this point see Sabri Sayarı, "The Turkish Party System in Tran-

documented empirically by Özbudun and by Ergüder[11] prompting both to label the 1970s as "critical," in V.O. Key's terms.[12]

The "predominant party system" classification seems to fit the Turkish case in the period that started with the elections of 1950 and ended with those of 1973. Thanks to the electoral support they received from many groups across society, the DP, and its successor the Justice Party (JP), were able to stay in power by themselves during this era although their electoral success was not of the same magnitude as that of, for example, the PRI in Mexico, a classic and extreme case of a "predominant party system."[13] Even though there is some evidence that class-based politics was becoming relevant in the 1970s with the JP being identified with propertied interests,[14] this "predominance" at the polls was based on the enduring center/periphery cleavage which helped to broaden the spectrum of that party's appeal to include less privileged groups with traditional values, notably the peasantry and the urban marginals.

The 1961 elections, which followed the coup, did not produce a governmental majority, as three parties (Justice Pary, New Turkey Party, and Republican Peasants Nation Party) were competing for the support of the adherents of the outlawed DP. The issue of succession was settled in 1965 when the JP received 53 per cent of the total votes cast. The party system reverted to its predominant character. Both the electoral and parliamentary majorities, however, were not as comfortable as those of the 1950s.

The 1973 elections signaled the end of the "predominant" party system in Turkey. The JP suffered its worst performance, receiving only 30 per cent of the votes. The RPP did much better, with 33.3 per cent. It shifted

---

sition," *Government and Opposition* 12 (1978), pp. 39-57; Üstün Ergüder, *Seçim Sistemleri ve Türk Demokrasisi* (Istanbul, Boğaziçi University, Publication 1982), pp. 97-138. For a slightly different interpretation of Sartori's typologies, see Ergun Özbudun, "Political Parties and Elections," in *Südosteuropa Handbuch: Türkei*, edited by Klaus-Detlev Grothusen (Göttingen, Vandenhoeck and Ruprecht, 1985), pp. 262-281. On fragmentation and polarization of the Turkish party system see Ergun Özbudun, "The Turkish Party System: Institutionalization, Polarization and Fragmentation," *Middle Eastern Studies* 17 (April 1981), pp. 228-240.

11 See Ergun Özbudun, *Social Change and Political Participation in Turkey* (Princeton, Princeton University Press, 1976), pp. 129-209; and Üstün Ergüder, "Changing Patterns of Electoral Behavior in Turkey," *Boğaziçi Üniversitesi Dergisi* 8-9 (1980-1981), pp. 45-81. See also Ergun Özbudun and Frank Tachau, "Social Change and Electoral Behavior in Turkey: Toward 'A Critical Realignment'?" *International Journal of Middle East Studies* 6 (1975), pp. 460-479.

12 V.O. Key, Jr., "A Theory of Critical Elections," *Journal of Politics* 17 (1955), pp. 3-19.

13 The only exception within this period is the period that started with the military take-over of 1960 that led to the banning of the DP. Elections held in 1961 did not return a majority to the National Assembly, and Turkey was governed by a series of coalition governments until the elections of 1965.

14 Özbudun, *Social Change and Political Participation in Turkey, passim.*

towards an ideology of social democracy under the leadership of Bülent Ecevit in an attempt to change its long-standing image as champion of both the state elites at the center and the traditional landed interests in the countryside. But the RPP did not capture enough seats to form a government. The 1973 elections ushered in a new period of coalitions and governmental crises.

The curious aspect of the party system that emerged after the 1973 elections is that it had all the trappings of Sartori's[15] "moderate pluralism," in which alternating coalition governments around major parties are the rule of the day. In "moderate pluralism," the system is center-oriented in the sense that support for ideological poles is weak, both in terms of electoral support and parliamentary representation. Moderate pluralism somewhat resembles the British two-party system, with its moderation and lack of polarized or extremist politics. The major difference is in respect to alternation of governmental power. "Moderate pluralism" is characterized, as in contemporary West Germany, by alternative coalitions of governmental power revolving around two major parties, rather than alternation of power between two major parties, each governing alone when in power.

There was little electoral or parliamentary strength at the ideological poles in Turkey during the 1970s. The Unity Party of Turkey (UPT), the only party to the left of the RPP which participated in the 1973 elections, received only 1.1 per cent of the total votes, and it captured only one seat in the National Assembly. It should also be mentioned here that the UPT was a party based on sectarian differences appealing to the Shiite elements living in different parts of the country as well as being a party of the ideological left. In 1977, the combined percentage of the parties to the left of the RPP did not exceed 0.5 per cent of the votes, with no representation in the Assembly.

The situation to the right of the JP, however, was more severely fragmented. The National Salvation Party (NSP) and the Nationalist Action Party (NAP) introduced an uncommon level of ideological dispute into Turkish politics. The NSP, focusing on fundamentalist Islamic issues and appealing to the Sunnite elements in various parts of the country, polled 11.8 per cent in 1973 and placed 48 deputies (out of a total membership of 450) in the National Assembly. The NAP, appealing to an extreme right ideology, with its emphasis on discipline, leadership, and militant party organization, stressed nationalism (with overtones of racism) and anti-communism. It polled 3.4 per cent in 1973 and placed 3 deputies in the National Assembly. In 1977 these same parties polled 8.6 and 6.4 per cent, winning 24 and 16 seats, respectively.

---

[15] See Sartori, *Parties and Party Systems*, pp. 173–185.

In 1973, the other parties in the Assembly were the Democratic Party (DemP) and the Republican Reliance Party (RRP), with 11.9 per cent (45 deputies) and 5.3 per cent (13 deputies), respectively. These personality parties were not identified with ideological polarization. Each polled 1.9 per cent in 1977, while the DemP gained 1 and the RRP 3 deputies.

The Turkish party system of the 1970s, however, performed much like Sartori's "polarized pluralist" systems[16] despite the fact that the ideological distance was not great between the two major parties. Governmental instability and parliamentary immobility increased even more after the 1977 elections, when the system, paradoxically, approximated more closely the formal aspects of "moderate pluralism," with the representation of ideological parties to the right of the JP being trimmed and the other minor parties of the right (the RRP and the DemP) virtually disappearing in terms of electoral support.

Throughout the 1970s, ideological intransigence increased in the parliament, with growing inability of the major parties to come to terms on the basic rules of the game - despite the visible threats to the continuation of a competitive system. Concessions were bargained away allowing minor parties coalition participation far disproportionate to their electoral strength, especially by the NSP and the NAP.[17]

Party discipline seemed to break down as defections from one party to another, making and unmaking coalition governments, became increasingly rewarding. Consequently, governmental leadership based on secure parliamentary majorities, critically important for dealing with mounting economic problems as well as with rising social and political unrest, virtually disappeared. The behavior of the Turkish party system was reminiscent of Germany during the Weimar Republic, a classic case of polarized pluralism. The conditions appeared increasingly threatening to the ideological fabric of the Turkish Republic, extolling a powerful state, making especially the military elite quite apprehensive.

Polarization of political parties and their leaders is not a new phenomenon in Turkey. In fact, the breakdown of the democratic system in 1960, prior to the May military intervention, could be partially explained by the intransigence of the DP leadership toward the opposition and to the extreme oppositional stance assumed by the RPP. Such postures virtually eliminated that consensual politics so critically important for a viable par-

---

16 *Ibid.*, pp. 131-145.

17 See Metin Heper, "Bureaucrats, Politicians and Officers in Turkey: Dilemmas of a New Political Paradigm," in *Modern Turkey: Continuity and Change,* edited by Ahmet Evin (Opladen, Leske and Budrich, 1984), pp. 64-83; İlkay Sunar and Sabri Sayarı, "Democracy in Turkey: Problems and Prospects," in *Transition From Authoritarian Rule: Experiences in Southern Europe,* edited by Guillermo O'Donnell, Philippe C. Schmitter and Laurence Whitehead (Baltimore and London, The Johns Hopkins University Press, 1986).

liamentary democracy.[18] Novel in the 1970s was the increasingly ideological tint this polarization assumed, especially between the RPP and the JP.

In contrast to polarization, fragmentation of the party system is of more recent origin, increasing gradually during the 1960s, when compared with the earlier period, and growing through the 1970s. In the 1960s, the evidence was an increased number of parties in the Assembly (4 in 1961, 6 in 1965, and 8 in 1969), along with increasing difficulty in keeping party discipline. This fragmentation, however, did not have a major impact on the party system, since the JP was able to maintain its predominance in the elections of 1965 and 1969, returning parliamentary majorities each time.

The destabilizing impact of fragmentation in the party system came into full force with the 1973 elections when no party could return a governing majority to the National Assembly. The 1977 elections provided no cure. In an atmosphere of hightened volatility, polarization and fragmentation came to tear the Turkish party system asunder.

While always noting the effects of formal electoral rules and individual leaders' behavior, the search for causes of fragmentation in the Turkish party system has almost always overlooked one other important factor: the impact of military interventions. Each military intervention, while ostensibly responding to political misbehavior, creates a period of uncertainty and fragmentation in the party system. The banning of the DP in 1960 ushered in a four-year period of coalition governments in the Assembly and a disorganized scramble for votes among the electorate, especially among groups seeking to inherit the mantle of the Democrat Party.

Even through no specific punitive action was taken against any of the political parties after the 1971 military intervention, the elections that followed in 1973 brought in the DemP, the NAP, and the NSP as electoral contenders.

The military intervention of 1980 and the electoral/party arrangements that followed were designed to end the fragmentation of the party system which, as already noted, the military identified as a culprit in Turkish political problems. Paradoxically, the banning of the old parties and leaders, and the emergence of new ones, coupled with an electoral system designed to limit the number of parties in the Assembly, might usher in yet another period in which fragmentation of the parliamentary party system will be reduced while fragmentation of the electoral party system will be

[18] Mardin provides a good account of the social and cultural roots of oppositionalism and intolerance which have been traditionally ingrained in Turkish social psychology and which were manifest in the party system during the 1950s, undermining its moderation. (See Mardin, "Opposition and Control in Turkey," passim.) His analysis provides a plausible explanation of the lack of accommodation between key actors in what appeared, on the surface at least, to be a classic two-party system.

increased, at least until patterns of partisanship stabilize. This is a limitation on our ability to project systemic consequences from the first election under the new rules.

Volatility, fragmentation, and polarization of the party system help explain the gross instability of the Turkish political system during the 1970s. They also explain the frame of mind of the military in pushing a constitutional overhaul to limit office-seeking and reshape the party system so that the 1980s would not be molded in the pattern of the 1970s.

On the other hand, a close look into changing patterns of party support not only provides an explanation for the woes of the 1970s, but it also sheds light on possible outcomes with respect to party support during the 1980s, with brand new parties and leaders competing. It is our contention here that what made the Motherland Party electoral coalition possible in 1983 was the fact that the Turkish electorate of the previous decade was already groping for a new centrist solution to the maladies of the party system.

To provide a more accurate analysis of the 1983 elections, it is necessary to construct some quantitative benchmarks of partisan structure in the preceding two decades. Such quantitative findings will serve to illustrate and validate the foregoing discussion of the party system.

3 Measuring Post-1961 Partisan Structure

By analyzing the patterns of party performance in the Turkish provinces, a more accurate picture of the dimensionality running through the electoral history may be obtained. It would be most useful to have a series of surveys to identify the bases of individual partisanship and persistence of electoral behavior. Unfortunately, such data are not available in anything approaching consistent form. Reliable and quite relevant aggregate data are available, however, for the 67 provinces.

Our use of provincial data is not wholly a compromise. If there is any persisting pattern to recent Turkish politics, it is reasonable to assume that the pattern is related to an organizational and socio-economic context measurable with provincial-level aggregate data.

Turkish provinces *(iller)* are not comparable to states in a federal system. They are administrative units, more similar to French *departements* rather than to American states or Swiss cantons. Nevertheless, each jurisdiction does represent some degree of socio-economic coherence. They serve as units for the delivery of public services. And they constitute, for most parties, a unit of organization. Given the rather high quality of social, economic, and political statistics in Turkey, provincial data at a minimum capture a good portion of any major geographic variance. Given Turkey's geography, that variance is of no mean consequence.

To take advantage of cross-provincial variance as an aid to gaining insight into the patterning or structruing of pre-1980 Turkish politics, we conducted a pooled factor analysis of party voting percentages across the provinces for four national parliamentary elections: 1965, 1969, 1973, and 1977.

Several minor parties were grouped together, given that individually their performance was quite skewed, even if highly variant across provinces, while their absolute percentages were very small. Two groups of minor parties were incorporated into the analysis: (a) minor left parties and (b) minor personalistic parties. In addition, the individual provincial percentages for the JP, NAP, NSP, and RPP were included (see Table 1).

The results of the factor analysis are presented in Table 2. The first factor is a close approximation of Lipset and Rokkan's conception of a *periphery/center* cleavage.[19] The modernizing, more or less free market JP anchors the scale at the center end, followed closely by the equally mod-

Table 1 Party performance in Turkish National Assembly elections (1965-1977)

Party	1965		1969		1973		1977	
	% Vote	Seats	% Vote	Seats	% Vote	Seats	% Vote	Seats
Justice	52.9	240	46.5	256	29.7	149	36.9	189
Republican People's	28.8	134	27.4	143	33.3	185	41.4	213
National Salvation	–	–	–	–	11.8	48	8.6	24
Nationalist Action	–	–	3.2	1	3.4	3	6.4	16
Minor Personalistic[a]	15.4	62	17.6	40	21.8	65	6.2	8
Minor Left[b]	3.0	14	5.5	10	–	–	0.5	–

[a] Republican Reliance Party, Republican Peasants' Nation Party, Democratic Party, Nation Party, New Turkey Party, Independents

[b] For 1965, Turkish Labor Party. For other elections sum of Turkish Union Party and Turkish Labor Party

[19] Lipset and Rokkan, "Cleavage Structures, Party Systems and Voter Alignments: An Introduction," pp. 9-13.

Table 2 Structure of Turkish party system: factor analysis of party performance, 1965–1977

Factor loadings/party-election					
Periphery/Center		Left/Right		Anti-System	
Min-Pers'69	0.92	RPP'73	0.86	NAP'77	0.91
Min-Pers'77	0.79	RPP'77	0.85	NAP'73	0.75
Min-Pers'65	0.77	Min-Left'69	0.66	NSP'73	0.68
NSP'77	0.76	Trk Lab'65	0.60	Min-Left'69	0.37
Min-Pers'73	0.73	RPP'65	0.57	Min-Left'77	0.31
NSP'73	0.30	Min-Left'77	0.56	Min-Pers'65	0.13
Trk Lab'65	0.17	RPP'69	0.47	NSP'77	0.09
RPP'65	0.12	NAP'77	0.06	Min-Pers'69	0.01
Min-Left'69	0.03	NAP'73	−0.03	JP'65	−0.04
NAP'77	0.00	Min-Pers'69	−0.14	JP'69	−0.07
Min-Left'77	−0.02	JP'65	−0.17	Trk Lab'65	−0.07
NAP'73	−0.09	Min-Pers'65	−0.20	RPP'77	−0.09
RPP'73	−0.28	NSP'73	−0.20	RPP'73	−0.13
RPP'69	−0.38	Min-Pers'77	−0.23	JP'77	−0.15
RPP'77	−0.39	NSP'77	−0.24	Min-Pers'73	−0.18
JP'73	−0.70	Min-Pers'73	−0.33	RPP'65	−0.20
JP'77	−0.80	JP'69	−0.37	RPP'69	−0.21
JP'69	−0.85	JP'73	−0.45	Min-Pers'77	−0.25
JP'65	−0.88	JP'77	−0.48	JP'73	−0.32

Min-Pers = Minor Personalistic parties (see Table 1); NSP = National Salvation Party; Trk Lab = Turkish Labor Party; RPP = Republican People's Party; Min-Left = Minor left parties (see Table 1); NAP = Nationalist Action Party; JP = Justice Party

ernization-oriented RPP. Only in 1965 did the RPP slip below any party-election other than the JP on the periphery/center factor. At the peripheral end of the scale are the minor personalistic parties, along with the heavily Islamic-oriented NSP.

The strength of the peripheral parties is concentrated along the Syrian-Iraqi border away from coastal areas. This is not only the most geographically inaccessible and topographically harsh part of Turkey, but also the region where there is the highest concentration of ethno-linguistic minority groups. The only apparent deviations are the central Anatolian provinces of Konya and Kırşehir, which have been bastions of religious dissent for centuries, most notably focused around the Mevlevi order of dervishes.

Unlike their proximity on the modern or center end of the first factor, the RPP and the JP became polar opposites on the left/right dimension, the factor most comparable to the dominant Western party cleavage. The left/right dimension is the most difficult to capture with aggregate data because, by its very definition, it is territorial and more class relevant than is the center-periphery dimension.[20] Those familiar with Turkish social geography will see that, first, the industrial commercial centers support the left (e.g., Istanbul, Izmir, Adana, Ankara). Second, support for the left comes from provinces which had, in the 1970s, experienced *Alevi/Sünni* conflicts.

Repeated iterations of the data consistently supported our observations indicating the necessity for accommodating a third factor into the analysis. Turkish electoral politics has been more than a two-dimensional rotation around a durable periphery/center and an emerging left/right cleavages. These conflicts take place more or less within the generally accepted structure of the regime, even if producing vigorous dissent from certain rules and tendencies of that regime. Even the spokespersons of the minor personalistic parties, so strongly anchored at the peripheral end of Factor 2, insisted upon their allegiance to the Turkish state. But there are, within recent history and in the contemporary setting, persons and groups who have not been so clear and firm in their acceptance of the national regime.

Elements of Pan-Turanism (an ideology which seeks to unify all Turks on the basis of ethno-linguistic identity, including more people outside the boundary of the Turkish Republic than within) persist just below the surface of many disputes in today's Turkey. The Young Turk movement of the early years of the century was led by the Pan-Turanist Enver Paşa.

Notably, Factor 3, which we have labeled *anti-system,* is one-tailed in its composition. The Nationalist Action Party dominates this dimension, followed by the National Salvation Party in one election, and a set of minor left parties. It is the proximity of these minor left parties to the "ultra-rightist" NAP that has convinced the present authors of the value of the index as a measure of anti-system political leanings. The negative (or "pro-system") variance is modest, being anchored by the Justice Party in 1973. But most of the pro-system variance in the total matrix of elections and parties was concentrated in the first two factors: periphery/center and left/right.

The factor analysis produces scores that are uncorrelated with each other ("orthogonally rotated"). Thus, the score of a province on one factor is computed holding constant the other two factors. A high score on periphery/center, therefore, does not mean that there are no anti-system or left/right elements located there. Rather, it reflects the relative amount of anti-system behavior, controlling for the extent of the other two dimensions. Geographically we see that the degree of anti-system voting, rela-

[20] *Ibid.*

tive to either periphery/center or left/right behavior, was highest in the central Anatolian plateau, but extending from Afyon in the west of Anatolia to Erzurum in the east.

Across the four elections (1965, 1969, 1973, and 1977) included in the factor analysis, it is interesting that there is no apparent time trend in the loadings. Parties which earlier scored high on one end or the other of the center-periphery dimension do not move, in later elections, to a different factor. To the extent that aggregate data can reveal such a change, these findings suggest that there was no major realignment of electoral behavior in the decade and a half prior to the 1980 military take over. Rather, there was a complex process of deterioration in system capacity.

4 The 1983 Election: Reinstatement or Reform?

An interesting aspect of the 1983 elections is that it came in the wake of a constitutional referendum which may have had all the trappings of a regime endorsement. The question in November 1983 was: will the electorate continue to support the military leaders by endorsing political parties favored by them or would *politics* and old political cleavages become once again salient? The voters in 1983 have reverted from regime issues to *politics,* but the efforts of the military rulers to reshape and restructure politics appears at least tentatively to have had an impact.

Previous efforts by Turkish military governments to alter the structure of the party system have a mixed record. The banning of the Democrats in 1960 did not prevent a reincarnation in the form of the Justice Party. On the other hand, the reforms in electoral systems embodied in the 1961 Constitution almost certainly accelerated, especially in the 1970s, the fragmentation and polarization of Turkish politics - a hardly intended, even if predictable, outcome of the constitution writers' efforts.

Did the conditions imposed on the elections of 1983 actually bring about a realignment along a newly dominant cleavage? One event does not make a trend, of course, and it will not be possible to confirm a pattern until much more time has passed. The elections of 1961 proved to be a poor predictor of future patterns, since the supporters of the ousted DP were casting about among several groups seeking to inherit the DP mantle. The 1983 elections could appear to be an equally poor predictor.[21]

We think not, however, given the controls imposed upon the available options. All previous parties were banned, and their supporters' choices

---

[21] The 1983 results are compounded in their complexity, not only by their recency, but also by the presence of a very popular head of the party which won the elections. Özal's popu-

were limited to three options: the Motherland Party, the Populist Party, and the Nationalist Democracy Party.

The returns from 1983 certainly do not conform to the old pattern, not even as it could have been predicted to evolve from the trends in place in the late 1970s. By many standards, the results in 1983 deviate from the past even more than in the volatile, fragmented conditions evolving under the pre-1980 system. A review of the conditions and participation rules of those elections is in order here. Recall that the military government had taken several steps to break the old pattern:

- Disbanding and prohibiting the reformation of all parties from the previous period
- screening all potential parties and proscribing all but three from participation in 1983: the Motherland Party (headed by Turgut Özal, the current prime minister), the Populist Party (thought by some to be a potential successor to the RPP), and the Nationalist Democracy Party (given tacit support by the leaders of the military government)
- Proscribing from standing for parliamentary seats a specific list of named politicians from previous governments
- Imposing an electoral system designed to decrease the number of minor parties in the TGNA

The results gave Özal's Motherland Party (MP) 45 per cent of the popular vote and 211 seats out of a total of 400 in the new National Assembly. This is Turkey's first majority government since 1969. President Evren ac-

---

larity, at the time of the elections, may be analysed in terms of his relationship to pre-1980 parties and leaders as well as his contribution to successful economic policies during both the pre- and post-1980 periods. First, Özal, while never being closely associated with the Justice Party, served under Süleyman Demirel in a technocratic capacity on several occasions. He also had close ties to the NSP, as his brother was one of the influential members of the party. While flirting with it, he never became a member of the NSP. In terms of former political associations he was occupying a space in Turkish politics somewhere between the moderate and more secular right of the JP vintage and the religious right of the NSP. Second, in terms of policy performance, he was in responsible positions during two important junctures in Turkish economic history. He was heading the State Planning Organization, in 1969, when the Demirel government took important measures to stem the economic crisis of the day. It was then that Özal started to build his reputation as an economic miracle worker. More importantly, Özal and Demirel are known as the major architects of the controversial but, in terms of short-term economic indicators successful, January 24th, 1980 measures to deal with the severe economic crisis and the triple-digit inflation of the late 1970s. Demirel was deposed by the military during the 1980 takeover, but Özal stayed in power as the major economic brain behind the policies of the new military backed-government. The policies were a continuation of the January 24th measures. He resigned his post almost a year before the 1983 elections and was not a member of the government when economic performance appeared to be heading towards rough seas once again.

Table 3 Relationship (r) between 1983 election and prior patterns: 67 Turkish provinces

	Motherland	Populist	Nationalist Democracy
Periphery/Center	−0.32	0.02	0.38
Left/Right	−0.36	0.68	−0.31
Anti-System	0.50	−0.20	−0.39
1973 and 1977 Elections			
JP '77	0.36	−0.24	−0.15
JP '73	0.18	−0.18	0.01
RPP '77	−0.29	0.68	−0.39
RPP '73	−0.38	0.69	−0.30
NAP '77	0.44	−0.17	−0.35
NAP '73	0.36	−0.11	−0.30
NSP '77	−0.06	−0.34	0.42
NSP '73	0.47	−0.38	−0.18
Min-Pers '77	−0.27	−0.13	0.47
Min-Pers '73	−0.20	−0.21	0.45
Min-Left '77	−0.07	0.32	−0.24
Min-Left '73[a]			

[a] The minor left parties obtained an inconsequential number of votes in 1973, nearly all endorsing the RPP

cepted the results gracefully and Özal, as the Prime Minister designate, formed the governing cabinet.

The Populist party placed second, with 30 per cent of the vote and 117 seats. The blessing of the military government was insufficient to enable the Nationalist Democrats to play a major role, with 24 per cent and 71 seats.

As interesting as the absolute results are the extent to which any or all of the parties participating in 1983 seemed to replace parties from the pre-1980 period. There is little question that the JP, by 1965, was appealing to the same voters of the same socio-economic groups as had the Democrats of the pre-1961 period, despite the banning of the DP in 1961. The RPP had carried the banner of Atatürk consistently since the single-party period before 1950 up to the banning of parties in 1980. Some speculated that the Nationalist Democrats would draw from the more right-wing periphery, if not the anti-system parties.

Table 3 presents the correlations between the 1983 votes and the factor scores of the three dimensions of partisanship. The most important message of Table 3 is that the MP is not the anchor of any pre-existing partisan cleavage. It comes closest to the center end of the periphery/center cleavage, but not with anything like the strength of association of the now-outlawed Justice Party.

The volatility of the performance of Turkish parties - the lack of consistent support among voting groups - makes assessment of continuity or change quite risky. It is difficult to sort the signals from the noise of pre-1980 electoral behavior. Without assuming what we wish to investigate, namely the continuity or change in the bases of support of the new parties compared to the old ones, it is risky to draw conclusions from the correlation of the 1983 elections with specific party figures in prior years. To the extent that there was any stability in the pre-1980 period, we are persuaded that it is captured better by the three factors (periphery/center, left/right, anti-system) than by votes in specific elections. Therefore, while noting the correlations of the 1983 results with particular parties in prior elections, we have the most confidence in the relations of 1983 to the provincial scores on the three factors.

Turgut Özal's Motherland Party, while capturing nearly a majority of the votes (47 per cent) and an absolute majority of the seats in the newly constituted National Assembly, is not the reincarnation of any single pre-existing partisan entity. It is moderately anchored on the center end of the periphery/center dimension ($r = -0.32$), as well as to the right of the left/right factor ($r = -0.36$). Most important, however, is the 0.50 correlation with the anti-system dimension of 1960s and 1970s.

The initial temptation is to read a gloomy message into the correlation between the 1983 returns for the MP and the anti-system parties of the pre-1980 period. We are more inclined, however, to see the glass as half full. The fragmentation of the party system of the 1960s and 1970s, coupled with the absence of an acceptable center, in effect pushed some elements of the electorate to the edges of the system. Özal's party, if it can be viewed as a centrist, moderate force, has served to draw back into the mainstream those who were formerly engaged in anti-system protest. The 0.36 and 0.44 correlations between the MP and the Nationalist Action Party in 1973 and 1977, respectively, provides further confirmation of this observation. The open question is: were the anti-system voters of the 1960s and 1970s forced into that stance before 1980 by the conditions of that time, or were forced by the military government's banning of options in 1983 into support of the MP?

Optimists will accept the former interpretation. Whether the formerly discontented elements stay within the fold of a centrist party will, in all likelihood, hinge upon perceptions of the performance of Özal's party in office.[22]

[22] The Turkish local elections of March, 1984, free from many of the restrictions placed on

Less difficult to interpret is the performance of the Populist Party. Its support seems solidly anchored on the left of the left/right dimension ($r=0.68$). Recalling that the party most strongly associated with that dimension was the RPP, it is not surprising also that the Populists' vote in 1983 correlates positively with the RPP percentage in the two last elections before 1980 ($r=0.68$ and 0.69, respectively).

While drawing moderately from the periphery ($r=0.38$) as well as from the right ($r=0.31$), the Nationalist Democracy Party - favorite of the military in the 1983 elections - did not capture the anti-system vote ($r=-0.39$). It did, however, capitalize on some carry-over from the fragmentation of the pre-1980 period, being most closely associated with the minor personalistic splinter parties of 1973 ($r=0.45$) and 1977 ($r=0.47$).

When faced with a moderate option, disassociated from the tarnished politics of the past, the Turkish electorate seems to have responded positively. In the campaign of 1983, Turgut Özal ran on a platform stressing economic growth and fiscal caution. He advocated de-emphasis on state economic enterprises. He has described himself as a devotee of supply-side economics. His program would have placed him comfortably within the range of many Western right-of-center parties. He also stressed the need to enhance Turkey's place within the Middle Eastern economic network. Sometimes described as a Muslim technocrat, he seems to appeal to traditional values without giving them ideological pre-eminence over the need to bring Turkey into the international competitive marketplace. A comparison to Ronald Reagan is not wholly out of place. Reagan's appeal to Christian values, anti-abortion interests, etc., enables him to absorb traditional elements of the electorate without sacrificing his prime emphasis on modern issues - the market over the state, investment and

---

the 1983 general elections, provided support for the former, more optimistic interpretation. The Motherland Party repeated its electoral success at the polls, with about 42 per cent of the votes. The MP also captured 52 mayoral positions out of 67 provincial centers. The other post-1980 parties blessed by the military did poorly at the polls. The Populist Party and the Nationalist Democrats did no better than 9 and 7 per cent, respectively, of the total votes cast. One of the more surprising results of the March, 1984 local elections was the failure of the True Path Pary (TPP), specifically organized as a successor to the JP and competing for the first time in a post-1983 election, to make widely expected inroads into the electoral support of the MP. The TPP received about 14 per cent of the total votes. A second but somewhat more expected outcome was the success of the Social Democracy Party (SDP), with about 24 per cent of the votes. SDP was organized to replace the RPP. It, however, had not received the blessing of the military in the 1983 elections. In the 1984 local elections, SDP seems not only to have taken over fully the mantle of the RPP, but it virtually eclipsed the Populists, who had been allowed by the military to participate in 1983. After March, 1984, only the Motherland Party, among the new "blessed" organizations (i.e., allowed to participate in 1983) appeared to remain as a major force with substantial electoral support.

growth over income maintenance programs, etc. Those who support Reagan for his economic policies may wince at, but tolerate, his moral preachings in the quest of a winning coalition. Özal's public stance on traditional morality (clad in an Islamic garb) has, if anything, been notably more muted than that of his American counterpart. Özal would seem, therefore, to be moving toward an absorption, and thus a diminution, of the impetus toward fragmentation on the periphery.

During the 1970s, while there was some fragmentation on the left, the RPP had moved toward, what appeared to be, a class-based foundation in the electorate.[23] It was increasingly similar, in rhetoric and electoral appeal, if not in policy accomplishments, to a left-of-center social democratic party, with minimal relevance to more traditional lines of cleavage. What fragmentation there was on the left was probably due to immoderation of specific leaders, plus facilitation by the electoral system. The new Populist Party of 1983 continued to capitalize on the growing coherence of the left-of-center elements of the electorate.

Although the left splinter groups were often dramatic in their ideological pronouncements and protest behavior, their numbers and institutional strength were less than the fragmentation on the right. That is, the match between the RPP, as a substantively moderate left party, and an enduring set of electoral interests was greater than for any single entity to the right of center. It was on the right that the most threatening fragmentation had become most institutionalized.

Modernization in a competitive democratic framework cannot be accomplished by a social democratic force alone. The right and the periphery, too, must have legitimate options *within the system*. Özal's Motherland Party may have provided a broadly acceptable, pro-system alternative, neutralizing (for the time being, at least) and reintegrating, if not eliminating, the anti-systemic tendencies on the right and the periphery.

---

[23] See Özbudun, *Social Change and Political Participation in Turkey,* 220-221; Özbudun and Tachau, "Social Change and Electoral Behavior in Turkey: A 'Critical Realignment'?" *passim;* and Ergüder, "Changing Patterns and Electoral Behavior in Turkey," *passim*. The empirical evidence suggests such a shift towards class-based foundation for the RPP. Others, however, point out that aggregate and survey data used in these analyses do not control for the impact of ethnic and religious factors on voting behavior. Former Prime Minister Süleyman Demirel has pointed out to one of the present authors during an interview that Alevis (a religious minority in Turkey closely associated with Shiism) normally vote Republican and that they also happen to constitute an important element of the working class in major urban areas. For cross-cutting cleavages in Turkish politics see Sayarı, "The Turkish Party System in Transition," *passim,*

5 Developments Since the Elections of 1983

The results of the early general elections held on 29 November 1987 suggest that important developments have taken place in Turkish politics since November, 1983. As far as political parties are concerned, the True Path Party (TPP), claiming to be a successor of Justice Party, has emerged as an important contender on the right under Süleyman Demirel's[24] leadership. The TPP's performance in November 1987, however, did not live up to the expectation of its leaders. With 19.1 per cent of the vote, 59 TPP deputies were elected to the Grand National Assembly.

The Nationalist Democracy Party (NDP), the other party of the right formed before the 1983 elections, was dissolved, with its members joining ranks either with the TPP or the MP. The remaining parties of the right competing in the 1987 elections were the Welfare Party (WP) and the Nationalist Work Party (NWP). The WP, claiming to succeed the Islamic fundamentalist NSP, received 7.2 per cent of the vote. The NWP, claiming inheritance from the militant nationalist NAP, was able to garner only 2.9 per cent of the vote. Both parties were unable to return any deputies, since the electoral system[25] introduced in September, 1987, is heavily biased against minor parties.

There were two important developments on the left. The first was the merger of the Social Democracy Party (SODEP), a party which was not allowed to participate in the 1983 elections, with the Populists. The move was engineered by Erdal İnönü, the leader of SODEP, and Aydın Güven Gürkan. The new party, Social Democratic Populist Party (SDPP),[26] emerged as a contender for political power under the leadership of Erdal İnönü. The SDPP, with 24.7 per cent of the vote, returned 99 deputies to

---

[24] Süleyman Demirel, a former prime minister and the leader of the Justice Party was among those who were banned from politics by the military for a period of ten years. Demirel is not even a member of the TPP. The party is officially led by Hüsamettin Cindoruk, a trusted lieutenant of Demirel. Cindoruk makes it no secret that he is just filling in for the time being.

[25] The system is basically d'Hondt version of proportional representation with national (10 per cent) and local thresholds. Especially the system of local thresholds, determined by dividing the total number of votes in a constituency with the number of seats to be allocated in that constituency, has been highly controversial. Moreover, the same law stipulated that the divisor could not be any greater than 5, even in constituencies where 6 seats (maximum size) would be allocated. Consequently the local thresholds in November, 1987, elections ranged from a maximum of 50 per cent of the votes for the smallest three constituencies to a minimum of 20 per cent for the largest 48 constituencies. With its further provision that in 46 constituencies 1 deputy would be elected by simple majority, the system heavily penalized minor parties and was engineered to produce one party majorities in the GNA - a reaction to the unstable coalition governments of the 1970s.

[26] The acronym used for the Party in Turkish is SHP which stands for Social Populist Party.

the GNA. The other significant development on the left has been the formation of the Democratic Left Party (DLP) under the leadership of Bülent Ecevit, the leader of the RPP and a former prime minister. The DLP, while emphasizing some continuity with the past through the Ecevit name, differentiated itself as the forerunner of grass-roots left in Turkey. Attempts by the SDPP leaders to include the DLP in the merger was cold shouldered by the Ecevits. The DLP, with 8.5 per cent of the vote, suffered the fate of the WP and the NWP and was unable to return any deputies to the GNA.

An important concern of Turkish politics between 1983 and 1987 was the developments at the right of center. Will the MP, under Özal's leadership, be able to hang on to the major party status of the right? How successful would it be in continuing as a melting pot, as our findings point out, of the diverse elements of the right? What will the impact of the efforts of the TPP and Demirel be on the MP? The MP received 36.3 per cent of the vote and, aided by the tendency of the new electoral system to create governing majorities, returned 292 deputies to the GNA in November 1987. A cursory analysis of the election results suggests that the MP has carved out a place for itself at the center right, at the expense of the other parties of the right. It may also, at this early stage, be cautiously argued that it has even received some support from the center left.

During the period between the two general elections there was a dominant tendency to equate the fortunes of the MP with the ups and downs of the economy. The assumption was that the MP had the right set of policies (backed internationally) to address Turkish economic problems in the early 1980s. Failure to control inflation, rising levels of unemployment and a worsening income redistribution would eventually weaken the MP at the polls. A high inflation rate, ranging between 30 to 50 per cent (1987), but accompanied by a high growth rate of around 7 per cent per annum, has not produced the expected impact on the MP. Under heavy competition from the successors of the old parties under old leaders, the MP has managed to join the Turkish political scene as a major party.

It may be argued that there was really more than an economic mission as far as the future of the MP in Turkish politics is concerned. The MP came up with measures to reduce the burden of bureaucracy on the citizen. Furthermore, there was a concerted effort to emphasize service delivery to the citizen along with a well conducted campaign to show the relation between taxes paid and services delivered. The MP attempted to revolutionize, with some success, the concept of government and citizen, and the attitudes of one to the other. Especially at the municipal level there emerged energetic MP mayors, casting an image of "getting things done" and "listening and being responsive" to the demands and problems of citizens. Some of them are attempting to change the face of Turkish cities.[27]

The challenge that came from the TPP was not on issues concerning economic policy. After all the January 24, 1980 Economic Measures adopted by Demirel's last JP government have been the basis of Özal's economic policies. Judging by past JP policies, a TPP government might be more sensitive to the fortunes of the agricultural sector as opposed to the urban emphasis of the MP. Perhaps income redistribution and unemployment might carry more weight with the TPP leadership. The differences in terms of economic policy, however, do not appear to be crucially important.

The major challenge from the TPP came on constitutional issues and more generally on civil-military relations, an area where the platform put forward by Demirel and the TPP was expected to appeal to constituencies beyond the right as a rallying point for those who would like to limit the role of the military in Turkish politics. The Constitutional Referendum of September 6, 1987 on the issue of the restoration of the political rights of political party leaders of the 1970s somewhat defused the importance of this constitutional issue. The country was almost divided evenly, with only a slight majority approving the lifting of the ban. All the parties, except the MP, campaigned for a *yes* vote to end the ban. The MP campaigned actively for a *no* vote, and the close vote was treated as a political success by the MP leadership[28] prompting a decision for early elections in November 1987.

The evolution of Turkish politics between the elections of 1983 and 1987 tends to lend support to our findings that the MP may have emerged as a new party taking advantage of the void created by the absence of the old parties and of the electorate's wish to have a democratic and relatively grass-roots, center-right alternative, given the choice they had in 1983. By steering clear of ideological and partisan conflict and by addressing new sets of issues in a changing and urbanising Turkey through dynamic leadership both at the national and local levels, the MP has become a major party of the right despite strong opposition from the old guard.

---

[27] See Üstün Ergüder, "Decentralization of Local Government and Turkish Political Culture," in *Democracy and Local Government: Istanbul in the 1980s*, edited by Metin Heper (Walkington, England, Eothen Press, 1987).

[28] Turgut Özal repeated on several occasions that the Referendum helped the MP prove that it was a political party.

Chapter 8
Political Leadership in Turkey: Continuity and Change

Frank Tachau

1 Introduction

This chapter provides an analysis of the social and political background of the members of the Grand National Assembly, or parliament, of Turkey (TGNA). Some comparisons with pre-1980 parliamentarians are also presented, thus highlighting continuity and change in political leadership.

Social and political background data provide useful insights concerning elite groups. In a sense, such data provide a snapshot of the structure of the political elite at a certain point or points in time. The analysis need not be static, however. One can get a sense of the dynamics of change by comparing similar data from different points in time and noting the changes which appear. At the very least, such changes indicate the shifts in the character of the elite. One may also infer that they reflect changes in career paths to the top of the political system. Changes of this sort may or may not coincide with other indicators of change in the political and/or social system, such as voter alignments or class cleavages.

If shifts in background characteristics of elites coincide with such other indicators of change, our understanding of the dynamics of social and political change will be enhanced. If they do not coincide (that is, if elite background characteristics change but such other indicators as aggregate voting alignments remain stable), we may infer that such surface indicators as aggregate measures, which show stability, are misleading. In other words, instead of merely observing the placid surface of an apparently calm sea, we may put on our social science snorkel, as it were, and observe the remarkable complex of shifting social and political elements below the surface. As Rustow observed in comparing elite analysis to the study of political institutions: "while constitutions and other formal arrangements would project a false image of stability, individuals and groups can be seen as a 'binding link' from regime to regime."[1] The reverse may also be true, of course: there may be sharp shifts on the surface (for example, in the electoral balance between right and left parties) while background characteristics of the elite remain stable. Such a combination of indicators would suggest elements of continuity in an apparently unstable system. In short, it is inadequate to simply observe aggregate voting statistics and conclude that the Turkish political system has not changed in 35 years simply because the current balance between right and left parties remains approximately what it was when democratic politics began in 1946. It is also important to note the limits of background analysis. As I have stated elsewhere:

> The weakness of analysis based solely on such [background] data is that it cannot in and of itself explain value commitments or policy outcomes to which the elite members in question may contribute, nor the behavior patterns to which they adhere. Therefore, social background data must be linked with available evidence concerning the value commitments of elite members. Where direct evidence is not available, patterns of socialization and recruitment, particularly through formal educational institutions, may provide indirect indicators which are more readily available, particularly in societies where such institutions possess fairly well defined cultural and behavioral norms of their own, and where they provide clear channels of access to elite status.[2]

Significantly, one of the hallmarks of social and political change in Turkey over the last 40 years is reflected precisely in the institutions referred to here, and in their relationship to the political elite of parliamentarians. In the first two decades of the Republic, the membership of the TGNA was dominated by former civil servants or bureaucrats. A large proportion of these individuals had been educated at the Political Science Faculty in Ankara (Siyasal Bilgiler Fakültesi). The socialization impact of this institution on its students and alumni was magnified by the fact that it was an elite institution in a system in which there were only a very small number of institutions of higher education of any kind. In more recent years, by contrast, former bureaucrats have no longer predominated among members of the TGNA. Moreover, the Political Science Faculty became only one among a much expanded number of institutions through which TGNA members had passed, reflecting the massive expansion of the entire system of higher education. Consequently, the membership of the

---

[1] Dankwart A. Rustow, "The Study of Elites: Who's Who, When and How," *World Politics* 18 (1966), pp. 690–717.

[2] Frank Tachau, "Introduction: Political Elites and Political Development in the Middle East," in *Political Elites and Political Development in the Middle East*, edited by F. Tachau (New York, John Wiley, 1975), p. 10.

TGNA reflected great changes in the socialization patterns of Turkish society; and these changes were also reflected in the regime changes in 1950, 1960, 1971, and 1980.

The following analysis reflects these changes only in abbreviated form. Our data do not provide indicators of the value commitments or behavior patterns of TGNA members. Such indicators were not available when these data were gathered. Fortunately, however, the work of Ersin Kalaycıoğlu, as exemplified by his contribution to this volume, helps mightily to fill this gap. Although it is clearly misleading to infer a direct causal link between changes in social backgrounds and the kind of unruly behavior he documents, one may infer that the failure of the TGNA to develop stable institutional norms (which is cited by Kalaycıoğlu as a probable underlying cause of unruly behavior) is not unrelated to changing social patterns among the members.

2 The 1983 Grand National Assembly

The Grand National Assembly elected in November of 1983 differs from earlier Assemblies in several respects. First, unlike the parliaments of the 1960s and 1970s, the new Assembly is once again a unicameral body, as was the TGNA from 1920 to 1960. This makes little difference for purposes of analysis, since the defunct Senate was much less salient politically then the "lower" house; moreover, no personal background data on members of the Senate have thus far been collated and analysed. Second, the size of the Assembly has been reduced from the previous 450 seats to 400. This should not significantly affect our analysis, either. Third, some of the more populous provinces were subdivided into two or more constituencies. Since this change involved primarily the larger urban areas, it may have affected the balance of urban/rural representation. Such effects might have manifested themselves in electoral outcomes (which are the subject of the chapter by Ergüder and Hofferbert), but they could also conceivably have impinged on the nature of the membership of the TGNA. Our data have not yet been analysed in sufficient depth to reveal such effects. Finally, and most important, the election of the members of the 1983 TGNA was hardly an exercise in unfettered democracy. The details of that election need not detain us here. Suffice it to say that the military junta maintained tight control over the entire process, beginning with the certification of the parties, as well as their lists of candidates, and including the regulation of the campaign. (In fact, General Evren committed his personal prestige at the very end of the campaign in an apparently futile effort to affect the outcome directly.) Even after the election had taken place, it was unclear for a brief period whether the junta would permit the newly elected parliamentarians to convene. These constraints may well have affected the nature of the membership of the new TGNA, as we shall have occassion to point out.

We turn now to an examination of the composition of the 1983 TGNA. One of the indicators of social background is occupation. We have grouped occupational categories under four over-all rubrics, three major and one residual. The results are shown in Table 1.

Table 1 Occupations

Occupation	Number	Per cent
Professional	174	44
Official	145	36
Economic	154	39
Other	52	13

Notes: Numbers exceed actual membership and percentages total more than 100 due to the fact that the foregoing were calculated from a base of multiple responses. Occupational categories are: Professional: medicine, law, engineering, pharmacy, architecture; Official: military, civil service, education, judge and prosecutor, diplomat; Economic: all private enterprise; Other: miscellaneous, including journalism and union officials. These results differ from those reported by Kalaycıoğlu ("Elites, Political Culture and the Political Regime in Turkey," paper presented at the Annual Meetings of the Middle East Studies Association, San Francisco, 1984), possibly because of his inclusion of economists in the professional category and his identification of religious functionaries as a separate category.

In the 1983 TGNA, the proportion of professionals remained roughly the same as in all post-1950 sessions (except 1957).[3] However, lawyers were considerably less prominent (down from 26-34 per cent between 1961 and 1977 to only 17 per cent, while engineers rose to about one-sixth (16.6 per cent); they are the second most numerous occupational category, virtually equal to the number of lawyers. By contrast, those in official positions increased to the highest level since 1946. While civil servants constituted the largest single group in this category (63, or 16 per cent), those involved in education remained at roughly the level they had attained during the 1970s (46 or 11.5 per cent in 1983 vs. 13 per cent earlier). Religious functionaries almost disappeared from the 1983 TGNA; they had

[3] Frank Tachau, "Parliamentary Elites: Turkey," in *Electoral Politics in the Middle East: Issues, Voters and Elites,* edited by Jacob Landau, Ergun Özbudun and Frank Tachau (London, Croom Helm, 1980), pp. 205-242 and Ergun Özbudun, "Parliamentary Elites: Comparisons," in *Ibid.*, pp. 299-313.

accounted for 4-5 per cent of the membership during the 1970s. It is also worth noting that the proportion of former military officers appears to have risen in the 1983 TGNA: while only 25 (5 per cent) report a military career, a total of 42 (11 per cent) report having attended military educational institutions. Economic occupations rose to the highest level in the history of the TGNA, as did the remaining miscellaneous occupations.[4]

Educational experience provides another rough indicator of social background. The data for the 1983 TGNA are shown in Table 2.

Table 2 Educational backgrounds

Highest level attained	Per cent
Intermediate (0-8 years)	6
Secondary	15
Post-secondary	79
(University)	(67)

The figures in Table 2 show a slight shift in educational backgrounds from earlier sessions. Since the establishment of the TGNA in 1920, university-educated deputies accounted for roughly 70 to 75 per cent of the membership of each session.[5] University-educated members of the 1983 TGNA account for a somewhat smaller percentage; but when all post-secondary institutions are included, the percentage is somewhat higher. This may reflect the growth of the Turkish educational system, specifically rising proportions of post-secondary-level institutions and graduates. Changes in the organizational structure of the educational system (such as the designation of economic and commercial academies as universities) may affect these figures in future sessions of the TGNA. The drop in the proportion of members with secondary or less education may also reflect the higher educational requirements specified for TGNA members in the new Constitution as well as the Evren regime's predilections (that is, the regime may have vetoed those who were perceived as deficient in this respect).

Educational background in Turkey today is not quite as reliable a guide to social status and structure as it was in the early days of the TGNA, when there were only a handful of institutions of higher education. Among these, the Political Science Faculty, which became part of the University of Ankara in 1946, was the undisputed leader in producing po-

[4] For comparisons see Tachau, "Parliamentary Elites: Turkey," p. 206, Table 9.1 and Frederick W. Frey, *The Turkish Political Elite* (Cambridge, MIT Press, 1965), p. 181, Table 7.5.

[5] See Tachau, "Parliamentary Elites: Turkey," p. 219, Table 9.4 and Frey, *The Turkish Political Elite*, p. 176, Fig. 7.2.

tential members of the political elite. It tended to predominate among members of the TGNA as well. Since those days, however, the system of higher education has expanded dramatically; concomitantly, the Political Science Faculty has receded as a producer of the political elite to the point at which its alumni constitute only a small proportion of TGNA membership. This is a reflection of the increasing complexity and fragmentation of the Turkish political elite. In the past, the products of higher education, small in number and the products of a single, rather unique, socialization experience, tended to form a cohesive social and political elite. Higher education today produces a much larger and more varied set of graduates who tend to form smaller, more discrete groups. In a real sense, Turkey now has a number of competing elite groups whose identities are only partially formed by their educational experiences.

By comparison with previous sessions, the 1983 TGNA is almost bereft of members with previous experience in the parliament or comparable bodies such as the Constituent Assembly of 1961 and the Consultative Assembly of 1981-1983 (Table 3).

Table 3 Previous membership in the TGNA

Session	Per cent	
	(GNA only)	(including other bodies)
1920	23	–
1931	71	–
1946	59	–
1950	19	–
1957	47	–
1961	16	30
1965	49	50
1969	47	51
1973	43	46
1977	53	53
1983	9	15

Sources: for 1920-1950: Frey, *The Turkish Political Elite,* p.164, Table 7.1; 1957: Kâzım Öztürk,
TBMM Albümü, 1920-1973 (Ankara, Önder Matbaası, 1973); 1961-1973: Tachau, "Parliamentary Elites in Turkey," p.224, Table 9.9; 1977-1983: data files

Table 3 shows that there is a far smaller percentage of members with parliamentary experience in the 1983 session than in any session in the history of the TGNA. This includes both the 1920 and 1961 sessions, both of which inaugurated new regimes, the former a revolutionary one. The 1973 session also stands out in that the percentage of members with no previous parliamentary experience dropped, though it rose again in 1977.

This undoubtedly reflects the "realignment" of 1973,[6] specifically the leftward swing and new leadership of the RPP as well as the appearance of two new parties on the scene. Apparently a significant proportion of these new deputies were re-elected in 1977.

The extreme outcome in 1983 undoubtedly resulted from the total ban imposed by the Evren junta on politicians who had been active in the last elected TGNA prior to the 1980 coup; by contrast, the National Unity Committee in 1961 barred only members of the Democrat Party of the 1950s from competing for national office. Perhaps of yet greater significance, even the revolutionary regime launched by Atatürk in 1920 included a leavening of individuals with previous experience in parliamentary bodies. It is possible that the Evren junta excluded candidates with previous parliamentary experience of almost any kind from competing in the 1983 elections through its veto power. Generally, it would seem unwise to exclude politically experienced individuals in such a systematic way. In fact, it is at least conceivable that the low level of political experience may have contributed to the authoritarian atmosphere of the new TGNA, at least during its first year of existence.[7] Kalaycıoğlu emphasizes this point also, noting the absence of virtually any political experience among the members of this session of the TGNA. As we have noted here, this is neither the result of "natural" political forces, nor even an unintended result of a political initiative designed to achieve some other objective. It is the direct consequence of a deliberate effort to exclude experienced politicians from playing an active role in the post-1980 Turkish parliament. We shall return to this point in our conclusion.

Age of TGNA members may be associated with previous parliamentary experience in that, by and large, more experienced deputies ought to be older than less experienced ones. This assumption suggests that 1983 TGNA members should be much younger than those of previous sessions. As Table 4 indicates however, the opposite is the case.

Table 4 indicates that new regimes in Turkey have generally brought younger men into the TGNA. This tendency was especially evident in 1920 and 1961.[8] Although it was not true of the TGNA as a body in 1973, two of the major parties in that session which particularly reflected the electoral realigment of that year did elect markedly younger deputies.[9] It

---

[6] Ergun Özbudun and Frank Tachau, "Social Change and Electoral Behavior in Turkey: Toward a 'Critical Realignment'?" *International Journal of Middle East Studies* 6 (1975), pp. 460–480.

[7] This at least was the perception of a TGNA member belonging to the Nationalist Democracy Party during the summer of 1984, as told to this writer.

[8] Frey, *The Turkish Political Elite*, p. 170, Table 7.2 and p. 172, Fig. 7.1; Tachau, "Parliamentary Elites: Turkey", p. 222, Table 9.7.

[9] *Ibid.*, p. 234, Table 9.16.

Table 4 Average age

Session	Average age	Session	Average age
1920	43	1961	43
1931	48	1965	45
1943	54	1969	45
1950	48	1973	45
1954	47	1977	46
1957	46	1983	49

Sources: for 1920-1954: Frey, *The Turkish Political Elite,* p.170, Table 7.2; 1957: Öztürk, *TBMM Albümü, 1920-1973,* 1961-1973; Tachau, "Parliamentary Elites in Turkey," p.222, Table 9.7; 1977-1983: data files

is also noteworthy that the age curve for TGNA members rose from the mid-40s to the mid-50s between 1920 and 1943, then sank gradually through the 1950s back to the mid-40s, where it remained throughout the 1960s and 1970s.[10] Thus, the average age of 1983 TGNA members is about the same as in the late 1940s and early 1950s. These figures do not support the conclusion that the Evren regime harbored an "age prejudice" when it approved the lists of candidates for election. In any event, the Turkish parliament has tended to have younger members on average than legislatures in other countries, including those in the Middle East.[11]

However, if we break TGNA members down by three rough age groups, a somewhat different picture emerges (Table 5). In Table 5, it appears that age prejudice may in fact have been at work in the composition of the 1983 session of the TGNA. The oldest age group (those over 60 at the time of election) are more prominent than at any time since 1961, while those in the middle age group (35-60 years of age) are less prominent. Interestingly, the youngest age group (those under 35) is of roughly the same proportion as during the 1960s and 1970s; only the 1961 session stands out on this score.

Thus, the 1983 session of the TGNA is not only the least politically experienced parliament in the history of the Turkish Republic, but also one of the oldest in terms of its members' ages. This is not an auspicious omen. Lack of political experience can be overcome through individual and collective learning processes. Older members, however, have less time to learn; they are more likely to leave the TGNA just as they will have acquired the experience requisite for the development of stable institutional norms. This underlines Kalaycıoğlu's observation (in this volume)

---

[10] *Ibid.*, p.306, Fig.12.1.

[11] Jean Blondel, *Comparative Legislatures* (Englewood Cliffs, N.J., Prentice Hall, 1973), Appendix C.

Table 5 Age groupings

Session	Over 60 per cent	35–60 per cent	Under 35 per cent
1961	6	76	19
1965	6	86	9
1969	4	88	8
1973	3	86	11
1977	4	86	10
1983	14	73	12

that the TGNA faces a prolonged period of institutionalization in the near future.

Turkey remains a marrying society, and the TGNA deputies reflect this characteristic, as they have since the beginnings of the institution.[12] Since 1950, more than 90 per cent of the members have been married; in 1983 once again, the figure is 95.2 per cent (to which we may add another 2.3 per cent who are widowed, for a total of 97.5 per cent who are or have been married).

Data on family size is a better indicator of traditionalism (or modernism). Large families are more common in traditional societies and therefore may be taken as an indicator of traditionalism. Whether or not individuals who head large families have more traditional values or attitudes than those who head smaller families is, of course, not certain. In the aggregate, however, it should not be surprising if a body such as the TGNA were to manifest values and policy preferences which reflected the social environment from which its members emerged. Family size may be a rough indicator of the character of that environment.

In fact, throughout the history of the TGNA, family size has fluctuated somewhat. The average number of children per member dropped from a high of 2.8 in the 1927 session to a low of 2.4 in 1954. From 1961 on, the figure rose again to 2.8 in 1973, dropping slightly to 2.7 in 1977. In the 1983 session, the average number of children has fallen back to 2.4.

Once again, if we divide the deputies into discrete groups, a clearer picture emerges (Table 6).

Large families were much more prominent in the early sessions of the TGNA than in later years. Significantly, the proportion of large families continued to decline until the 1969 session, when there was a sharp surge upwards, followed by renewed decline. By 1983, the proportion is back down to the level registered in 1961. Small families, on the other hand, declined consistently from 1961 on, reaching an apparent plateau just below

[12] Frey, *The Turkish Political Elite*, p. 174, Table 7.3.

20 per cent in 1977. At the same time, middle-sized families remained quite stable during the 1960s and through 1973, but then increased sharply to 62 per cent in 1977 and even further to 66 per cent in 1983. If this is an accurate indicator of elite behavior, and if elite behavior sets the tone for - or, conversely, reflects - mass behavior, we may observe here a trend toward middle-sized families of two to three children in Turkish society. In this sense, we may characterize the fluctuations in family size over the years as possibly reflecting a tension between values of modernism and traditionalism in society. It would, however, be rash to conclude that the 1983 TGNA is more "modern" than its predecessors simply because its members, on average, have smaller families. Among other things, we must remember that entry into this body was rather tightly controlled by an authoritarian elite at the outset.

Table 6 Family size

Session	Number of Children		
	0–1 per cent	2–3 per cent	more than 3 per cent
1927	–	–	31
1946	–	–	26
1950	–	–	21
1954	–	–	17
1961	33	52	15
1965	26	53	13
1969	27	52	22
1973	23	54	24
1977	18	62	20
1983	19	66	15

Source: for pre-1961 sessions: Frey, *The Turkish Political Elite,* p. 175 n

Finally, with regard to this variable, there is evidence that family size among parliamentarians may be related to the level of socio-economic development of these constituencies; it takes the form of a clear association between family size and the level of development in the constituencies. Moreover, the difference between more and less developed constituencies increased over time between 1961 and 1973. Thus, we are able to say that the increase in the average number of children per deputy from 1961 to 1973 was largely due to representatives of less-developed constituencies. This would seem to reinforce the point we have just made regarding the relation between parliamentarians' family size and the character of the society which they represent.[13]

[13] Tachau, "Parliamentary Elites: Turkey," p. 222, Table 9.8

Table 7 Localism

Session	Locally born (per cent)	Session	Locally born (per cent)
1920	62	1965	60
1935	34	1969	75
1950	60	1973	74
1954	62	1977	72
1957	66	1983	66
1961	69		

Source: for 1920-1957: Frey, *The Turkish Political Elite,* pp.187-9; 1961-1973: Tachau, "Parliamentary Elites in Turkey," p.221, Table 9.6; 1977-1983; 1977-1983: data files

Another interesting indicator is localism, defined as the proportion of deputies born in the constituency which they represent (Table 7).

As Frey has pointed out, the curve of localism reflects the development of the Turkish party system with remarkable accuracy. During the lifetime of Kemal Atatürk, the proportion of locally born deputies dropped by almost one-half. This was the period during which the one-party regime reached its apex. In Frey's words, this decline

> portrays the development and rise of the Kemalist movement, a modernizing elite resting heavily on officers and bureaucrats who were primarily national, nationalistic, and political in their social outlook. After the death of Atatürk [in 1938] the always latent opposition gathers enough strength to compel its reluctant recognition, and then finally breaks openly into power with the introduction of the multiparty system in 1946 and the victory of the Democrats in 1950. The change is reflected in the rising localism curve following the Fifth Assembly (1935). The dominant composition of the top political leadership now has become legal and commercial in occupation, local in origin, and localistic and economic in social outlook.[14]

Frey concludes that "as the parties have moved into a situation of true interparty competition - a situation of increased need for popular support and simultaneous uncertainty regarding this support - there has been an acute rise in localism within all the political parties of Turkey ..."[15]

Table 7 indicates that the upward curve of localism continued into the 1960s (with a temporary dip in 1965) and reached new peaks in 1969 and 1973. Seen in this context, the level of localism in 1983 appears to be about average for Turkish multi-party regimes, although it marks a sharp drop from the level of immediately preceding sessions. It is difficult to say

[14] Frey, *The Turkish Political Elite,* pp.188-189.
[15] *Ibid.,* p.192.

how influential the selection processes within the parties or the exercise of the regime's veto power were in determining this outcome. It appears, however, that the appeal to local interests remains strong in the Turkish electoral system.

It is also interesting to note that while Frey found that the more highly developed Western constituencies manifested a higher degree of localism during the one-party era than less developed ones, the reverse has been true since at least 1961. Frey attributed this outcome to a combination of factors involving the nature of the one-party regime, geographic distribution of elite elements, and the commitment or opposition of both elites and masses to the regime's modernization policies. Our figures for the period from 1961 to 1977 suggest that this explanation may not fully apply to this period. Nevertheless, there appears to be a link between localism and level of socio-economic development of constituencies, for these two factors are inversely correlated, especially in 1973. If this reflects, as it may, a continuing geographical maldistribution of elite elements, as Frey suggested for the earlier period, then the TGNA may in fact have harbored proportionately more "modern" individuals than society as a whole. Further analysis is required to determine whether this relationship persisted in 1983.

It is also notable that the relative standing of the parties in terms of localism remained unchanged between 1950 and 1969 (that is, the Democrat Party and Justice Party showed a lower level of localism during those years than did the RPP). In 1969 and 1973, the two large parties were roughly equally locally based; but it is perhaps significant that in 1973 for the first time, the JP had a higher proportion of locally born deputies than the RPP - or, for that matter, any other party. On this point, too, we have not been able to extend our analysis of the 1983 parliamentarians.

3 Conclusion

What can we conclude from these background data? Do they tell us anything about the degree of change or continuity among leaders in Turkey since the 1980 military coup?

First, to sum up our findings, the members of the 1983 TGNA do not differ radically from their predecessors. This is not to say that there are no observable differences in background characteristics. The 1983 session includes more representatives of business and commercial groups, more officials, is better educated, somewhat older, with more intermediate-sized families, somewhat less locally rooted, and has virtually no political experience. What do these differences mean?

Before we attempt to answer this question, we should note that significant changes in the background characteristics of elite groups may come about gradually, over extended periods of time. One might expect an exception in the case of a deep-seated revolutionary upheaval following a period of stability in an aging and entrenched elite. In such a situation, the old elite would not reflect changes in social background, values and attitudes, and behavior patterns which had occurred in society at large. Sharp differences could then be evident between the old elite and its replacements.

No such revolutionary upheaval occurred in Turkey in 1980. Hence it is not surprising that we find no great differences between the TGNA members elected in 1983 and those of prior years. The greatest change we have noted in this chapter is with regard to the deputies' previous parliamentary experience. As was already indicated, this probably reflects the Evren regime's deep antipathy against the politicians of the old order. General Evren himself used strong rhetoric when he portrayed these politicians as being primarily responsible for the chaos and disorder of the late 1970s.[16] But, as has been pointed out in the foregoing discussion, the Evren regime may have thrown out the baby with the bathwater. For political experience is essential to political institutionalization; and it is difficult to conceive of political stability without institutionalization. The regime was perhaps well advised to seek parliamentarians untainted by the bitter partisan divisions of the 1970s. But in applying a wholesale prohibition on *all* members of the 1977 TGNA, and possibly using its veto power selectively to ban others with previous parliamentary experience, the regime may well have undermined its own good intentions. Elected politicians have a strong defense against the charge that they were solely - or even primarily - responsible for the ills of the "bad old days": they were, after all, brought to power by the free will of the electorate, that is, they represented constituents. In other words, perhaps the political divisions in parliament were an accurate reflection of the political divisions of the society as a whole. The solution then would seem to be to remove the institutional obstacles to effective government, but not necessarily the individuals involved.

In most respects other than political experience, the members of the 1983 TGNA closely resemble their predecessors. There is even continuity in some of the trends observed earlier, particularly in the increased proportions of engineers and those with business and commercial backgrounds. This is, of course, epitomized by the current Prime Minister who, despite his earlier association with the quasi-traditional National Salva-

[16] Frank Tachau and Metin Heper, "The State, Politics and the Military in Turkey," *Comparative Politics* 16 (1983), pp. 17-33.

tion Party, projects a strong image of technocratic expertise, political pragmatism, and avoidance of ideological or partisan extremism. At the same time, his programs of bureaucratic reform and extensive scaling down of governmental control of the economy should resonate with the continuing rise in influence of the political periphery at the expense of the old center. Ironically, this program is being implemented under the aegis of the most forceful of the old centrist elite elements: the military.

This raises an interesting question: to what extent does the 1983 TGNA reflect the military's vision of the ideal parliament? One might assume, on the one hand, that it must be a group of individuals closely embodying such a vision, in as much as the regime had ample opportunity to veto objectionable candidates, and appears to have used that opportunity to a maximum. The virtual disappearance of religious functionaries and the reappearance of former military officers and civil bureaucrats among the parliamentarians suggest a military bias of this sort. On the other hand, the party which won an absolute majority in the new TGNA did so virtually in open defiance of General Evren personally. From this perspective, one might infer that the new parliament is not at all what the military expected or desired.

It may be helpful to recall that the military cannot be totally unaffected by the Turkish experience of democracy. After all, free competitive politics have been the rule in Turkey for three and a half decades. Thus, even the most senior military officers have served out virtually all of their careers under democratic regimes. Moreover, even though the military have experienced frustration in their attempts to solve some of the most critical problems of Turkish democracy, they have also gained a certain degree of political sophistication and skill of their own. So far, at least, they have retained a basic commitment to democratic norms and procedures. Their political preferences have also evolved to the point at which they no longer insist on the domination of the traditional statist economic and social policies of the earlier days of the Republic, despite the repeated and exaggerated evocation of the symbol of the great Kemal Atatürk. Perhaps this concatenation of factors explains General Evren's willingness to abide by the outcome of the 1983 elections, as it may explain his earlier continuing support of the economic austerity plan imposed by the Demirel government in January of 1980 and orchestrated by the same Turgut Özal who now heads the government.

But it is also important to recall that partisan politicians have not yet regained full control of the Turkish political system, and may not for many years to come. The military retains effective authority over national security and matters of public order as well as such critical institutions as the universities. Should new political crises arise, no one can predict with assurance the future behavior of the Turkish military. Should they lose faith in democracy as a guiding principle for political life in Turkey, then possibly the TGNA may survive as a formal political institution, but neither social background analysis nor attitudinal nor yet behavioral analysis will reveal much about the actual allocation of political authority.

Chapter 9
The State, Politics, and Religion in Turkey

Binnaz Toprak

1 The State and Civil Society in Turkey

The relationship of the state to civil society has been among the most salient issues for students of Turkish politics in the past few decades.[1] The state-society dichotomy has only recently been perceived as a serious political question in a country with a long tradition of a dominant state controlling the social fabric of a multi-religious and multi-ethnic empire. The patrimonial authority of the Ottoman state did not allow for the development of a civil society and the emergence of an autonomous class which could play a leading role in modernization. Rather, modernization efforts in the Ottoman and later in the Republican periods were carried out by the leadership of the military and civil bureaucratic cadres. The role of the state as a spearhead of modernization even extended to include the creation of a Muslim-Turkish bourgeoisie which would be dependent upon state economic activity and develop under its protective wings.[2] Given this background, the Ottoman as well as early Republican intellectuals and statesmen, with few exceptions, were more concerned with strengthening the state than with the question of bringing limits to state power.

---

[1] See, for example, Şerif Mardin, "Power, Civil Society and Culture in the Ottoman Empire," *Comparative Studies in Society and History* 11 (1969), pp. 258-281 and "Center-Periphery Relations: A Key to Turkish Politics?" *Daedalus* 102 (1973), pp. 169-190; Metin Heper, "Center and Periphery in the Ottoman Empire with Special Reference to the Nineteenth Century," *International Political Science Review* 1 (1980), pp. 81-105 and *The State Tradition in Turkey* (Walkington, England, Eothen Press, 1985); İlkay Sunar and Sabri Sayarı, "Problems of Democratic Politics in Turkey," *Transitions from Authoritarian Rule: Experiences in Southern Europe* edited by Guillermo O'Donnell, P. Schmitter, and L. Whitehead (Baltimore, Johns Hopkins University Press, 1986).

[2] See Zafer Toprak, *Türkiye'de 'Milli İktisat': 1908-1919* (Ankara, Yurt Yayınları, 1982).

Hence, the interest in the cleavage between the center and the periphery, between the state and civil society, and more recently, revived discussions of nineteenth-century Western liberal thought among the Turkish intelligentsia has something more to it than pure academic curiosity. After four decades of experiment with democracy, Turkish intellectuals had to face the question, which Metin Heper pertinently asks in his introductory chapter in this volume, concerning the difficulties involved "in the transition to democracy in those settings with a state tradition."[3] Intermittent military interventions and the ensuing reassertion, each time, of the state's dominance over many institutions of civil society has brought the question to the agenda of both scholarly and political debate.

This chapter will limit the wider discussion to only one institution of civil society, namely, that of religion.[4] Religion in Turkey, especially during the formative years of the Turkish Republic, has been the most important centrifugal force with a potential to challenge the state. It is partly for this reason that the separation of religion and state was never attempted in its Western version as orthodox Islam was put under state control and made subservient to state authority.[5]

That, however, is only part of the picture. Although orthodox, Sunni institutions became appendices of the state apparatus with their personnel functioning as civil servants, the state was unable to control folk Islam organized around various *tarikats* (religious orders) despite the legal ban on their existence since 1925. Hence, religion has been an important issue for the state elite throughout the single-party period (1923-1946) as well as during the years of party competition after the inception of democratic politics in 1946 and up to this day. In fact, not only religion but ethnicity and class conflict have also been among the priority list of concerns for the state elite, who view group solidarity as a potential cause for the disintegration of the state. For example, under republican solidarism as state ideology, the legitimacy of class interests was for long years denied,[6] and the state would not officially recognize ethnic or sectarian groups.

Such fear is not totally unfounded as the near-civil war situation prior to the 1980 military intervention attests. However, the military's frequent

---

[3] See Chap. 1 in this volume.

[4] For an interpretation of Islamic politics in Turkey from the vantage point of the state and centralist elites see İlkay Sunar and Binnaz Toprak, "Islam in Politics: The Case of Turkey," *Government and Opposition* 18 (1983), pp. 421-441.

[5] On the question of the separation of religion and state in the Turkish Republic see Binnaz Toprak, *Islam and Political Development in Turkey* (Leiden, E.J. Brill, 1981), Chap. 3.

[6] See Zafer Toprak, "2. Meşrutiyette Solidarist Düşünce: Halkçılık," *Toplum ve Bilim* 2 (1977), pp. 92-123; and "Halkçılık İdeolojisinin Oluşumu," *Atatürk Döneminin Ekonomik ve Toplumsal Sorunları*, edited by İktisadi ve Ticari Bilimler Akademisi Mezunları Derneği, (İstanbul, Murat Matbaacılık, 1977), pp. 13-31.

involvement in politics and the subsequent change of regimes, constitutions, and laws work to the detriment of civil society and install a yet stronger state-dominant polity. The result, as would be expected, has been a setback for the development of an open and democratic system, the smothering of the nascent civil society, and the reinforcement of a political culture where individual expectations are geared toward the state.

2 Religion and the State in Turkey

As Şerif Mardin points out, the religious heterogeneity of the Ottoman Empire was a constant source of concern for Ottoman statesmen.[7] The Ottoman bureaucrats attempted to control dissident religious movements through cooptation, deportation, or outright suppression. At the same time, orthodox Sunni Islam was put under state control. As early as the Classical Period (fourteenth to sixteenth centuries), the Ottoman *ulema* (Doctors of Islamic Law) were incorporated into the state bureaucracy through a vast network of central and provincial offices. Within the administrative structure of the Ottoman state, the *ulema* occupied important educational, judicial, and religious posts.[8]

Beginning with the nineteenth century, the Ottoman state began to disengage itself from the authority of Islam and its clergy. As Pierre Birnbaum argues, the separation of church and state in France after the Revolution, including secular control over education, was an important step in the building of the French state and the inception of what he calls a "state political system".[9] Similarly, secularization attempts of the Tanzimat era (1839-1876) gradually weakened the authority of the *ulema* and of Islam in the socio-political life of the Empire, particularly at the level of the westernized elite cadres. The process culminated in the complete withdrawal of power from the *ulema* after the establishment of the Turkish Republic in 1923. This meant, in effect, that the only alternate locus of power to state authority was now under the control of a sovereign state.

In general, the Ottoman patrimonial bureaucracy was careful to keep

---

[7] Şerif Mardin, "Religion and Secularism in Turkey," in *Atatürk: Founder of a Modern State,* edited by Ali Kazancıgil and Ergun Özbudun (London, C. Hurst, 1981), pp. 191-219.

[8] See Niyazi Berkes, *The Development of Secularism in Turkey* (Montreal, McGill University Press, 1964), pp. 9-10.

[9] Pierre Birnbaum, "State, Centre and Bureaucracy," *Government and Opposition* 16 (1981), pp. 58-77.

institutions of civil society under control the moment those institutions began to attain some autonomy from the state. As Şerif Mardin has argued, the attitude of the Ottoman bureaucracy toward kinship and other social groups was to see them as sources of disintegration. Hence, group solidarity was viewed with suspicion and any source of power that could potentially become differentiated was stopped short of gaining greater autonomy.[10]

The secularization process of the Turkish Republic strengthened state authority and control over orthodox Sunni institutions and religious functionaries. One of the major aims of the Kemalist reforms was to substitute Western culture for the Islamic/Ottoman, and in so doing, Kemalism tried to break down both the institutional strength of Islam and the symbolic structure of society. The authoritarianism of the single-party years was conducive to introducing reforms from above, and indeed, the institutionalization of secularism at the level of the polity was firmly established by 1946.[11]

Since the establishment of the Republic, the organization of orthodox Islam has been under the jurisdiction of the Presidency of Religious Affairs (PRA: *Diyanet İşleri Başkanlığı*). The President of Religious Affairs is appointed by the Council of Ministers upon the nomination of the Prime Minister. The PRA has offices *(müftülük)* both at the province *(il)* and subprovince *(ilçe)* levels. The *müftüs* control the administration of the religious institutions under their jurisdiction and supervise all religious services. The teachers, textbooks, and curricula of all religious schools, whose graduates staff the PRA, are under the supervision of the Directorate-General of Religious Education *(Din Eğitimi Genel Müdürlüğü)* which is a separate office within the Ministry of Education. Hence, as civil servants, approximately 52,000 personnel of the PRA function under direct state control.

The Turkish state also tries to prevent religious propaganda through various statutes. Articles 14, 24, and 68 of the 1982 Constitution; Articles 163, 241, and 242 of the Turkish Criminal Code; and various articles of the Political Parties Law of 1983 and the Law of Associations of 1983 forbid the use of religion for political purposes or for private gain as did the provisions of earlier constitutions and laws. A large number of individuals have received court sentences for violating Article 163 of the

---

[10] Mardin, "Power, Civil Society and Culture in the Ottoman Empire,", p.276.

[11] For the institutionalization of secularism in the Turkish Republic see Binnaz Toprak, "Die Institutionalisierung des Laizismus in der türkischen Republik," in *Jahrbuch zur Geschichte und Gesellschaft des Vorderen und Mittleren Orients: 1984 Thema: Islam und Politik in der Türkei,* edited by Jochen Blaschke and M. van Bruinessen (Berlin, Express Edition, 1985), pp.95–108, translated by Jutta Aumüller.

Criminal Code[12] and five political parties have been outlawed since the establishment of the Republic for violations of these various laws.[13]

3 Development of Democratic Politics

The strict secularization program of the single-party period led to a partial relaxation after the inception of democratic politics in 1946. Between 1945 and 1950, eight political parties were established with explicit religious themes in their programs.[14] All, except the Nation Party (NP: *Millet Partisi*) were obscure organizations which disappeared from the political arena by 1950. The 1946-1960 period was characterized by the conflict over the interpretation of secularism between the Republican People's Party (RPP: *Cumhuriyet Halk Partisi*), in power during the single-party years, and the Democrat Party (DP: *Demokrat Parti*) which won the first free elections in 1950 and stayed in power until ousted from office by the military in 1960.

Throughout the 1950s, the Democrats were accused by the opposition for their policies alleged to undermine the secular principles of the Republic in an effort to gain votes. The minor revisions of policy that they implemented, such as the lifting of the ban on the recital of the *ezan* (call to prayer) in Arabic, the broadcasting of Koran readings over the state radio, the establishment of religious schools, and the expansion of the PRA's budget, were heavily criticized by both the secular press and the RPP leaders as major steps toward the establishment of a non-secular state.

Such concerns were shared by foreign observers, similar to the current fashion, who talked of a "revival of Islam" in Turkey as witnessed by an unprecendented increase in religious publications, in visits to local shrines, in mosque attendance, and in the pilgrimage to Mecca.[15] Perhaps

---

[12] For a list based on official statistics see the series of articles by Mehmet Cemal, "Yüzaltmışüç," *Milli Gazete*, April 10-30, 1974. Based on his calculations, 1,971 people were sentenced for violating Article 163 between 1949 and 1972.

[13] The Progressive Republican Party in 1924, the Free Republican Party in 1930, the Nation Party in 1954, the National Order Party in 1972 and the National Salvation Party in 1980.

[14] See Tarık Zafer Tunaya, *İslamcılık Cereyanı* (İstanbul, Baha Matbaası, 1962), pp. 190-192.

[15] See, for example, Bernard Lewis, "Islamic Revival in Turkey," *International Affairs* 28 (1952), pp. 38-48; Lewis V. Thomas, "Recent Developments in Turkish Islam," *The Middle East Journal* 6 (1952), pp. 22-40; Uriel Heyd, *Revival of Islam in Modern Turkey* (Jerusalem, Magnes Press, 1968), pamphlet; Howard A. Reed, "Revival of Islam in Secular Turkey," *The Middle East Journal* 8 (1954), pp. 267-282. For a different perspective, see Dankwart A. Rustow, "Politics and Islam in Turkey, 1920-55," in *Islam and the West*, edited by Richard Frye (The Hague, Mouton, 1957), pp. 69-107.

the most serious of such accusations was the rumored support that the *Nurcus* gave to the Democrat Party and the government's lenient attitude toward the order, which became a major issue of Turkish politics during the early part of 1960.[16]

This controversy over the politicization of Islam continued after the 1960 military intervention with the establishment of the Justice Party (JP: *Adalet Partisi*) in 1961, which now replaced the DP as the target of secularist attack during the first half of the 1960s. The 1961 Constitution had allowed genuine associational freedom which resulted in the mushrooming of organizations throughout the decade, including religious ones. Religious forces were finally able to establish a political party of their own in 1970 under the name, the National Order Party (NOP: *Millî Nizam Partisi*) which, however, was outlawed in 1972 by the Constitutional Court. The NOP leadership quickly reassembled and founded the National Salvation Party (NSP: *Millî Selamet Partisi*) which, as it turned out, would play a crucial role in the political arena during the 1970s.

The rise of the National Salvation Party coincided with a period in Turkish history when, for the first time, institutions of civil society were beginning to develop considerable autonomy. Labor unions, professional organizations, the universities, the press, and even the state-owned radio and television network had gained unprecendented autonomy from state control. Indeed, in the latter part of the 1970s, apprehensive voices were being heard which complained of the disappearance of state authority altogether. This was, in fact, one of the major themes of the post-1980 military government to bestow legitimacy to the intervention. In any case, in the liberal atmosphere of the 1970s, the NSP was able to make considerable inroads into party competition.[17]

State control of religious institutions, coupled with westernizing reforms, had met with armed resistance during the early years of the Republic.[18] However, by the time the transition to democratic politics was

---

[16] For details see B. Toprak, *Islam and Political Development in Turkey*, pp. 71-90.

[17] On the National Salvation Party see Jacob M. Landau, "The National Salvation Party in Turkey," *Asian and African Studies* 11 (1976), pp. 1-57; Binnaz Toprak, "Politicization of Islam in a Secular State: the National Salvation Party in Turkey," in *From Nationalism to Revolutionary Islam*, edited by Said Arjomand (London, Macmillan, 1984), pp. 119-133; "Milli Selamet Partisi," *Cumhuriyet Dönemi Türkiye Ansiklopedisi*, No. 67, pp. 2104-2110; and *Islam and Political Development in Turkey*, Chap. V; Türker Alkan, "The National Salvation Party in Turkey," in *Islam and Politics in the Modern Middle East*, edited by Metin Heper and Raphael Israeli (London and Sydney, Croom Helm, 1984), pp. 79-102; Mehmet Ali Ağaoğulları, *L'Islam dans la vie politique de la Turquie* (Ankara, Ankara Universitesi Basımevi, 1982) Part III; Ali Yaşar Sarıbay, "Die Nationale Heilspartei," in *Jahrbuch zur Geschichte und Gesellschaft*, pp. 255-298 and *Türkiye'de Modernleşme, Din ve Parti Politikası: "MSP Örnek Olayı"* (Istanbul, Alan Yayıncılık, 1985).

[18] See B. Toprak, *Islam and Political Development in Turkey*, pp. 67-70. For a more detailed

made in 1946, the authoritarian single-party governments had for long established a firm control of the religious opposition. After 1946, however, the role of Islam in Turkish society had again become a major political dispute with the emergence of mass parties such as the DP and its successor, the JP. These parties seemed to receive the religious vote by following more relaxed policies on secularism. The founding of the NSP in 1972 was the final outcome of this process as the legitimacy of religious demands and the right of religious groups to organize was at last accepted by the state elite. In particular the RPP, which had been historically the bulwark of secularism, softened its stand in the early 1970s and accepted the NSP as a coalition partner in 1974.

The NSP was a neo-Islamic party whose major concern was the partial retraditionalization of Turkish culture along Islamic precepts. However, it placed this concern within a modern context by emphasizing rapid industrialization. In the NSP view, these two issues were related: Turkey had a distinguished imperial past which was attributable to its success in combining military power with the building of an Islamic civilization. The statesmen of the Tanzimat, however, had made the erroneous assumption that the decline in military strength was correlated with Islam, and as a remedy, began to westernize Ottoman society. This process of westernization, according to the NSP, signalled the end of grandeur for Ottoman society. The road to world leadership for Turkey, therefore, had to pass through the abandonment of reliance on the West both in cultural and economic terms. The "National Outlook" *(Milli Görüş)*, as the NSP called its ideology, promised a country which would be fully industrialized through economic cooperation with the Muslim world, the prerequisite of which was the return to Islam as the basis of social organization.[19]

The NSP became an indispensible partner in three coalition governments between 1973-1978.[20] It polled 11.8 and 8.6 per cent of the total votes in the 1973 and 1977 elections, respectively. No doubt, this relative success was partially due to the NSP's organizational network, especially its rumoured ties with the *Nakşibendi* order. It also had a powerful youth organization, the *Akıncılar* (Raiders) with approximately 600 branches

---

analysis of these rebellions see Çetin Özek, *Türkiye'de Gerici Akımlar ve Nurculuğun İçyüzü* (İstanbul, Varlık Yayınevi, 1964).

[19] See B. Toprak, "Politicization of Islam in a Secular State," pp. 123-127.

[20] The Republican People's Party/The National Salvation Party coalition government was formed in January 1974 and lasted until September 1974. The first Nationalistic Front Government of Süleyman Demirel was formed in March 1975. It included the Justice Party (JP), the National Salvation Party (NSP), the Nationalist Action Party (NAP) and the Republican Reliance Party (RRP). It ended in June 1977. The second Nationalistic Front Government of Demirel was formed in August 1977, with the participation of the JP, the NSP and the NAP. It ended in January 1978.

throughout Turkey; an affiliated labor union, the *Hak-İş* Confederation; the Organizations of the National Outlook in Germany *(Milli Görüş Almanya Teşkilâtları)* with approximately 170 branches in various German cities; a party daily, *Millî Gazete;* and organic ties with several professional organizations.[21] The NSP also built a considerable patronage network through placing the NSP sympathizers in various ministerial and other governmental positions.

4 Intervention of the Military

Following the military intervention of 1980 the NSP, along with all the other political parties, was outlawed. The aim of the military government was to strengthen the state and to restructure Turkish politics through the establishment of a new legal-institutional framework. The 1961 Constitution was replaced by a new constitution drafted under military auspices.[22] The 1982 Constitution was designed to correct, among other things, what the military saw to be a costly weakness of the 1961 Constitution, namely, the guarantee of unprecendented individual and group rights and liberties in the absence of properly drawn limits. According to this analysis, the cost was the excessive politicization of groups and institutions which had led to the anarchy on the street, the ideological divisions within the state apparatus itself including the police force, and the government's inability to control violence.

Hence, the new Constitution put extensive limits on basic rights and liberties, which could now be curtailed by law for the protection of national or public concerns. It also put restrictions on the organization and activities of political parties and voluntary associations. Political parties could not establish women's, youth and other affiliated organizations, nor could they have organic ties with interest groups. In a similar vein, voluntary associations could not engage in political activity nor could they cooperate, financially or otherwise, with political parties. Separate articles on labor unions specified the same limitations on labor union activity.

---

[21] For details see B. Toprak, "Politicization of Islam in a Secular State," p. 128. The *Hak-İş* Confederation had in 1984 approximately 12,000 members and is still one of the biggest unions. See *Cumhuriyet*, January 18, 1984.

[22] The 1982 Constitution was adopted by a referendum which resulted in an overwhelming 91.5 per cent of affirmative votes. Voting in the referendum was mandatory. Failure to do so was punishable by a TL 2500 fine and the cancellation of the right to vote, for five years, in the national or municipal elections to be held under the new Constitution. In addition, campaigns against the ratification of the Constitution were not allowed.

The 1983 Election Law changed the electoral system with a view to correct the stalemate of coalition or minority governments which had become a characteristic feature of the pre-1980 period. Although the proportional representation system was kept, a percentage barrier was introduced on the basis of which a party that failed to receive 10 per cent of the total vote could not send representatives to the Assembly. In addition, in order to gain a seat in a given electoral district, parties had to pass a second barrier at the district level.[23] This arrangement, of course, works to the disadvantage of minor parties and was designed to push the system into a two-party model. It was accordingly hoped that the new electoral law would help secure stable governments with clear majorities in the Assembly and would drive extremist parties, including the religious ones, out of the political arena.

As already noted, all existing parties at the time of the military takeover had been closed down by a 1981 law. The 1983 Political Parties Law also banned their top administrative cadres from party activity for ten years. It imposed the same limitation for five years on all members of the pre-1980 Grand National Assembly. In addition, the founding of new parties under the same names and emblems was outlawed.[24]

Taken as a whole, the 1982 Constitution and other post-1980 legislation represent a significant attempt toward depoliticization coupled with greater state control over both the legal arena and the institutional framework of the nascent civil society in Turkey. As already noted the new Constitution rejected a major premise of pluralist democracy, namely, the representation of interests through links between political parties and interest groups. It also rejected the principle, which was implicit in the 1961 Constitution, that institutions of civil society are, by definition, autonomous from the state.

However, despite the military's emphasis on a fresh start, the national elections of November 1983 and the municipal elections of March 1984 showed that there is a continuity of electoral preferences in Turkish politics. As soon as party activity was allowed in 1983, and especially after the elections, it became apparent to political analysts that there were significant linkages between old political parties and new ones.

One continuity of electoral alignments since the mid-1960s is the structuring of the political spectrum on a center-right and center-left axis. This

---

[23] A party had to receive more votes than the number to be found by the division of the valid votes with the number of representatives to be elected from that district. See *Milletvekili Seçimi Kanunu,* Law Number 2839, Date of Ratification, 6/10/1983, Articles 33 and 34. An amendment passed in 1987 made it even more difficult for smaller parties to get their candidates elected in some districts.

[24] See *Siyasi Partiler Kanunu,* Law Number 2820/K., Date of Ratification 4/22/1983, Provisional Article 1 and Article 96.

continuity became apparent after the 1983 national and 1984 municipal elections. The gap in the center-right after the closing of the Justice Party was filled by the Motherland Party (MP: *Anavatan Partisi*) of Turgut Özal which won 45.2 per cent of the total vote in 1983 with an absolute majority of seats in the National Assembly and formed the government. The gap in the center-left after the closing of the Republican People's Party was originally shared by the Populist Party (PP: *Halkçı Parti*) and the Social Democracy Party (SDP: *Sosyal Demokrasi Partisi*) although the latter could only participate in the municipal elections and therefore had no representation in the Assembly. In late 1985, the PP and the SDP merged under a new name, the Social Democratic Populist Party (SDPP: *Sosyal Demokrat Halkçı Parti*). There are other contenders on both the center-right and the center-left which are now under the leadership of former politicians.

As the Turkish electorate realigned itself under the major parties, a new neo-Islamic party, Welfare Party (WP: *Refah Partisi*) was founded in 1983 to fill the gap after the closing of the National Salvation Party. The WP emerged on the political scene to realign the "Muslim vote." It was unable to acquire legal status before the 1983 national elections and was left out of the competition.[25] It was, however, able to participate in the municipal elections of March 1984 and received 4.8 per cent of the total votes.

Reminiscent of the "National Outlook" of the NSP, the Welfare Party calls its ideology "National Consciousness" *(Millî Şuur)*. Again like the NSP, it defines development as a combination of material and spiritual welfare, the latter indeed being a prerequisite for the former. By "spiritual development" the WP understands a return to indigenous sources of culture and interprets the modernization efforts of the last two hundred years as a failure. According to the WP, Turkey has remained behind the industrial world because of a misplaced emphasis on "foreign ideas and resources." Such emphasis has led to a spiritual crisis as witnessed by the unprecedented increase in amoral behavior.

In the WP view, the emphasis on material growth that has embraced most countries of the world has resulted in wars, oppression, terror, injustice, poverty, and famine. Mankind is in a spiritual void. As statistics suggest, prostitution, alcoholism, drug addiction, and mental diseases have afflicted most societies. Values which men have cherished for centuries such as love, kindness, truth, piety, affection, altruism have all but disap-

[25] In order to compete in the national elections of 1983, a party had to complete its organization in 34 out of 67 provinces and to have its list of founding members approved by the National Security Council (NSC) before August 24, 1983. The series of vetoes of the NSC concerning the Welfare Party's list left the Party out of the 1983 elections.

peared. What is needed, therefore, is a new consciousness which will place material wealth under the umbrella of higher values. Although the WP is cautious enough not to specify Islam as a source of such values, it is clear that this new "national consciousness" will mean a partial return to Islam as a way of life.[26]

Like the NSP, the Welfare Party declares the establishment of heavy industry in Turkey to be one of its major goals. It emphasizes, however, that industrial growth will be carried out with a view to correct regional imbalances and disparities between income groups. The WP also points out the need to develop an independent foreign policy which will enable Turkey to fully use its own manpower and resources. In this context, it calls for close relations with countries that have a common "spiritual" (to be read religious) and historical background, i.e., the Muslim Middle East.[27]

The vision is simple yet powerful. It promises prosperity and wealth without the all-too-familiar pains of rapid industrialization: an industrial country where a sense of community, of belongingness, mutual help and love of brothers reigns; above all, a country of the faithful who have a common purpose to build a system which reflects divine design.

The emphasis on religion by Welfare Party is implicit only if one reads party literature in between the lines. Otherwise, some of this material is impressive in terms of revealing the extent of research that party think-tanks are engaged in. For example, the opening speech of Ahmet Tekdal, a lawyer and the WP ex-leader, in the First Congress of the party is a carefully prepared document mostly devoted to the critique of the MP government. The use of extensive statistical data to criticize Özal's policies is striking.[28] In fact, the WP's appeals for social welfare, social justice, and political freedoms led one commentator of Turkish politics to point out that the WP is probably attempting to reach civil servants and workers as potential party supporters.[29] If this is indeed the case, it is in sharp contrast to the clientele of the defunct NSP which was mostly made up of small merchants, traders, shopkeepers, and artisans.

---

[26] See Refah Partisi, *Refah Partisi Büyük Kongresi: Genel Başkan Ahmet Tekdal'ın Açış Konuşması, 30 Haziran 1985* (Ankara, Elif Matbaası, 1985), pp. 4, 36.

[27] *Ibid.* Also see *Refah Partisi Programı* (Ankara, 1983) and Emin Çölaşan's interview by Ahmet Tekdal in *Milliyet,* July 7, 1985.

[28] See note 26 above.

[29] Tanıl Bora, "Politikanın Müslüman Kanadı: Refah Partisi," *Yeni Gündem* (July 16-31, 1985), p. 13. For the WP's emphasis on political freedoms, see the interviews by Ahmet Tekdal in Yankı (July 8-14, 1985), p. 22 and *Nokta* (July 4, 1985).

5 Growth of the Influence of Islam

After the First Congress of the Welfare Party which was held in June 1985, the Turkish press unanimously commented that the WP would play a significant role in future Turkish politics. Journalists who observed the Congress were impressed by the discipline, the crowds, the excitement.[30] Uğur Mumcu of the daily *Cunhuriyet,* for example, wrote that he had not witnessed a party congress of similar magnitude in the last 25 years.[31] Yet, a public opinion poll conducted two months later showed that if the elections were to be held in 1985, the WP would muster a meager 2.2 per cent of the votes.[32]

The results of the poll should not indicate that 2.2 per cent is the total strength of religious forces in Turkey. The Welfare Party is rumored to have connections with the *Nakşibendi* order, as did its predecessor the National Salvation Party. However, the WP and earlier the NSP connection with the *Nakşibendis* is apparently confined to only the followers of the late *Nakşibendi* sheikh Mehmet Efendi in Istanbul. Part of the *Nakşibendis,* especially an offshoot of the order, *Süleymancıs,* are rumored to have connections with the ruling Motherland Party, including prominent leaders within the MP. The *Nurcus,* on the other hand, are known to support the True Path Party (TPP: *Doğru Yol Partisi*) as they previously supported the Justice Party and the Democrat Party.

In comparison to these various orders which have chosen to operate within the existing party spectrum, there is a radical fundamentalist movement which refuses to engage in party activity. This movement sees party politics as a cooptation, views Islam as a revolutionary anti-imperialist force within a Third World paradigm, and confines itself at present to intellectual pursuits.[33] Indeed, the number of formerly leftist or secular intellectuals who have turned to Islam is said to have been on the increase

---

[30] See *Cumhuriyet, Milliyet, Tercüman, Günaydın, Güneş, Milli Gazete,* July 1, 1985, *Yankı* (8-14 July 1985), pp. 20-21.

[31] Uğur Mumcu in *Cumhuriyet,* July 1, 1985.

[32] See the *Milliyet-Siar* public opinion poll, August 1985. For results see *Milliyet,* August 19, 1985.

[33] The *İnsan Yayınları* is among the most important publishing houses of the Muslim intellectuals. For some representative studies see, for example, Rasim Özdenören, *Müslümanca Düşünme Üzerine Denemeler* (İstanbul: İnsan Yayınları, 1985); İlhan Kutluer, *Modern Bilimin Arka Planı* (İstanbul: İnsan Yayınları, 1985). The *İnsan Yayınları* has also translated and published a number of books by Muslim and other thinkers. The *Dergâh Yayınları* is a second publishing house which puts out serious research on Islam. There are other publishers although not of the same intellectual quality. In fact, in an exhibit on published material on Islam organized by the *Türkiye Diyanet Vakfi* (May, June 16, 1985), over 40 publishing houses participated which publish exclusively on Islam.

in recent years.[34] The opposition of this movement to party politics seems to be of considerable concern for the WP leaders who find it important to emphasize, in various press interviews, that the road to power for the believers passes through party organization.[35]

One factor that accounts for the low electoral support of the WP, therefore, is the competition between the Islamic groups. An equally important factor is the split of the previous NSP support between the WP and the Motherland Party. In fact, the daily *Millî Gazete* which formerly supported the NSP and now backs the WP, wrote an editorial on local politics in the Şanlıurfa province (where the mayor was elected on a WP ticket) in which the point was made, although in an exaggerated tone, that the Motherland Party sees the WP as its major competitor.[36] The NSP clique within the MP, headed by the party's vice-president Mehmet Keçeciler, has considerable strength.[37] Turgut Özal himself is known for his religousness as well as affinity with the National Salvation Party[38] and his apparent backing of the Keçeciler group as against the supporters of the defunct ultra-Right Nationalist Action Party (NAP: *Milliyetçi Hareket Partisi*) within the Motherland Party,[39] has caused quite an uproar during its First Congress in April 1985.[40]

Until late 1985, the strength of the NSP sympathizers within the MP leadership was also evident in their control of the Ministry of Education, Youth and Sports which has always been considered a key ministry by Islamic groups. The former Minister, Vehbi Dinçerler, was said to be a member of the *Nakşibendi* order and was a center of attention in the Turkish press for his unprecedented decisions. The most controversial of these concerned his ban on the teaching of Darwin's theory in primary and secondary schools.[41] Equally striking was his imposition of what came to be

---

[34] See, for example, the article in *Nokta* which was entitled "Turkey's Garaudys," ("İslami Dalga - Ateizmden Müslümanlığa: Türkiye'nin Garaudy'leri") *Nokta* (August 11, 1985) pp. 52-55. For some tentative suggestions on the reasons for the resurgence of Islam among the educated in Turkey see Metin Heper, "Islam, Polity and Society in Turkey: A Middle Eastern Perspective," *The Middle East Journal* 35 (1981), pp. 361-362.

[35] See *Milli Gazete*, July 24, 1985 and March 18, 1985.

[36] *Milli Gazete*, February 1985.

[37] See Teoman Erel in *Milliyet*, March 5, 1985 and June 19, 1985.

[38] He was an NSP candidate in the 1977 elections, but lost. For his apparent connections with Islamic groups see the interviews by Yusuf Türel, the President of the Society for the Propagation of Knowledge *(İlim Yayma Cemiyeti)* which has organic ties with the NSP, in *Nokta* (June 16, 1985), pp. 20-21.

[39] This clique is headed my Mustafa Taşar, the Secretary-General of the MP and Halil Şıvgın, the ex-vice-president of the party. Another strong man within this group is Veysel Atasoy, former Minister of Communications and now a Minister of State.

[40] See *Milliyet*, April 14, 1985: *Cumhuriyet*, April 14-16, 1985.

[41] See *Cumhuriyet*, April 8, 1985.

called "long shorts" for female students during the national Sports Day of May 1984.[42] Although not within the jurisdiction of his Ministry, Dinçerler was also the key man behind the ban of beer advertisements on national radio and television.[43] Beer had become a religio-political issue during the RPP-NSP coalition government of 1974 when the NSP's Minister of Interior had banned its sale in places without a permit for alcoholic beverages.[44] Moreover, a new law was enacted in 1984 which forbade the opening of bars within 200 meters of schools, student dormitories, sports clubs, and mosques.[45] Dinçerler's decision to include Arabic language courses in the curriculum of secondary schools[46] and his suggestion that religious instruction in primary and secondary schools should henceforth be converted to "applied" courses to teach the performance of the *namaz* (daily prayers) to students all met with a major controversy in the press.[47] Also controversial was his decision to have textbooks rewritten for which he formed commissions during the summer of 1985. These commissions were directed to censor modern Turkish words, to emphasize "national" history and geography with particular attention to the leading political and military figures of the early Republican period who were known for their religious opposition to the Kemalist regime,[48] as well as to introduce Muslim philosophy in the texts. In this context, the use of modern Turkish has long been a political issue due to the opposition of

[42] The sports shorts for female students has been a controversial religio-political issue for a long time. For the religious who believe in *tesettür* (Islamic precept for the covering of women's bodies and hair) the wearing of shorts is, of course, sinful. The "long shorts" solution was a compromise. On the controversy over this decision see Oktay Akbal in *Cumhuriyet*, July 15, 1984.

[43] See *Hürriyet*, July 5, 1984. The beer companies, of course, reacted to the decision and published full-page ads in major newspapers which denounced the government's decision as reactionary and contrary to the secular principles of the Republic. For the controversy that followed see Hasan Pulur in *Hürriyet*, June 12, 1984 and Teoman Erel in *Milliyet*, June 16, 1984.

[44] See B. Toprak, "Politicization of Islam in a Secular State," p. 125.

[45] See *Günaydın*, July 10, 1984.

[46] The alphabet was changed from the Arabic to the Latin script in 1928. The use of the Arabic script is laden with religious symbolism in Turkey because of the sacred quality attached to Arabic as the language of God (See B. Toprak, *Islam and Political Development in Turkey*, pp. 41-42). In line with the 1928 Alphabet Reform, Arabic was dropped (along with Persian) from the curricula of all secondary schools by an order of the Ministry of Education in 1929. The controversy in 1984, therefore, had religious overtones. However, there are a number of secular intellectuals in Turkey who approve of the teaching of Arabic in schools either to encourage young students to engage in historical research or to aid in commerce with the Arab world. For this controversy see the editorials by Nazlı Ilıcak in *Tercüman*, July 8, 1984; Mümtaz Soysal in *Milliyet*, July 4, 1984; and Mehmet Barlas in *Milliyet*, July 4, 1984.

[47] See Hasan Pulur, in *Hürriyet*, July 12, 1984.

[48] See *Nokta*, (August 11, 1985), pp. 22-23.

Islamic and ultra-nationalist groups to the change of the alphabet and the language. A faction within the MP has sided with these groups on this point and succeeded in banning the usage of a long list of words from state radio and TV programs.[49] Dinçerler 's decision to include several Islamic publications as suggested readings to primary and secondary school students finally prompted the opposition parties to press the government for his replacement.[50]

The religious group within the Motherland Party has also drawn some attention as a result of the government's decision to build places of worship *(mescit)* within both the Grand National Assembly and various ministries. The building of *mescit* or mosques inside the campuses of several state universities in Ankara (e.g., Hacettepe, Ankara, and Middle East Technical Universities)[51] and the firing of a lycée director and two teachers in Izmir (by an order of the Ministry of Education, Youth and Sports) who were against the building of a *mescit* within the premises of the school,[52] added to the list of concerns of the secularist camp in Turkey.

Indeed, like in the 1950s, there has been much talk of a revival of Islam in Turkey in recent years. The entrenchment of the Islamists within the government, the existence of an Islamic party, the wealth of Islamic publications and periodic press reports about several incidents involving Islamic groups has once again put the question of religion on the agenda of the Turkish secularist intelligentsia. One such incident concerned the mayor of a town in the Konya province who reportedly participated in *Nakşibendi* rites inside the Town Council building, banned the public breaking of the fast during *Ramadan,* and fined a citizen who acted otherwise.[53] Another involved a civil servant working in the Bureau of Marriage in Ankara who systematically enforced a religious marriage in addition to the civil.[54] Several reports about private Koran courses,[55] which were supposed to be terminated after 1980, indicated that they were still in operation under different names and had become an arena in the fight for control between the *Süleymancı* and *Nurcu* orders.[56] The reports also included a *Nakşibendi* sheikh, accused of giving the *fetva* for the murder of a *müftü* in Istanbul who was against operating Koran courses without official per-

---

[49] *Cumhuriyet,* January 10, 1985.

[50] *Cumhuriyet,* August 30, 1985.

[51] See *Nokta* (July 21, 1985), pp. 29–30; and Talat Halman in *Milliyet,* June 1984.

[52] See *Nokta* (June 30, 1985), pp. 53–54.

[53] See *Nokta* (July 7, 1985), pp. 26–27.

[54] See *Nokta* (June 30, 1985), pp. 22–23.

[55] These are courses financed by citizens or local communities where the recital of the Koran is taught to students.

[56] See *Cumhuriyet,* August 10, 12, 1985 and *Nokta* (July 21, 1985), pp. 26–28.

mit from the Presidency of Religious Affairs.[57] Another involved fourteen *Nakşibendis*, including the powerful *Nakşibendi* sheikh Raşit Erol, who were accused of cooperating with a fundamentalist organization in Saudi Arabia, the *Rabitat-al-Alem-al-Islam,* in order to start an armed uprising with the aim of establishing a "theocratic state" in Turkey based on the *Shari'a.*[58] The concern over the *tarikats* and folk Islam even prompted the weekly *Nokta* to publish two cover stories on this topic.[59] The much publicized issue of female students who believe in *tesettür* (Islamic precept for the covering of women's bodies and hair) and who refuse to lift their scarfs during school hours,[60] was yet another example of Muslim militancy for the secularists.

There are, of course, critical differences between these cases in terms of their implications for secularism. For example, a government official who imposes on the public the observance of a religious practice through using the authority of his office clearly violates the concept of a secular state. A Muslim woman who believes in *tesettür,* on the other hand, intrinsically poses no threat to the secular foundations of the state. Indeed, on the basis of present Republican laws, whereas the first case would result in legal action, the second would simply involve administrative sanction, only if the woman in question is a civil servant or a student. These demarcation lines, however, are seldom drawn by the secularist elite who have been historically sensitive to the role of Islam in Turkish society. This sensitivity has at times led to an exaggerated vigil over secularism and a disposition to interpret any display of religiousness as an example of obscurantist advance. This is partially due to the inseparability in Islam of state and religion and the subsequent problems that this particular predisposition poses for the very concept of a secular state.

---

[57] The *Nakşibendi* sheikh in question is Mahmut Ustaosmanoğlu known also as Sultan Mahmut Efendi. For the story see *Nokta* (March 3, 1985), pp. 32-33.

[58] See *Nokta* (June 16, 1985), pp. 30-31.

[59] See "Tarikat Olayı," *Nokta* (March 3, 1985), pp. 26-34; and "Büyü, Üfürük, Fal," *Nokta* (June 23, 1985), pp. 44-52. *Nokta* is a weekly magazine. Its orientation is secular. Its cover stories are based on the research of its own staff rather than summaries of previous press reports. It follows a liberal democratic line and often includes reports on "unconventional" topics such as feminism, homosexuality, environmental problems, and the like.

[60] See *Milliyet,* July 12, 1984. An *İmam-Hatip* Lycée (Prayer Leader and Preacher School) in Istanbul published a Yearbook in which *tesettür* was advocated for all Muslim women. The press gave the news as an example of "reactionary trends" in modern Turkey. See *Milliyet,* July 5, 1985. Of course, the Islamic literature has always advocated *tesettür* for women.

6 Conclusion

As the foregoing discussion illustrates, the case of Islam points to the precarious nature of the relationship between the state and civil society in Turkey. Above all, it points to the limits of state power even in a state-centered polity. Despite half a century of attempts to put religion under state control, the role of Islam in Turkish society and politics remains influential.

Part of the reasons for this influence lie in the shaping of voter alignments in Turkey. As is the case in most democracies the choices of the voter have been historically crystallized. Indeed, the trends in Turkish politics can be mapped through cleavage clusters in Turkish society which shape not only the behavior of the voter but also the structuration of politics itself. Hence, despite legal and institutional changes designed for a fresh start, a good part of the historical structure remains. It contains feelings, loyalties, and attachments toward specific politial symbols that emerge from the past and the cleavages inherent in that past which mould the outlook of the voter and the politician, the limits within which legal-institutional arrangements operate, and the nature of the political action itself. In short, there is a patterned political spectrum in Turkey which survives attempts to restructure party politics and electoral behavior.

As I have attempted to point out, Islam as a political force is an integral part of this patterned spectrum. However, the electoral fortunes of Islamic parties in Turkey also demonstrate that Islam, by itself, is not a sufficient catalyst for mass mobilization. The Turkish case seems to differ significantly from other Muslim countries. Both the economic development of Turkey, and the implementation of strict secularist policies over a long period of time, have pushed the issue of religion to the background of electoral politics.

The very factors which have led to the waning importance of Islam in the voter's choice also account for its apparent vitality in Turkish society. The economy has increasingly become the primary concern of the voter at a time when urbanization and economic growth have turned the individual from his traditional milieu. As Sabri Sayarı aptly points out, Islamic re-traditionalism has much to do with "the separation of the individual from collective entities"[61] which results in a feeling of homelessness. Thus, for some, religious movements offer solace and security in the midst of rapid change. For others who have been pushed to the margins of industrial society - such as small merchants, traders, shopkeepers and artisans - they

[61] Sabri Sayarı, "Politicization of Islamic Re-traditionalism: Some Preliminary Notes," in *Islam and Politics in The Modern Middle East*, edited by Metin Heper and Raphael Israeli, pp. 119-128.

offer a channel of protest. And for a small minority, fundamentalism represents a revolutionary force which might lead to the reestablishment of a Muslim state and a society that follows Islamic traditions. In any case, the Islamic "movement" within present-day Turkey represents a counter-culture. During the early years of the Republic, religious reaction was confined to groups who were predominantly rural, uneducated and outside the ruling elite. It is now a counter-culture which has extended itself to the more prominent sectors of urban society such as the civil service, free professions, political parties and the press.

Part IV
The Military, the State, and Politics

Chapter 10
Military Interventions: Army-Civilian Relations in Turkey Before and After 1980

Kemal H. Karpat

1 Introduction

The purpose of this chapter is to analyse the process that brought a gradual disintegration of the Turkish ruling coalition. In fact, the military interventions mark the progressive breakdown of the grand socio-political coalition that had ruled Turkey since 1923. The 1980 takeover was, in fact, the final phase of the dissolution of the alliance between the military and the various civilian statist groups and the beginning of a new period of modernization with a new "division of labor."

2 The Background of the First Military Intervention

The military takeover of 1960 was a turning point in the relationship between civilian and military elites that had governed the country since 1923. Justified as a step necessary for the preservation of democracy, the action appeared to be chiefly designed to answer a threat (if there actually was one) to the Republican People's Party (RPP), which had governed Turkey from 1923 to 1950.

Strains within the civilian-military coalition had begun to develop as early as 1946, with the establishment of the opposition Democrat Party (DP). During a talk with the late İsmet İnönü some years ago, I asked whether he had set any conditions for allowing the establishment of opposition parties in 1945-1946. In response, İnönü said that he had told Celâl Bayar, the leader of the proposed new party, that his group would be free to debate and challenge any of the principles of the ruling party except the Kemalist tenets of republicanism and secularism.

The DP sought electoral support among the masses by offering economic incentives, such as credit, subsidies, road building programs, etc. The Democrats' interjection of economic issues into party politics was accompanied by an open display of animosity toward the military's informal linkage with the RPP, particularly on the part of Adnan Menderes, who had been a member of the RPP himself.

In fact, Menderes' attitude toward the military was rather ambiguous. He was aware and appreciative of the military's historical role as the defender of the state; he, nevertheless, also thought that the military had become mainly a guarantor of the highly centralized, statist-elitist system since the founding of the Republic and that it was unfriendly to landed notables and other groups favoring a degree of administrative decentralization. Moreover, he felt that the military was a non-productive group that demanded a larger-than-legitimate share of the national income. For example, he was cognizant of the fact that wartime budgets, which were always increased, continued to be presented to the legislature by the military even after 1945 and were usually approved.

Menderes appeared to reflect the chief interests and fears of the leading social groups in small towns and among rural farmers. In contrast to the urban bureaucratic stratum, which had undergone an ideological and cultural transformation while it sought modernization through imitating the West, the non-urban elites had maintained their cultural and religious roots and felt a strong sense of continuity with their past. They were dismayed by the secularist-statist turn taken by the government between 1938 and 1945. The DP emerged as a coalition of these groups.

In the summer and fall of 1946, it became obvious that within the ranks of the DP there was considerable difference of opinion regarding how to proceed. After a period of ideological ferment and argument (called the *"46 ruhu,"* "the spirit of 1946"), the party leaders ousted a group of Islamist-populist militants who were advocating open warfare against the military-civilian bureaucratic coalition and against the secularist-elitist ideology. The ousted members accused Bayar and Menderes of being basically the same in spirit and mentality as the group they appeared to be fighting against.

This accusation of the bureaucratic coalition by the DP radicals had much truth in it. Despite promises made during his years in opposition, Menderes did not try to amend the Constitution of 1924 when the DP came to power in 1950, for he did not really disapprove of its provisions. In fact, he made use of the Constitution to concentrate power in his own hands. He did try to downgrade the role of the military and the bureaucracy while he worked diligently to increase the power and influence of the nascent entrepreneurial groups, businessmen, and the special class of countryside merchant-landowners. This policy led to the rapid growth in size of the new economic middle class and to an inflation that not only reduced the purchasing power but also diminished the prestige and influence of the military-civilian bureaucracy. The DP's actions vis-à-vis the military during its ten years in power, however, were not sufficient in themselves to have provoked the 1960 intervention. In fact, the DP tried to respond to the military's important basic demands by rejuvenating the upper echelons of the army and modernizing its weapons and training systems, especially after Turkey entered the NATO alliance. Thus, the professionally rooted complaints of the military against the DP would not seem to be strong enough to engender a rebellion.

Rather it seems that party politics, which perhaps inevitably began to reflect changes brought about by the DP's policies, were the crucial ingredient in precipitating the army's action. The RPP did not take kindly to being out of power. It saw a fairly large number among the members of groups formerly dominant in the ruling coalition (such as former civil servants and retired army officers) defect to the ranks of the DP. This defection was often a purely expedient, and perhaps temporary, change in party alignment, as these "converts" to the Democrats' side retained their basic political philosophy even after they had switched parties. Nevertheless, some of the more orthodox statist-elitists among the Republicans considered such defections as betrayal.

Until the elections of 1954, the RPP maintained its old posture as the party that "represented the entire nation" and was the guardian of Atatürk's legacy and reforms. It should be remembered that the six basic principles of Kemalism (republicanism, nationalism, secularism, populism, reformism-revolutionarism, and étatism) had been incorporated into the RPP's own official ideology. Although the RPP continued to hold the same positions after 1954, in practice it identified itself increasingly with the new generation of intellectuals and their ideology, which began to acquire social-economic overtones that manifested themselves in a more radical definition of economic statism leading some intellectuals to socialism.

The relative success of the RPP in the elections of 1957 (when its parliamentary representation soared from 31 to 173 seats, while that of the DP decreased from 490 to 419 despite an increase in the total votes cast) convinced the RPP leaders that the taking of a strong Kemalist-secularist ideological line with the incorporation of new socio-economic ideas held the promise of future success and reinstatement of their party in power. The ideas in question were put forth by social-democrats, pseudo-socialists, and orthodox Marxists, all of whom were also "secularists" except that they regarded religion as subject to market forces: thus their brand of "secularism" was actually materialism.

Meanwhile, the DP was losing membership and Menderes was losing his prestige and influence within the party. Dissension was ripe. Some of the dissidents broke away to form the Freedom Party, after which there was a vote of no confidence in the Parliament (although, on demand, the Prime Minister was personally exonerated). Menderes was particularly vexed by the fact that so substantial a number of young professionals of the new generation, many of whom owed their new status to education in DP-established schools, opposed his party. But the problem was that since the DP did not have a cadre of intellectuals working on party ideology, it was unable to come up with new principles or new theoretical bases to replace the old ones and thus it could not have any appeal to the new educated elites. However, Menderes failed to see this and attributed the DP's misfortunes to the machinations of the RPP and, especially of İnönü, whose influence with the army and among the intelligentsia he feared greatly.

Menderes had expected the RPP to accept the new leadership developing in the ruling coalition in the same way that the entrepreneurs, agrarian groups, conservatives, Muslim fundamentalists, etc. had accepted the leadership of the secularists, Kemalists, statists, and the military in the past, although they had held their own views. To Menderes, this was the meaning of democracy. The Democrats had not, since coming to power, disturbed the foundations of the republican form of government or sought to destroy the legacy of Atatürk (except for a few institutions, such as the People's Houses and Village Institutes that were holdovers from the single-party days and seemed ideologically suspect). Menderes was not prepared for militant opposition from the Republicans.

However, to the new generation of RPP members, the DP ideology and policies were unacceptable; and, in its new posture as the party representing the aspirations of this rising intelligentsia, the RPP challenged the Democrats forcefully with mass demonstrations as well as political speeches. Menderes responded with harsh measures to quell the opposition and threats to close down the RPP. His fatal mistake was to use the army against some demonstrations (partly just to show the Republicans, and İnönü especially, that the military was controlled by the government). At this point İnönü decided, or was persuaded, to issue his famous statement calling vaguely for the intervention of the army to "save democracy" (that is, the RPP) from the wrath of the DP leadership. The inside story of this phase is still to be told. These events occurred shortly after Sygman Rhee, the strongman of South Korea, was ousted by the military, and what İnönü in effect said publicly was that when necessary the Turkish army would act no less patriotically than had the South Korean army.

Now with the hindsight gained through twenty-five years of study of the documents related to these events and discussion with civilian and military leaders in Turkey, I have come to the conclusion that Menderes and Bayar and İnönü were issuing threats in pure bluff. The evidence in the records of the courts that tried the DP leaders and deputies in 1960–1961 indicates that Menderes and Bayar did not truly intend to close down the RPP in 1959–1960 but hoped that by suggesting closing as a possible measure they could compel the party to forego mass demonstrations. İnönü's declaration in turn was intended to remind the DP that if it actually went so far as to close the RPP, the army, the cutting edge of the statist-Kemalist-secularist forces, would not permit it. Neither party appeared to believe that the army could or would act.

In the first place, as previously pointed out, it did not appear that the DP's relations with the military were so antagonistic as to engender support for a takeover. A variety of small, so-called secret, associations had existed within the military since 1954, but these were basically social organizations that were promoted as "revolutionary societies" after 1950, when anti-DP activities acquired an aura of heroism and patriotism. Furthermore, in view of the army's old tradition of political neutrality, which had been reinforced by Atatürk's firm opposition to military involvement in politics, it seemed unlikely that the army would choose to intervene.

However, in 1960 accompanied by hosannahs from the statist intelligentsia a handful of officers did decide to act, proclaiming (not entirely truthfully) that the takeover represented the desire of the entire military establishment and that they were safeguarding democracy and the state, and protecting the legacy of Atatürk.

3 Aftermath of the 1960 Intervention

Following the intervention except for the relatively short period until the ousting of the "radical fourteen," there was no real military junta installed in power. In fact, by the fall of 1960 the government was virtually in the hands of the RPP once more, although there were military personnel in a number of important positions. The chief effect of the intervention was to raise some members of the radical statist-secularist wing of the RPP (including the pseudo-socialists) to posts of influence in the government.

The arrest and trial of the Democrat Party deputies, the detention of landlords in special camps, the establishment of a committee (soon deactivated) to inquire into the source of the wealth of DP members and of its sympathizers, and a variety of other measures with such an ideological-political bent as to remind one almost of class warfare were put into effect by the radical wing of the military and their civilian advisors. Once again it should be emphasized that the military rule of 1960, unlike the intervention of 1980, was wide open from the beginning to cooperation and intercourse with civilians, and these civilians belonged overwhelmingly to the RPP.

Having precipitated the takeover, the top leadership in the Republican People's Party, headed by İnönü and his associates of the time, now tried to defuse the charged atmosphere and to extricate the military from politics altogether. The ousting in the summer of 1960 of the fourteen officers supposedly of radical bent (with the exception of one who seemed to have some peculiar relations abroad, none was a true socialist or Marxist; rather they were secularist-nationalist-statists) prevented the further radicalization of the military rule, and eliminated the officers opposed to RPP. It also had the effect of keeping the ideologically oriented young radicals in the party from gaining direct access to government power.

The majority of the radicals in the RPP (whose views came to be expressed in *Yön*) were strongly statist; that is, they wanted expanded control of the economy by the state, but also sought rapid economic development through accelerated investments and the rationalization of the economy. They were also nationalists, in the sense that they wanted a more independent foreign policy, and, naturally, secularists, although their attachment to the principles of secularism was generally limited by the extent to which this secured party and army support for their goals. In the last analysis ideology of the radical wing in the RPP amounted principally to a typical bureaucratic-intellectual reaction to the rise of the entrepreneurial business-oriented class and to the threat of erosion of the traditional statist-elitist values.

The Constituent Assembly was convened late in 1960. All former members of, and even voters for, the defunct DP were excluded by law from becoming members of the Constituent Assembly. The Constitution of 1961 was almost exclusively the work of the RPP. The main debate in the Assembly was between the statist-radicals (who were in the minority but, because of their superior education and their knowledge of tactics, exerted great influence) and the majority group of conservative, old-time Kemalists-secularists. İnönü, as usual, played the role of powerbroker, although on balance he appeared to have sided more with the radicals than the conservatives.

Unlike the Constitution of 1924, which accepted pluralism but failed to provide the mechanism for achieving it, the Constitution of 1961 did openly recognize the existence of some social groups, such as labor, and acknowledged workers' right to organize themselves politically on the basis of occupation and interest.

The 1961 Constitution represented, in fact, a compromise between the radical-statists and the socially conservative but economically somewhat liberal leadership of the RPP by recognizing the aspirations of both groups. In effect, it promised a wide range of economic and social programs, which could be carried out only by a strongly socialist state, and at the same time, espoused free enterprise and extensive political freedom, which called for far less governmental intervention in the affairs of society. The two sides agreed on a weak executive, not only because it would prevent the emergence of a "strongman," but also because each group felt that it would be more able to promote its own views and enhance its position without interference from above.

The new regime, with its legal paraphernalia in question, was expected to endure for a long time. The old ruling coalition was restored to power and the expectation was that it would soon acquire the *de jure* right to rule the country. The only task remaining was the legitimization and perpetuation of the revived elitist apparatus through the ritual of the elections demanded by the Constitution. The trouble, of course, was that the millions of ordinary Turks saw all the machinations that preceded the creation of the new Constitution and government not as matters of intellectual interest only but as the manipulation of their own lives and traditions.

The elections of 1961 held with the expectation that they were to give the RPP a comfortable majority, that is, a form of popular mandate to enforce the new Constitution, did not go as planned. The Justice Party (JP) and the New Turkey Party (NTP), both of which were successors to the Democrat Party, together won 238 seats representing a majority in the 450 member Assembly. In effect, the voters returned to power the party ousted by the military only the previous year. Nevertheless, the RPP was entrusted with the task of forming the cabinet under İnönü's leadership.

In connection with Turkish election results since 1961, it has been said that the period until 1980 has been the era of coalitions. The statement is true only for the period after 1973 when the electorate became highly fragmented and political parties proliferated. During the period 1961–1973, the JP won the majority in all the elections, either by itself or with the NTP. However, the Justice Party was prevented from forming a government until 1965. Instead İnönü formed a series of weak coalitions, ostensibly in order to ensure the implementation of the socio-economic provisions of the Constitution so as to achieve rapid economic development and an egalitarian distribution of income, although the GNP of Turkey would be adequate support for only a fraction of the benefits which the Constitution promised to the citizens.

Furthermore, even though the Justice Party won the majority of votes itself and formed its own independent governments in 1965 and 1969, it was effectively prevented from exercising full authority by a series of well-planned strategies of the radical wing of the RPP. In fact, the study of these tactics provides an illuminating view of the mentality of statist-radical intelligentsia and a primer on how to prevent an elected government from exercising its mandate. First, there were delaying tactics in the parliament, ranging from the introduction of endless amendments to bills to debates amounting to a sort of filibuster. Second, there were constant challenges to the constitutionality of laws, and often the Constitutional Court, would oblige by striking down JP legislation, since a good part of its personnel sympathized with the RPP and its radical social views. Third, through the Council of State the bureaucracy, although officially neutral, could in subtle ways block the administrative decisions of the JP government. The JP could only respond by complaining meekly that it was being prevented from carrying out the mandate given to it by the national will *(millî irade).*

The internal politics in Turkey, now more than ever, was being decided essentially through the struggle of the same two groups as before (despite some overlapping): the statist-elitist intelligentsia and bureaucracy, on the one hand, and the entrepreneurial, free-economy-oriented group, the power of which had begun to reach into the larger towns and cities, on the other. After 1961, however, the strategies and goals of each side changed markedly. The social-democratic (statist-socialist) groups in the RPP had acquired considerable influence and were no longer interested in rebuilding the old ruling coalition on behalf of the ideas of Kemalism and secularism, but wished instead to achieve the political and ideological supremacy of its own cadres in order to carry out schemes for economic development and social welfare.

The secularist-republicanist-Kemalists within the RPP, bound to the party by personal loyalty and family traditions, initially went along with their more radical colleagues, often on İnönü's advice. The military stood by as the silent guardian of the Constitution and the faithful supporter of the RPP, which was still regarded as the sole party that understood and could implement the Constitution of 1961 and maintain the principles of Kemalism.

The Justice Party was preoccupied chiefly with obtaining amnesty for the imprisoned Democrat Party leaders and deputies rather than with basic issues facing the regime. On the one hand, it claimed, in order to soothe the military, that it was a new party and not the continuation of the Democrat Party and that it sought no revenge on behalf of the DP, on the other hand, in private it extolled the memory of Menderes and the socioeconomic legacy of the DP.

In 1963, İnönü made a decision on an issue that both sides saw as the key to greater state control desired by the radicals. In question was the scope of the responsibility and authority of the State Planning Organization (SPO). The Constitution provided for a "mixed economy" *(karma ekonomi)* that accorded more or less equal recognition to private and state enterprises (although in practice the state enterprises were favored by both special legislation and by the continuous infusion of capital from the national budget). Many of the authors of the law which established the State Planning Organization were social-democrat-statists who were openly critical of capitalism and private enterprise. They sought to place the SPO above the parliament by making its decisions immune to parliamentary amendment, approval, or rejection. İnönü accepted the supremacy of the SPO in principle; however, hard pressed to form a coalition government that would keep the RPP in power, he finally agreed, after considerable bargaining, to limit the SPO's autonomy by placing it under the authority of the government as an advisory body on economic matters, as demanded by Ekrem Alican, the leader of the New Turkey Party and the RPP's new coalition partner. Thus a vital issue was settled in favor of private enterprise. The decision marked İnönü's first major break with the statists and young militants in his own party.

The next major development, one that proved fatal to the regime, came after the elections of 1965, with the spillover of the intergroup ideological-political struggle (which had therefore been confined largely to the parliament) to the society at large. The catalyst for this new development was the JP victory in an election from which the Labor (LP) Party emerged as the true spokesman for the leftists. The LP, an avowedly Marxist conglomeration of workers, intellectuals, and a variety of marginal groups that held no seats in the Assembly in 1961, won 15 seats in 1965, although its vote was a mere 3 per cent of the total cast. Meanwhile the number of seats held by the RPP, despite the military's silent support - or in part because of it - and despite its leftist posturings, fell from 173 to 134. The radicals within the RPP blamed the party's electoral failure on a half-hearted commitment to social democracy, while the conservative wing blamed it on the party's alliance with the left. The issue of the direction the RPP was to take was settled in favor of the left wing, headed by Bülent Ecevit, who became Secretary General. A new principle of the left of center *(ortanın solu)* was adopted and the party platform redrafted. Thereupon the liberal and middle-of-the-road group, headed by Turhan Feyzioğlu, resigned and formed its own Reliance Party (RP) in 1967.

The repercussions were extreme and far-reaching. Now dominated by the statist social democrats, the RPP sought to attract all sorts of leftist voters by becoming gradually the champion of all leftist causes, especially on economic issues. It claimed at times to have undermined even the communists' appeal, including that of the Labor Party. It sought to bring in groups outside the parliament, even the trade unions, which previously it had regarded as solely professional associations. However, even as the RPP sought to establish itself solidly among the working class, Ecevit was forced to acknowledge that it was basically a petty bourgeois party.

Leftist currents of all shades experienced an enormous upsurge between 1961 and 1965, but, in general, the groups were not openly militant in character. After 1967, and especially after 1968, the left became very militant, and the LP split up into a variety of radical organizations under the leadership of new, hard-driving, and seemingly professionally-trained leaders, many with connections abroad. The LP was fragmented by differing views of the Soviet occupation of Czechoslavakia. The Kurdish issue became a central theme of leftist propaganda, as many of the new leaders of these new militant groups promoted the Kurdish separatist claims.

The so-called right-wing groups - that is, the ethnic nationalists and Islamists who had lent support to the DP and JP in the past - finally responded to the upsurge of the left by forming their own organizations such as the Grey Wolves, and eventually their own parties, although the Islamists had a much earlier start in 1961. This development among the rightists, occurring primarily after 1968, was fully tolerated, if not encouraged by the JP government, which sought support outside the Parliament in order to counteract the RPP and the more militant leftists, whose activities were carried out in towns and villages.

Thus, the spread of Marxism to some university circles, trade unions, the press, and professional associations was accompanied and counteracted by even a more vigorous resurgence of active nationalist-Islamic-Ottoman feeling, which had long been quiescent under official disapproval but had not been stamped out. This development has been called a Turkish identity crisis, the elements of which were the continuing historical ties to the Ottoman political and cultural past (which during the decades of official non-recognition seemed to have become even stronger and acquired wider public acceptance) and the newly reaffirmed religious identity of the Turks as Muslims. According to the more moderate religious groups, this revived Islam was impregnated with a heavy dose of Turkishness and modernism. The two political parties of the right, the Nationalist Action Party (NAP) and the National Salvation Party (NSP) were not responsible for the national-Islamic-Ottoman resurgence but were to some extent its beneficiaries. They sought rather unsuccessfully to channel and use these popular currents of feeling to attain their own political ends. Toward the end of the 1960s, however, the JP was able to undermine the appeal of the two rightist parties and attract many of their followers. The NAP in turn attempted widening its popular appeal by accepting Islam as a basic part of the Turkish legacy while amending its bylaws to allow for rapid modernization, and the militant activities increased. The NSP, unlike the NAP, did not involve itself in violence.

In conclusion, one may state rather categorically that the grand ruling coalition which had in one form or another governed Turkey since 1923 had vanished, to a large extent because it could no longer accommodate all the conflicting new ideologies and the new social groups. What was needed was a coalition put together with some degree of selectivity but broad enough to encompass all the new forces and ideas, and able to bind these together through some sort of supra-parliamentary mechanism. Indeed, the political history of Turkey after 1971 is the history of the final collapse of the old coalition with the military emerging as the supreme arbiter above political parties and social groups.

4 Interlude: The Takeover of 1971

The takeover of March, 1971 drew its impetus from the old tradition of the army's association with the statist-elitists and the RPP, although it was a rather premature, only half-thought out action. Once more its ostensible aim was the preservation of secularism and the legacy of Atatürk; in addition it was supposed to speed up the implementation of the social economic reforms decreed by the Constitution. It produced no lasting results.

The military, as usual, tried to rule through a National Security Council that was superior to the civilian parliament and a cabinet headed by a "neutral" figure, who, in this case, was Nihat Erim, a liberal-minded old-timer among RPP leaders. Once more the RPP was given preference in the army's arrangement for governing the country as shown by the recent memoirs of General Muhsin Batur, a member of the ruling junta who subsequently joined the RPP.[1]

For the second time a properly elected JP was ousted and its premier, Süleyman Demirel deposed. This time the move was welcome to some people, who where glad to see the military come to grips with the spreading violence and anarchy. İnönü reluctantly gave his public endorsement to the intervention, while Bülent Ecevit denounced it as a blow to the RPP effort to transform itself into a mass social-democratic party. The eventual outcome of this dispute between the RPP leaders was the victory of Ecevit-backed candidates over those put forward by İnönü for the party elections. Ecevit himself was elected Secretary General and, subsequently, İnönü resigned as party chairman. Ecevit was elevated to the chairmanship in 1972.

After the natural death of İnönü in 1973, the RPP gradually discarded Kemalism as an ideology and took a position opposed totally to the basic tenets of the republican regime: it tended to reject the concept of nation *(millet)* and the idea that Turkey was a *national* state. It sought for a solid social foundation on the basis of which it could call itself a true socialist

---

[1] *Anılar ve Görüşler: Üç Dönemin Perde Arkası* (İstanbul, Milliyet Yayınları, 1985).

mass party. This search for a cause led Ecevit to describe the *Alevis* as an "oppressed" minority and to enlist their support. Ecevit's position was not representative of that of the entire RPP but only of the two groups that had captured the leadership of the Party Council. The first group consisted of the secularist-elitist-statist followers of Ecevit (who called themselves social-democrats and many of whom were culturally alienated from society), and a variety of intellectuals, academics, former bureaucrats, etc; the second one consisted of a smaller number of Marxists and radical statists opposed to the capitalist system and this group included such persons as Süleyman Genç and Mustafa Ok (both of whom were former army officers). The third group, although far larger than the other two and representative of the views of the bulk of the RPP members, was inarticulate and incapable of effectively opposing the top leaders. In most cases this group silently deferred to the decisions of the party secretary and council, as had been the case during the days of the single-party rule. The acceptance of decisions from above remained a characteristic of the RPP membership until its end.

It is clear that the deviation of the RPP to the left, its rejection of the Kemalist principles, and its espousal of a hodgepodge of minority and potentially explosive causes (for example, Kurdish nationalists found favor with the party) alienated the military from the RPP in general and from Ecevit in particular. The economic stagnation that set in after 1976, the rampant anarchy and disorder with armed battles between the leftists and rightists, and finally, Ecevit's disastrous coalition government (formed with the help of ten deputies claimed to be "bought" from the JP) of 1978-1979, which followed on the heels of the ineffective but equally ideological coalition of the rightist parties in 1975-1977, removed the possibility of reconciliation among Turkey's political parties. In the autumn of 1979, the RPP suffered a total defeat in the partial elections when it lost five seats contested in the National Assembly. Demirel then established a minority government which, in January of 1980, introduced the economic stabilization program recommended for years by Turkey's foreign creditors. He could not, however, initiate successful measures to curb the anarchy. The entire political edifice erected by the Constitution of 1961 had deteriorated beyond repair.

5 Final Intervention: Characteristics of the 1980 Takeover

In the preceding analysis of the events following 1960 I have sought to focus attention on the profound changes which took place in the structure of the ruling coalition of Turkey and to emphasize a crucial development, namely, the gradual alienation of the military from the RPP. While the military intervention of 1960 brought about a de facto identification of the military with the RPP via the reforms and the Constitution, that of 1971 not only failed to arrest but actually accelerated the process of alienation primarily because it brought into the open the divergence of opinion between the party and the military on social classes, Atatürk, nationalism, secularism, and reformism, which had hitherto been glossed over. The breach between the military and the RPP was detrimental to the development of democracy in Turkey, and for that breach, Bülent Ecevit himself was mainly responsible. On the eve of the 1980 takeover, Kemalism as a state philosophy had no longer a formal, organized representation.

The first outstanding feature of the intervention of 1980 that sets it decisively apart from the 1960 action was that it had been planned well ahead of time by the General Staff in consultation with the field commanders. In a recent work, Mehmet Ali Birand has pointed out that there had actually been a sort of planning staff that not only worked toward achieving the consent and cooperation of all the leading military field commanders but also designated individual officers to perform specific tasks during the takeover and after.[2] Also quite unlike its predecessors, the military seem to have determined in detail the basic constitutional principles that would be enacted, the type of institutions that would be established, the division of labor between the "state" and the government, and the sort of mechanisms that would be needed to ensure smooth functioning after the return to civilian rule.[3] General Kenan Evren declared that the takeover had been carried out in accordance with Article 34 of the military by-law, which charged the military with the defence of the Turkish republic and that it was an act taken on behalf of the entire nation, a claim given substance by later acts.

It appears certain that, in common with the previous takeovers, this one was not envisaged as a permanent military regime but aimed toward the eventual re-establishment of civilian parliamentary rule once the army had put the government house in order. Süleyman Demirel and other politicians claim, however, that had the military adequately used its martial law authority to put down the anarchy prior to 1980, the government could have managed to put its own house in order. Demirel's view (which he reiterated at our meeting in June 1985 in Ankara) is that the military deliberately failed to use its power to stabilize the situation in order to discredit the civilian government and bring the populace to such a point of desperation that the intervention would be welcomed and the orders of the military regime followed without dissent.

---

[2] *12 Eylül: Saat 04: 00* (İstanbul, Karacan Yayınları, 1984).

[3] *Ibid.*, passim.

It is true that under the martial law the military has great discretionary authority to quell disturbances; and it is also true that the military has an extensive intelligence network superior to any such civilian apparatus. However, the full co-operation and participation of the police and other civilian bodies would have been necessary. But Premier Ecevit had invoked a new principle - *eşgüdüm* (coordination) - whereby the martial law authority's decisions had to be approved also by the government. Meanwhile, the police, infiltrated by rightist and leftist "moles," had been divided along ideological lines and become totally ineffective.

It is essential to remember that the military's plans for the takeover, and for the civilian regime that would emerge afterwards, did take into consideration public opinion. Indeed, unlike the military chiefs of 1960 and 1971, the leaders of 1980, showed their concern for the public. Evren succeeded in becoming very influential, not only because of his rather effective speaking ability but also because he conformed to the average Turk's image of a leader, seeming to combine both traditional and modern characteristics. First, he attempted to speak on behalf of the nation as a whole, without attacking by name the old leaders or the political parties but merely condemning the politicians' ineptitude and their disregard for the national interest. He was also able to convey to the public his feelings of trust, respect, and consideration for them by keeping them informed about the important developments concerning the nation as a whole, giving them, for example, the news about his trips abroad. In sum, Evren's reserved and dignified manners, his caring attitude toward the public, his ability to rise above political parties and individual concerns in the name of the nation cast him in the image of a charismatic father figure.

The wide approval of the military by the people was particularly necessary in 1980 because, unlike the interventions of 1960 and 1971, this one did not have the organized support of a political party or a social group. The most significant aspect of the takeover was the lack of identification with any specific civilian or bureaucratic group. Under the military's plan for governing the country, basic decisions were made by the National Security Council (NSC), which included the Chief of the General Staff, Commanders of the Army, Navy and Air Force, and Secretary General of the Council - altogether some six people - whereas the junta of 1960 consisted of 38 officers, to which were added a series of other formal and informal military bodies. The arrangement of 1971 was similar to that of 1960.

In 1980, the participation of the military establishment in the government was limited greatly. The views of the military commanders were passed on directly to the Council without being reviewed by any intermediaries. There were, of course, occasions when the officers expressed dissatisfaction with the actions or attitudes of the NSC. One major objection expressed by a large group of officers was to the relatively lenient policy toward the leftists. Eventually this resulted in a shift of the right followed by a correspondingly ambiguous change of personnel in the NSC, which will be taken up below. In another instance, officers outside the NSC forced the partial abandonment of liberal economic measures and were instrumental in obtaining an increase in the benefits of the public servants. However, the NSC's position toward Necmettin Erbakan and especially, Alparslan Türkeş, the leaders of the NSP and NAP, respectively, remained uncompromising, despite considerable sympathy for the latter among some officers.

The best yardstick for measuring the seriousness of a conflict between the NSC and the rank-and-file officers was the frequency of General Evren's visits to troops to try to persuade them to support the NSC's action. This system was designed to keep decision-making hierarchical, to prevent decisions from being made on the spot by any officer desiring to exercise power, and it was, in great measure, successful. Although there were military officers occupying a variety of positions in the government bureaucracy, their access to and participation in the decision-making process at the top was so limited as to be almost non-existent. Recommendations from the army were normally passed up through hierarchical channels, leaving the ultimate decision to the discretion of the top leaders. This procedure seemed to have been planned well in advance in order to prevent the rank-and-file from becoming directly involved in politics. Its ultimate purpose was to prepare the ground for the permanent extrication of the military from the political arena, a goal repeatedly emphasized by the leaders themselves.

The NSC initially did not abolish the two major political parties (RPP and JP) or arrest deputies, although a few party leaders were detained temporarily and some deputies associated with radical groups and Kurdish separatists were taken into custody. The initial plan was to have a cabinet composed entirely of civilians. However, Turhan Feyzioğlu, the leader of the Reliance Party, was replaced at the very last minute, as prime minister designate, by retired Admiral Bülent Ulusu, ambassador to Rome, because some officers objected to giving the premiership to another politician. The NSC did its best to insulate itself from direct civilian influence and from personal prejudice within the army. Oddly, the isolation from outside influence seems to have increased the popular respect for the military. One can assume that the few army commanders in whose hands the power was concentrated with no intermediaries between them and the populace, were seen as incorruptible and dedicated to the national good.

It may be argued that the administrative apparatus set up in 1980 was not different in essence from that employed in 1960 and 1971. While such an argument is essentially not incorrect, the concentration of power in the NSC, the level of centralization as well as the separation of the decision-makers from the population in 1980 was greater than in the previous military government. It was the type of government that conformed to both the traditional Ottoman pattern and Atatürk's philosophy of government, despite the difference in the goals pursued by the Sultanate and the Republic. It may be added that there is a close resemblance between the methods used by Evren and Atatürk in dealing with the public. The dominant philosophy in both eras was that governmental authority should be exercised strictly in conformity with the political requirements of rulership, eschewing social, economic, or ideological considerations. The ruling of society, according to this philosophy, was a political art. Power and authority were to be reposed in a supreme and wise authority, which might be even a single person so long as that person exercised this authority faithfully for the welfare of the nation and the community.

Atatürk, it should be remembered, saw himself as the total embodiment of the nation and, as such, acted to secure the nation's welfare. The sultan also had been the ultimate repository of state authority. This resembled the Western idea of absolutist but enlightened government, although in the Ottoman-Turkish case, there was an intricate mechanism that defined the limits of authority and the nature of the relations between the ruler and the ruled: it was a popularly supported absolutism that relied upon the populace for legitimacy rather than upon "divine right" or naked power. With such as background in mind, it was obvious that the new regime would incorporate a dominant executive, as had always been the case in Turkish history except in the 1960-1980 period.

The military's view of the civilian sector as an undifferentiated nation-mass and the categorical segregation of the ruler from the ruled, at least in the initial phase of the takeover, determined its actions with regard to the political parties. A substantial number of the army officers as well as the extreme rightists and leftists, viewed the political parties as either hotbeds of strife and dissension or simply as convenient means of achieving power. In 1980 the prestige of the parties was at an all time low due to their pitiful performance in the years from 1960 to 1980. In general, the military considered that political parties should be instruments of national unity, order, and stability rather than vehicles for the expression of special interests of social or economic groups or particular regions of the country.

Yet, the military did not immediately abolish the middle-of-the-road parties. However, when Süleyman Demirel and Bülent Ecevit, despite restrictions imposed on political activities, appeared determined to hold on to the leadership of their parties and perhaps use them to carve roles for themselves in the new government, both the JP and the RPP were summarily abolished.

The closure of these two established political parties, needless to say, was of overwhelming importance for the political life of Turkey. The decision was made after the nationalist wing among officers favoring stronger military rule gained the upper hand. General Necdet Ürüğ became the Secretary and Co-ordinator of the NSC, while General Haydar Saltık, rumoured to have demanded lenient treatment for leftists not involved in violence, was sent to complete his field duty as commander of the First Army in control of Istanbul, the Straits, and Thrace.

One of the first acts of the military rulers was to revive the doctrine of Atatürkism, which had always been the salient ideology of the military, and make it the basis of the regime. To put it in the simplest terms, Atatürkism rests on the ideal that Turkey is a nation-state and that its form of government is republican. These were the fundamental principles enunciated by the Constitutions of 1924 and 1961 and reiterated in the Constitution of 1982. Secularism in its old form was to the military also an inseparable aspect of Atatürkism, while among the traditional Kemalists and some Islamic-nationalist groups, Atatürk's co-operation with the religious elites during the 1919-1922 period is emphasized. (One of these Islamists, of a group still in the minority, said to me in a discussion concerning this question: "We want to show that Atatürk's greatness stems first from his faith, Islam, which he saved and helped to gain a new vigor and vitality.") The issue of definition of "secularism" has since become moot, the meaning of the term having undergone considerable adjustment. However, there is no question but that Atatürkism is a strictly state ideology with no claim to reflect the social, cultural, or economic ideologies of society at large.

To promote the goal of a return to Atatürkism and, as well, to foster national unity, to revitalize the memory of the War of Independence and the establishment of the Republic, the military made much of the Atatürk centennial in 1981. The various national institutions, such as the Historical Society, the Language Society, and assorted Atatürk institutes, were consolidated in one central Supreme Atatürk Society. In June, 1985, I was told that its chief purpose was to train an elite body of intellectuals to be the vanguard of Atatürkism who would disseminate it throughout the country. The textbooks on the history of the Republic were revised in accordance with this new-and-old doctrine.

Meanwhile, as tranquility and public order were restored and the economy began to revive, the military's popularity reached a new peak. In 1981 a timetable for the return to civilian rule was announced. The decision at this point to settle upon a timetable was no doubt hastened by the relentless pressure from Turkey's western allies.

In the same year, a Consultative Assembly was convened, charged with drafting a new constitution. The Assembly members were carefully selected from among thousands of applicants. The constitution drafted by the Assembly, which was, in turn, put into final form by the NSC, established a two-tiered regime. The state *(devlet)* is represented by the President, who has the authority necessary to maintain the territorial integrity and security of the state and the modernist features of the regime and to exercise a mild form of tutelage over the Parliament. The second tier of the regime consists of the Parliament, the Cabinet, the bureaucratic apparatus, and several other institutions and it is designed to carry out the day-to-day functions of the government within the framework set by the state.

The new constitutional system is basically democratic, having preserved intact the general suffrage in free and regular elections, leading to the establishment of government by the winning party, and the whole spectrum of individual freedoms and rights despite some limitations. The Constitution turned out to be fully satisfactory to the average voter in Turkey, as demonstrated by the overwhelming acceptance of it in the popular referendum held on November 6, 1982, and by the endorsement of Kenan Evren as President. Voter participation was 91.27 per cent; 91.37 per cent of the votes were affirmative, while only 8.63 per cent were negative. I believe that the average Turkish citizen accepts as natural the state-government duality and the extensive state powers granted to the President because these conform to the traditional Turkish patterns of government, and are to a large extent outside the citizen's immediate concern.

The Constitution defines political parties as the "indispensable elements of the democratic political system" (Article 68) but prohibits the formation of class-based parties and the establishment of youth branches and the like. As already noted, the political parties are not regarded as channels of popular participation in the decision-making process, but chiefly, as vehicles necessary for the achievement of popular consensus and acquiescence to the regime. However, political parties, have their own dynamics and their own laws, and are difficult to confine within preordained bounds. Thus, the first and the gravest crisis encountered by the military was caused by the emergence of new parties, which also marked the first encounter between the military and freely established civilian political organizations since the takeover.

It appears that the overwhelming approval of the Constitution and the endorsement of Kenan Evren as President led him to assume that he enjoyed unqualified popular support even in *political* matters per se. What Evren failed to realize was that the citizens were predisposed to support a constitution which endowed the state with strong authority for looking after the "high interests of the nation" but not an authoritarian regime which would dictate the day-to-day activities of the citizens.

The issues was dramatized by the events that followed the granting of freedom to form political parties. The NSC, which ruled the country until a duly elected government took the power, used a variety of measures to prevent the etablishment of political parties or the election to the Assembly of individuals who were unwilling to agree with the military and carry out its mandate. At the end, only the Nationalist Democracy Party of General Turgut Sunalp, who had been picked by the NSC for the job, the Populist Party of Necdet Calp, a former provincial governor trusted by the military, and the Motherland Party of Turgut Özal, the Deputy Prime Minister for Economic Affairs between 1980 and 1982, were allowed to participate in the elections. Of these three, only Özal's party appeared to be a genuine political organization, relatively free of subservience to the military. Consequently, despite a variety of difficulties, it rapidly won wide popular support to the detriment of the two other parties. President Evren made a last minute effort to help Sunalp win the elections by launching a personal (and unconstitutional) attack on Özal. Yet, all this interference did not prevent Özal from securing a solid victory in the elections of October 1983, winning 211 seats in the 400-member Assembly, which enabled him to form a majority government.

The elections were a turning point in civilian-military relations, creating a new and unanticipated situation that necessitated the establishment of a new type of dialogue between the state and the government. President Evren accepted the popular verdict and, perhaps, unwillingly entrusted the leadership of the almost completely new ruling coalition to the popularly chosen Motherland Party and its chairman Turgut Özal.

6 Conclusions: Outlook for the Future

The military rule ended by creating a new ruling coalition in which a conglomeration of social groups from the middle classes, ranging from small entrepreneurs to capitalists and from moderate traditionalists to activist nationalists and Islamists finally gained the upper hand. This was the process begun in 1950 but interrupted, thwarted, and forced into ideologically chosen directions by the RPP in alliance with the military in 1960 and, partly, in 1971. As already noted, the fact is that the traditionalist but economically liberal middle class parties consistently had the majority of votes in the elections from 1961 on, although the winning parties were kept from exercising the mandate except when the JP won an absolute majority. The 1980 military intervenors finally created, unwittingly, the constitutional mechanism necessary to permit the political victory of the middle classes in a division of labor that suits both sides. At the upper level, the state interests are embodied in the presidency and are safeguarded by the extensive state powers given to the President.

The Presidency is the symbol and repository of the ideals and ideologies of the state and of the regime as a whole as these are understood by the military (e.g., nationhood, Atatürkism, secularism, and modernism) despite the rather distinct difference between the popular-traditionalist and the elitist interpretation of these terms. However, the difference in interpretation between the military and the civilians narrowed considerably in the last year or so. The key ideological change has occurred in the meaning attached to "modernism." Today, the cultural and political emulation of the West is no longer the axis of modernism. It is, rather, economic development, technological advancement, and material progress in all its forms. The reconciliation with the Ottoman past and the reshaping of the national identity in the light of the Turks' own national cultural and religious ethos have broadened the scope of modernization in such a way as to relegate the West, without abandoning it, to a secondary position, while giving priority to a new historically rooted socio-cultural Turkish identity. In large measure this has been achieved by reinterpreting "secularism" in such a way as to permit the reconciliation between the past and present without damaging the foundation of the Republic.

The conservative, middle class groups, needless to say, have won the final victory through the democratic processes after a thirty-year tenacious struggle against the elitist bureaucratic early reformists who had separated themselves from society. The military appears reconciled to accept these changes as long as they do not pose a threat to the republican regime or to Atatürkism. In fact, many military men appear to welcome the conservative traditionalist trends and regard them as bolstering national unity and building social solidarity, all of which are essential to assure the nation's survival and society.

There are, of course, various groups, which include even some of the middle-aged and older officers, that favor a much stricter policy of Atatürkism and secularism. This view is supported by the old guard of the RPP, a variety of leftist groups, and large numbers of westernized intellectuals, but as a whole, these constitute a small (though influential) minority. There are of course extreme rightist and religious groups within the ruling Motherland Party that are clamoring for a distinct nationalist-Islamist policy. In fact, at a recent private meeting held in Istanbul (June 1985), a nationalist group asked Prime Minister Özal to adopt a more genuine Islamist-nationalist policy even though this may disturb the military.

The key factor in the social realignment of the political system and the ruling coalition of Turkey has been the ideological transformation of the RPP, beginning with its deviation to the left, İnönü's loss of power and death, and the demise of the power of the Kemalists within the party. The transformation of the party to a so-called leftist organization also alienated most of its socially conservative but loyal members who had played important mediating roles in the past in achieving a degree of accommodation with the Justice Party and other middle-of-the-road parties on various economic and social issues. In 1978–1979 the party also lost a major part of its popular support because of the economic debacle and the anarchy that came to be associated with the government headed by Ecevit. The closure of the RPP by the NSC after 1980 was the final act that sealed the fate of this party which had played a significant role in the history of the Republic. Unlike the DP and the JP, and the Motherland Party as well, which could easily be revived due to their continuous strong popular support, the RPP could not be reconstituted on account of a lack of popular basis. The RPP's strength derived from its association with the early history of the Republic and Kemalism, and its main support came from the civil bureaucracy and the intelligentsia, groups that had power far in excess of what was warranted by their numbers because of their control of government, the communications media, and the educational system.

The closure of the RPP ended the phase of modernization that had begun with the founding of the Union and Progress Party during the Young Turk era. The victory of the Motherland Party in the elections of 1983 and the acceptance by the military of the election results began a new phase. The overwhelming popular approval of the Constitution and the electoral majority gained by the government fully legitimized the constitutional system and the government as a democratically approved body. The fact that there was guidance from the top early in the process does not appear to vitiate the result, despite some minority opinion to the contrary. The current challenge to the system appeared to stem from a rather unexpected quarter, namely the True Path *(Doğru Yol)* Party headed until 1987 by Hüsamettin Cindoruk but in reality representing the views of the old leadership of the Justice Party, notably of Süleyman Demirel. The key contention of this party is that the military still exerts considerable influence in and out of the government so that the regime is not fully civilian and that economic development has been too slow. In the 1987 general elections the True Path Party could become only the third party, for Demirel's popular support was and is limited. Most of the lower-ranking and truly influential communal and political leaders of the old JP appear to support fully Özal's party. In a private conversation with me, Demirel claimed that the ideas of the Motherland Party are "our ideas" and that Özal and his associates are "our boys."

Actually this rift within the ruling coalition can be easily repaired, and the accusations of military influence in government can be swiftly answered through the full "civilianization" of the system. This could be achieved by electing Süleyman Demirel to the Presidency, provided that the military do not insist on keeping their hold on that office. Yet, as the President is elected by the Assembly, it is obvious that the political parties are legally entitled to elect whom so ever they choose. As far as the other political parties are concerned, the Populist Party has quickly lost ground. In August 1985 the party merged with the Social Democracy Party, leading to the creation of the Social Democracy Populist Party (SDPP). The Nationalist Democracy Party, too, rapidly lost what little attraction it had in the eyes of the electorate. The SDPP appears intent on capitalizing on the early political traditions of Turkey so as to attract the old RPP followers. In the 1987 general elections the SDPP was placed second and I believe that its chances for success are little unless it judges correctly and realistically the present social and political conditions in the country. The old RPP had resulted from unique political and historical conditions and cannot be revived.

In sum, the present political system in Turkey appears to conform to the Turkish traditions regarding power and authority and to represent the synthesis of various socio-economic forces, and, thus, it enjoys overwhelming popular support. For the first time in its history, Turkey appears to be on the verge of taking upon itself the true essence of democracy. The distribution of power between the state (President) and government (Premier) can assure the co-existence of modernism and "traditionalism" and guarantee the maintenance of order and security.

Chapter 11
Transition to Civilian Governments in Turkey: The Military Perspective

William Hale

1 Introduction

The coup of 12 September 1980 was the third occasion within thirty years on which the Turkish army[1] had overthrown an elected government. What was remarkable about these interventions was not that they occurred (the military coup is, after all, the common coin of third world politics), but that each of them have been followed by a return to civilian government after a relatively short period. As Dankwart A. Rustow has reminded us, incoming military regimes usually promise a quick return to civilian rule, but seldom live up to the promise.[2] The fact that the Turkish army has proved exceptional in this respect indicates that the conditions which have determined its actions have differed significantly from those of other countries.

The first part of this chapter aims to take this enquiry further, by discussing the modern historical legacies which appear to have wielded a fundamental influence over the Turkish army's political role. The second part examines the way in which they performed it during 1980–1983. Admittedly, the discussion is far from complete. Since there seemed to be no point in going over ground which is thoroughly and expertly examined by other contributors to this collection, I have confined myself to those top-

---

[1] Throughout this chapter, I have used the word "army" or "the military" to refer to all four armed services (the army, navy, air force and gendarmerie). This avoids alternative and cumbersome locutions, and seems justified by the fact that, in Turkey the army is easily the largest of the four.

[2] Dankwart A. Rustow, "The Military in Middle Eastern Society and Politics", in *The Military in the Middle East*, edited by Sydney Nettleton Fisher (Columbus, Ohio State University Press, 1963), p. 13.

ics on which there may be something new to be said. Large and important areas of the subject have been ignored. The result may be lumpy and unbalanced, but it is hoped that it may provoke others into a fruitful discussion.

2 Legacies, Plans and Proposals

The Turkish army's view of its political task in 1980 seems to have been conditioned by three main factors: firstly, its political inheritance from the Atatürk and earlier periods; secondly, Turkey's international situation; and thirdly, its own experiences during and after the two previous interventions of 1960 and 1971. Each of these deserves a short explanation.

Most discussions of the army's modern historical legacy start from the claim that Atatürk established the "firm principle that the army must take no part in politics" and that "the coup of May 1960 was the first significant break with the Atatürk tradition".[3] This raises the tortuous question of what the Atatürk tradition actually was.

Legally, the answer seems straightforward. Article 40 of the 1924 Constitution vested supreme command of the armed forces in the Grand National Assembly, "represented by the President of the Republic". Article 23 stipulated that "no person may be a deputy and hold office under the Government at the same time"; this, presumably, included the tenure of a military commission.[4] More specifically, a law passed by the Assembly on 19 December 1923 required all army officers to resign from active duty before running for parliament. This left those who were sitting in the legislature entitled to retain their commands, but in October 1924 Atatürk required them to apply the same rule.[5] This order was not based purely on considerations of general principle, since Atatürk was apparently suspicious at this time of an incipient "Pasha's plot" against him,[6] but it was rigorously applied. Although innumerable ex-officers have entered parliament since, they have all retired from the forces first.

---

[3] Geoffrey Lewis, "Turkey, the End of the First Republic", *World Today* 16 (1960), p.377; Daniel Lerner and Richard D. Robinson, "Swords and Ploughshares: the Turkish Army as a Modernizing Force", *World Politics* 13 (1960), p.21.

[4] For an English text of the 1924 Constitution, see G. L. Lewis, *Turkey* (London, Benn, 1955), pp.197-208.

[5] Lerner and Robinson, "Swords and Ploughshares," p.20.

[6] George S. Harris, "The Role of the Military in Turkish Politics", *The Middle East Journal* 19 (1965), part I, pp.56-59. See Dankwart A. Rustow, "The Army and the Founding of the Turkish Republic", *World Politics* 11 (1958-59), pp.513-552; Kemal H. Karpat, "The Military and Politics in Turkey, 1960-64", *American Historical Review* 75 (1970), p.1659, Nurşen Mazıcı, *Atatürk Döneminde Muhalefet* (İstanbul, Dilmen Yayınevi, 1984), pp.73-76.

While a clear ruling could thus be found in the Atatürkist canon to the effect that membership of the legislature and the armed forces are incompatible, it can hardly be claimed that it rigidly or totally excludes the army from politics. In Ottoman days, the civilian and military arms of the state were not distinguished. Moreover, the army had played a crucial role in the introduction of the first Constitution in 1876, and its re-implementation in 1908. This legacy had not lost its force with the proclamation of the Republic. As an indication of this, several former members of the National Unity Committee referred to it in conversations with the writer in 1985, when seeking to explain their own actions of 1960–1961.

As George S. Harris concludes, "Atatürk's main concern with the army was not to keep it out of politics, but to make sure it remained completely loyal to him and to the Republic".[7] Behind the scenes, Marshall Fevzi Çakmak, Chief of the General Staff from 1921 until 1944, exercised a powerful and independent influence.[8] On occasions, Atatürk encouraged the army officers to think of themselves as the vanguard of his revolution: in his words "whenever the Turkish nation has wanted to take a step up it has always looked to the army ... as the leader of movements to achieve lofty national ideals".[9] In his broadcast speech of 12 September 1980 General Evren referred to this wider version of the Atatürk legacy when he spoke of "the aim of 'raising our national culture to the level of contemporary civilisation ...' as laid down by the great Atatürk".[10] However, Atatürk's recognition of the army's missionary role left the Generals with the task of deciding when they were entitled to infringe the equally Atatürkist rule that serving officers were not to be responsible for the government of the country. By merely referring to Atatürk's legacy, they were not solving the dilemma which it posed.

A second, and possibly crucial factor in determining the Turkish army's political attitudes may be the fact that, alone among the Near Eastern countries, Turkey is a member of NATO and the Council of Europe, besides having an Association Agreement with the European Community which is supposed to lead eventually to full membership of the Community. This involves it in formal obligations to respect democratic principles which do not affect the leadership of most developing countries. Although it is very hard to substantiate this point clearly, it seems extremely likely that the army has on several occasions been aware of the serious external problems which would be created if it were unable to convince the

---

[7] Harris, "The Role of the Military in Turkish Politics", p. 56.

[8] Rustow, "Army", pp. 549–550.

[9] Quoted, Harris, "The Role of the Military in Turkish Politics", p. 56, n. 4.

[10] English text in *12 September in Turkey: Before and After* (Ankara, General Secretariat of the National Security Council, 1982), pp. 225–233.

outside world that its interventions would be succeeded fairly quickly by the reinstallation of a democratically elected government.

In the case of the crisis which led to the intervention of 12 March 1971, we know that such considerations were important to the high command. As General Muhsin Batur, then the Air Force Commander, tells us, a group of officers had earlier approached him with a plan for the imposition of an outright military regime, which they wished him to lead. General Batur turned the idea down:

The Western world cannot accept this sort of system and procedure. It's just not good enough to say 'if they don't accept it, then so be it'. If we give way (i.e., adopt the proposed plan) we'll get support from the Eastern Bloc and Red China, but that would be a disaster for Turkey.[11]

It is hard to prove the importance of this factor in the Generals' decisions before and after 12 September 1980, but impossible to dismiss it entirely. Quite naturally, they were unwilling to admit that they bowed to pressure from abroad, since the very idea would have been unacceptable to most Turks. On the other hand, it was important to them to keep their relations with the western allies on as even a keel as possible. A crucial aspect of this was Turkey's relations with the Council of Europe, in which Turkey was suspended from membership of the Parliamentary Assembly after the 12 September coup. In his speech in the closing session of the Consultative Assembly in October 1983, the retiring Prime Minister Bülend Ulusu maintained that "the Turkish nation has adopted parliamentary democracy as her political system without any external influence."[12] Certainly, it would be a mistake to suggest that the government was entirely subservient to the Western allies. Nevertheless, the importance which the government attached to Turkey's readmission to the Parliamentary Assembly (which was achieved early in 1984) and the effort they put into tyring to convince the outside world that the regime established in 1983 met the democratic norms indicated that they were not entirely deaf to foreign opinion. They had to bear in mind that all sorts of groups and institutions in Western Europe - including trade unions, organizations such as Amnesty International, and politicians in the European Parliament as well as the national legislatures - took a much closer interest in Turkey's internal affairs than they had done in 1960-1961 or in 1971-1973.

A third and undoubtedly important influence on the army's political approaches has been the anxiety of the high command to prevent division within the army or any disturbance of the military hierarchy. In 1980, the

[11] Muhsin Batur, "Son 30 Yılın Olayı: Muhsin Batur'un Anıları", part 10, *Milliyet,* 12 May 1985.

[12] Quoted, *Newspot* (Ankara, Directorate of Press and Information) 21 October 1983.

Generals were also anxious to avoid having to intervene again after a few years. This danger had been bluntly referred to by İsmet İnönü, in a reported conversation with Bülent Ecevit in 1971:[13]

> From time to time Turkey enters a period of overhaul. Every time she enters such a period, the army intervenes; it stays (in power) for a time, and then withdraws. Time goes by and we politicians make a mess of things, so the army intervenes again. It will go on like this, and these periods of overhaul will gradually become more and more frequent.[14]

It was precisely because they wished to break this cycle of constant interventions that the military rulers of 1980–1983 tried to provide laws and constitutional machinery which, they believed, would prevent an eventual return to anarchy. The complaint against them is that, in doing so, they broke the democratic rules to which they claimed to be committed.

The need to preserve unity and the command hierarchy within the army was a connected priority. Eighteen days after the coup of 12 September, General Evren delivered these words to the cadets at the War Academy:

> Whenever the army entered into politics it began to lose its discipline and, gradually, it was led into corruption. We can observe its most basic example in our recent history, during the Balkan War. Therefore, I demand from you once again not to take our present operation as an example to yourselves and never to get involved in politics. We had to implement this operation within a chain of commands and orders to save the army from politics and to cleanse it from political dirt.[15]

Evren's remarks were probably inspired by the army's relatively recent political experiences, as well as those of the Young Turk period, to which he referred. Immediately after the coup of 27 May 1960, Cemal Gürsel had apparently expected that the relatively junior officers who had, of necessity, been recruited to the revolutionary team would quietly return to their barracks, leaving power in the hands of himself and his senior Generals.[16] But it was not to be. The National Unity Committee, which assumed power in Turkey after 27 May, was a large and unwieldy body which originally had 38 members, down to the rank of Captain. It faced a major internal split in November 1960 when 14 radicals, led by the then Colonel Alparslan Türkeş, were expelled from its ranks. Frustrated by their exclusion from power in 1960–1961, a small number of officers

---

[13] It will be remembered that at that time İnönü had supported the "12 March Memorandum" of 1971, whereas Ecevit did not.

[14] Quoted, Mehmet Ali Birand, *12 Eylül: Saat 04:00* (İstanbul, Karacan Yayınları, 1984), p.234.

[15] Quoted, *12 September*, pp.301–302.

[16] Feroz Ahmad, *The Turkish Experiment in Democracy, 1950–1975* (London, Hurst, for the Royal Institute of International Affairs, 1977), p.162.

supported Colonel Talât Aydemir in his two attempted coups of February 1962 and May 1963.[17] The challenge had been overcome, but repeated itself in 1970-1971. One of the senior Generals' main motives in issuing the *pronunciamento* of 12 March 1971 was to head off a prospective attempted coup by their more radical juniors.[18]

In the case of the 1980 intervention the Generals appear to have been extremely careful to avoid such complications. Unlike that of 1960, the 12 September coup involved no alteration of the command structure within the army. The National Security Council, a body established by the 1961 Constitution, simply took over as the ruling junta, having been purged of its civilian members.[19] General Evren, as Chief of the General Staff, became head of state. He agreed with his four force commanders that they would not make separate statements on political matters, and that he would speak for all of them,[20] a sharp contrast with the experiences of 1960-1961 when junior members of the National Unity Committee had regularly aired their separate views.

It can also be argued that the decision to confine authority to the five men at the very top of the armed forces had some important effects on the political direction taken by the regime during 1980-1983. In the first place, it probably gave it a more conservative political bent than its predecessors (particularly that of 1960-1961) granted that the radical officers - both of the left and right - tended to occupy the middle rather than the topmost ranks. This reinforced other factors leading to the gradual deradicalization of the army as a political force, such as the greater size of the civilian elite, which had undermined the army's previous position as the dominant radical force in Turkish society.[21] As a sign of this, after the 1960 coup there had been a good deal of rather loaded arguments as to

---

[17] See *Ibid.*, pp.165-172, 177-185; also Walter F. Weiker, *The Turkish Revolution, 1960-1961* (Washington, The Brookings Institute, 1963), pp.131-138, and C.H. Dodd, *Politics and Government in Turkey* (Manchester, Manchester University Press, 1969), pp.60-61.

[18] Ahmad, *The Turkish Experiment in Democracy, 1950-1975*, p.292; Batur, "Son 30 Yılın Olayı: Muhsin Batur'un Anıları", parts 10-14, *Milliyet*, 12-16 May 1985; Dennis Burnouf, "La situation en Turquie après les interventions du haut commandement dans les affaires politiques", *Politique Etrangère* 37 (1972), pp.104-105. According to Burnouf, Batur himself had prepared to launch a coup on the night of 9-10 March 1971, but was dissuaded at the last minute by Memduh Tağmaç, the Chief of the General Staff. Batur does not mention this in his memoirs: he tells us that a "secret organization" of officers had earlier asked him to head a radical coup, but he turned their proposal down. Nor does Cüneyt Arcayürek's blow-by-blow account support Burnouf's version of events: cf. Arcayürek, *Çankaya'ya Giden Yol, 1971-1973* (Ankara, Bilgi Yayınevi, 1985), pp.46-49.

[19] There was, admittedly, a change of title, which does not come out in English translation, from "Milli Güvenlik Kurulu" to "Milli Güvenlik Konseyi".

[20] Conversation with General Sedat Celâsun.

[21] Gerhard Weiher, *Militär und Entwicklung in der Türkei, 1945-1973* (Opladen, Leske Verlag für Deutsches Orient-Institut, 1978), pp.102-107.

whether it should be referred to as a "revolution". The coup of 1980 was officially dubbed an "operation" and the question of its claim to "revolutionary" status does not seem to have arisen.

Apart from this, the concentration of power at the top probably strengthened the decision not to continue the military regime indefinitely. The longer the army stayed in power, the greater was the risk of ideological or other divisions within the forces coming out into the open, and of a "coup within a coup" occurring. This combined with the factors mentioned earlier, deriving from Turkey's international position and the Atatürkist legacy (or at least a part of it) to ensure that there would eventually be a return to civilian government.

During the earlier part of 1980, there had been extensive discussions among senior military men about whether the army should take power, and, if so, what it should do afterwards. The planned coup, code-named the "Flag Plan", was originally scheduled for 11 July, but then postponed to 12 September.[22] There was some debate between what might be called the maximalist school of thought, which urged a total takeover, to be followed by radical social reforms, and the minimalists, who believed that changes should be restricted to the Constitution and laws affecting state security.[23] In the event, it was the minimalists who won the argument.

Six special study groups were set up to produce draft plans for the post-coup period. These were then submitted for discussion and approval by Evren and his four force commanders. Immediately after the coup, martial law would be proclaimed throughout the country, and exceptional powers given to the martial law commanders. Power would be assumed by the military members of the National Security Council (NSC). Special expert committees would be set up to prepare changes to the Constitution, the laws on political parties and elections, and reform of the trade unions and other organizations. All these proposals were outlined to the public by Evren, in his broadcast address of 12 September.[24]

An important feature of this programme was that it did not envisage the total exclusion of the old political parties from government. The Cabinet, which would have executive responsibility under the NSC, would be

---

[22] The reason for the postponement was that Demirel's administration won a vote of confidence on 28 June, and Evren decided that it would be injudicious to overthrow the government so soon after it had received the support of parliament. September 12th was chosen to coincide with joint NATO exercises, known as "Anvil Express", so that the unusual movement of troops would not arouse suspicion. Birand, *12 Eylül: Saat 04:00,* pp. 209-213.

[23] *Ibid.,* pp. 168-179.

[24] Text printed in *12 September,* pp. 225-233. See also Frank Tachau and Metin Heper, "The State, Politics and the Military in Turkey", *Comparative Politics* 16 (October 1983), pp. 26-27.

formed of members of the existing parties who were thought to be sympathetic to the army's ideas, as in 1971. However, parliament would be dissolved, and the Cabinet would be responsible to the NSC, not to the Assembly. (This arrangement was evidently inspired by the fact that, during 1971-1973, the programme which some of the commanders proposed had been frustrated by the refusal of the parties in parliament - notably the Justice Party - to go along with it.)[25]

Needless to say, these plans left some important questions unanswered. If it were decided that some permanent restrictions on civil liberties would be necessary, then the question would be raised as to whether such restrictions were so draconian as to make a mockery of the claim that Turkey's subsequent political system would be truly democratic. The future relationship between the military and politicians was also uncertain. If the existing parties refused to have anything to do with the military government, then should the military dissolve them, or leave them alone, in the hope that they would later have a change of heart? These issues were still in doubt at the time the coup was launched, and were to account for some of the most perplexing problems with which Evren and his colleagues were faced during the next three years.

On the other hand, a striking feature of the 1980 coup was that, in spite of these defects, the military appears to have formed a far clearer idea of what it wanted to achieve, and how to achieve it, than had been the case in 1960 and 1971. If nothing else, the army seems to have learnt much from its past mistakes.

3 The Military and the Politicians, 1980-1983

On 12 September, the army had set itself four main tasks: firstly, to suppress terrorism; secondly, to restore economic growth and stability; thirdly, to introduce a new Constitution and legal arrangements which, it was hoped, would prevent another lapse into anarchy; and, fourthly, to work out effective arrangements with the civilian politicians, both old and new. This discussion concentrates on the last of these themes. The first two, though obviously important, deserve a more lengthy and detailed description than can be given here. The constitutional and legal innovations of 1980-1983 have been well described and analysed elsewhere[26] and have

[25] Birand, *12 Eylül: Saat 04:00*, pp.249-251.

[26] Notably, by C.H.Dodd, *The Crisis of Turkish Democracy* (Walkington, England, Eothen Press, 1983), chap.5; John H.McFadden, "Civil-Military Relations in the Third Turkish Republic", *The Middle East Journal* 39 (1985), pp.70-73; Andrew Mango, "The Third Turkish Republic", *World Today* 39 (1983), pp.32-37.

also received expert attention from other contributors to this collection, so there seems to be little point in going over relatively well-cultivated ground. Certain of the provisions of the new Constitution and the laws on political parties nevertheless need to be referred to when discussing the regime's handling of its relations with the politicians.

On this score, it appears that the NSC were particularly influenced by their experiences immediately after 12 September. As we have seen, they had originally hoped that the existing parties would agree to co-operate in a Cabinet responsible to themselves. Their first choice for the job of Prime Minister was Turhan Feyzioğlu, leader of the Republican Reliance Party, which was originally a splinter of the Republican People's Party, and which had merely four seats in parliament then. Feyzioğlu was reluctant to take on the task, granted the smallness of his party, and offered to do so only if members of the Republican People's and Justice Parties were included in the Cabinet. Meanwhile, the only name for inclusion in the government to which the NSC were firmly agreed was that of Turgut Özal, who had been Demirel's economic supremo before 12 September. Özal was judged to have unrivalled experience and authority in the economic field, and virtually indispensable connections with overseas financial institutions. Unfortunately for the Generals, the moderates in the two main parties were dissuaded by their party leaders and colleagues from joining the Cabinet. In the Republican People's Party, Orhan Eyüboğlu, the Party's Secretary-General, told the NSC that he was ready to help, but that his party was suspicious of Feyzioğlu (who was, after all, a defector from their ranks). The RPP leaders feared that association with the military would not do them any good in the long run - an attitude which Ecevit had adopted in 1971-1973. Demirel apparently took a similar view, and prevented Kâmran İnan, the "moderate" favored by the military in his own party, from taking office under the army.

The NSC were aware of these toings and froings in the two main parties, since Ecevit and Demirel were both held in protective custody at a military camp at Gelibolu at the time and their telephones were being tapped.[27] Eventually, Evren's patience snapped. On 17 September he told his colleagues:

> All my trust in the politicians has been rubbed away. If they are all asking their leaders what to do, it means that in practice they will go on doing the same thing. We need people who really believe in us and will stick with us. Let's give up the idea of forming a government made up of the RPP and JP moderates.[28]

---

[27] Birand, *12 Eylül: Saat 04:00*, p.311.

[28] *Ibid.*, pp.306-311; Kenneth Mackenzie, "Turkey Under the Generals", *Conflict Studies* 126, January 1981 (London, Institute for the Study of Conflict), p.19.

After unsuccessful approaches to General Haydar Saltık (then Commander of the Aegean Army and later Secretary-General of the National Security Council) the NSC's choice fell on ex-Admiral Bülend Ulusu, who had fortuitously retired as Commander of the Naval Forces the previous month. Ulusu announced his Cabinet on 21 September: it contained 27 members, of whom six were retired Generals and the remainder were neutral bureaucrats or academics.

The fruitless discussions between the military regime and the politicians naturally delayed the formation of a Cabinet. It also had an important effect on the attitude of the NSC towards the old political leaders, since it raised the question as to whether their parties could be allowed to exist in the long run. As far as the two extremist right-wing parties were concerned, the NSC's policy was straightforward. Both Alparslan Türkeş and Necmettin Erbakan were held to have broken the law and Constitution on a number of points, and were placed on trial. Although both are now free men,[29] at the time, there seemed to be no question of their being allowed to re-form their parties. With Demirel and Ecevit, however, the Generals were forced to be patient, since they could not be proved guilty on any legal counts, and the NSC were probably aware of the danger of making martyrs of them, as had happened in the case of Adnan Menderes. For his part, Demirel did nothing to provoke the military. After his release from custody on 11 October, he remained quietly in his house in Ankara, awaiting an opportunity to engineer a political comeback.

Ecevit, however, presented a greater problem for the Generals, since he was not willing to withdraw entirely from the political stage, and had numerous friends in Western Europe who could be mobilized in his defence. He was released from custody, together with Demirel, on 11 October, and resigned from the Chairmanship of the Republican People's Party at the end of the month.[30] However, he then returned to journalism as editor of the weekly magazine *Arayış* (Search). Predictably, he was critical of aspects of the new regime[31] though he did not openly attack the necessity

---

[29] Erbakan was arrested in April 1981, and charged with working against the secularist principles written into the 1961 Constitution and Article 163 of the Penal Code. In February 1983 he was sentenced to four years imprisonment with subsequent confinement to the north-west of Turkey. He and his colleagues finally received a formal acquittal in September 1985. Türkeş was charged, together with 585 defendants from his party, with instigating civil war and murdering nearly 600 people between 1974 and 1980. He was eventually sentenced, but released on medical grounds in April 1985. Dodd, *Turkish Democracy*, pp. 45–46: *Milliyet*, 10 April 1985, 20 September 1985.

[30] The reason was that the parties had been banned from any active involvement in politics after 12 September 1980, but that this did not apply to Ecevit as an individual, once he resigned from his party.

[31] See, for instance, his editorials in *Arayış* of 2 May and 30 May 1981.

for the 12 September coup. An editorial he wrote on torture was banned by the military censors, and all copies of the issue concerned were confiscated.[32] Finally, on 2 June 1981, he was removed from the editorship of the magazine by Decree no. 52 of the National Security Council, which forbad any of the former politicians "to make verbal or written statements, write articles or hold meetings about the past or future legal or political system of Turkey".[33]

Ecevit was subsequently charged with violation of this Decree and sentenced to four months' imprisonment in November 1981. Soon after his release in April 1982 he was re-arrested for remarks he was said to have made to various foreign newspapers and broadcasting organizations. He was acquitted on these series of charges, but the following August he began a 34-day sentence for statements he had given to the German magazine *Der Spiegel*. By the end of the year, the cat and mouse game which the authorities had been playing with him appeared to have ended, as he was permitted to travel abroad to attend a conference in Stockholm. Whether this change of heart by the authorities was the result of pressure from his supporters in Western Europe, or whether it was simply decided that Ecevit's influence inside the country was waning, remains uncertain.

All these events appear to have pushed the military government to the conclusion that the party system would have to be restructured if their plans were to be carried through. At the time of the coup, all the political parties had been banned from political activities, though they had not been formally dissolved. It was not until October 1981 that this step was taken. Thereafter, the military made it clear that they would not allow the old politicians to re-enter politics for some time after civilian government was restored. This was spelled out in black and white in the Provisional Articles which were added to the Constitution by the NSC after its approval by the Consultative Assembly, and shortly before it was successfully submitted to a referendum in November 1982. The first of these provided that, if the Constitution were approved in the referendum, General Evren would automatically be elected President for the following seven years. Provisional Article 4 stated that the Chairmen, General Secretaries, and other senior office-holders in the former political parties could not form, join, or have "any kind of relations" with future political parties, or stand for election (even as independents) for ten years. Ex-deputies and senators could not form or occupy executive posts in any new parties for five years, though they could run for election as backbenchers. The hope evidently was that by 1992 most people would have forgotten about Ece-

---

[32] *Ibid.*, 18 April 1981, p. 13.

[33] Quoted, *Milliyet*, 3 June 1981.

vit, Demirel, and the other political leaders of the pre-coup period, so that their re-entry into politics would be practically impossible.

The form which the Generals wished the future party system to take became further evident with the promulgation of the new Political Parties Law in May 1983. This legislation repeated and strengthened provisions in the Constitution which outlawed Marxist, Kurdish separatist, and Islamic fundamentalist parties, and stated that parties should remain "attached to the principles and reforms of Atatürk". Their establishment was subject to the most elaborate bureaucratic procedures; parties required at least thirty founder members whose names and a plethora of personal documents had to be submitted to the Ministry of the Interior. Finally, the NSC was given the power to disqualify any founder members at its discretion, until the new Assembly was convened.[34]

On 28 April 1983, Evren had formally committed the regime to holding general elections on 6 November. The Political Parties Law gave the military government extensive controls over the prospective parties, but left open the question as to whether it would promote its own party. One option had already been foreclosed by the time the Political Parties Law had been issued - that General Evren should form his own party and run for the Presidency under its banner. By presenting his candidacy for the Presidency unopposed, and as an independent, Evren had in effect renounced the "Gaulleist option". His popularity in the country was such that he could probably have won the Presidency in a fair open fight, even though the democratic legitimacy of the actual form of the election was open to attack on a number of counts.[35] On the other hand, it is far from certain that his personal popularity could have been translated into support for an officially sponsored party. Moreover, the Constitution required that the President should not be a member of any party after his election, and the Turkish tradition (since 1961, at any rate) had been that the President should be a relatively neutral figure drawn from the top ranks of the armed services.

This still left the NSC with the option of giving official backing to one or more of the new parties. Past experiences on this score were not en-

---

[34] 1982 Constitution, Article 14; *Siyasi Partiler Kanunu*, no. 2820, Articles 4, 5, 8, 80-82, and provisional Article 4.

[35] These were (a) that there had been no competing candidates, (b) that Evren's election as President was considered to be automatic, on acceptance of the Constitution and (c) that campaining for a "no" vote in the referendum had been banned. Granted the conditions of the time, these objections could have been overcome if the voters had been asked separately whether they approved of the Constitution, and of Evren's election as President. Evren could then have served as President until the Assembly convened, at which time he could have re-submitted his name for election by the Assembly, as provided for in the Constitution (Articles 101-102).

couraging. In 1961 many Turks had treated the New Turkey Party as the group favoured by the army, but it had made little impact and faded away in the mid-1960s. During 1972–1973 the Republican Reliance Party had been fitted into the same role, but it had all but vanished by 1980. On the third occasion the military regime adopted a rather ambiguous attitude. Soon after the new Political Parties Law was enacted, ex-General Turgut Sunalp formed the Nationalist Democracy Party, whose policies clearly reflected the views of the military. President Evren was generally careful to avoid saying publicly that he favoured the party, but this was certainly the image that the public had of it. Similarly, the Populist Party, formed by Necdet Calp, a former provincial Governor and private secretary to two previous Presidents, was generally treated as an officially approved opposition of the moderate left.

Two other parties, formed on 6 June 1983, presented the military with greater problems. The Social Democracy Party (SDP) appeared at that time to be a fairly direct descendant of the Republican People's Party, although its policies generally reflected those which the RPP had espoused before its move to the left under Bülent Ecevit. In the opposing tradition of Turkish politics was the Great Turkey Party, which assumed the mantle left by the departed Justice Party. "A Great Turkey" had been one of Demirel's favourite election slogans; indeed he had used it as the title of a book he wrote in 1975.[36] The Chairman of the party was a retired general, Ali Fethi Esener, but its real organizer was Hüsamettin Cindoruk, who had been head of the Justice Party's provincial organization in Istanbul after 1960.

The Great Turkey Party, in particular, represented an open challenge to the military's determination that the old parties should be considered so dead and buried. According to a later statement by Demirel, Evren and Ulusu initially tried to persuade Esener to collaborate with Sunalp's Nationalist Democracy Party, but to no avail.[37] On somewhat dubious legal grounds, the Great Turkey Party was closed down by the NSC on 31 May 1983. Demirel was placed under detention at a military base in Çanakkale, together with the former Justice Party's deputy leader, Saadettin Bilgiç and the veteran JP Foreign Minister, İhsan Sabri Çağlayangil. For good measure, those detained at Çanakkale also included several ex-RPP personalities, notably Deniz Baykal. (In the event, the detainees were re-

[36] Süleyman Demirel, *Büyük Türkiye* (İstanbul, Dergâh Yayınları, 1975).

[37] In a message sent by Demirel from his detention camp in Çanakkale to *The Times* in London. Ironically, the boot is now on the other foot, as members of the NDP are anxiously trying to join up with the True Path Party, the successor to the Great Turkey Party.

leased on 30 September, by which time it was too late for them to have any influence on the results of the forthcoming elections.)[38]

A further dilemma for the military was the position of the Motherland Party, formed by Turgut Özal on 20 May 1983. Özal had resigned from the Ulusu Cabinet in June 1982 after disagreements with his colleagues over economic policy. However, the military could present no legal case against him (even if they had wished to do so and there is no evidence that they considered such action). Closure of his party could have produced serious repercussions abroad, and would have severely weakened the NSC's claim that Turkey was genuinely returning to democracy. Accordingly, they had to leave Özal free to carry on with what turned out to be a successful campaign, even though it sharply reduced Sunalp's chances of winning an overall majority in the elections.

SDP, however, received harsher treatment. On 23 June, using their powers under the Political Parties Law, the Generals vetoed 23 of 36 founder members of the party, including the Chairman, Erdal İnönü. The party then appointed replacements, but some of these were also vetoed. As a result, SDP was left without sufficient founder members on 24 August, the last date on which parties could officially enter the elections. Similar treatment was meted out to the True Path Party, which was a reincarnation of the Great Turkey Party, under the Chairmanship of Dr. Yıldırım Avcı. The outcome of all these restrictions was that Turkey entered the election campaign in October 1983 with five parties, of which only three - the Populist, Nationalist Democracy, and Motherland Parties - were permitted to run candidates. Of these, the Motherland Party had the ironic distinction of being the party least favoured by the military. SDP and the True Path Party occupied a still more ambiguous position, since they were legally allowed to exist as parties, but not allowed to compete in the elections.

Two other developments prior to polling day caused commentators to wonder just how democratic the elections would be. On 21 September, the NSC issued individual vetoes on 719 parliamentary candidates, 475 of whom were independents, 89 from the Populist Party, 81 from the Motherland Party and 74 from the NDP. The main motive, apparently, was the fear that some former politicians whom the Generals considered undesirable might get back into parliament as independents, plus the desire to appear even handed as between the parties. Finally, on the evening of 4 November, some 36 hours before polling was to begin, the President gave a television address in which he told the voters "I believe that you will bring in an administration which will continue the accomplishments

[38] See Andrew Mango, "Turkey: Democracy under Military Tutelage", *World Today* 39 (1983), pp. 431, 434.

of the NSC", an implied recommendation to vote for Sunalp's party. Later on in the same speech he delivered a veiled attack on Turgut Özal.[39]

Whether the President's intervention had a significant effect on the election results or not is open to dispute. The Motherland Party subsequently claimed that his speech had cost them five percentage points in the popular poll. Admittedly, in some areas in eastern Anatolia local officials may have used it to impress unsophisticated voters with the idea that they were obliged to vote for the NDP. On the other hand, it may well have strengthened support for Özal among middle class urban voters, who appreciated what the army had done for the country, but were also very aware of Sunalp's evident lack of political skills. Certainly, Evren's last minute intervention appears to have been one of his most serious mistakes. In particular it underlined the military's uncertain stance towards the new parties. Prima facie, they had adopted a neutral attitude to all of them, but had not prevented Sunalp from encouraging the popular idea that he was the army's choice. In this speech, Evren appeared to be stepping off the fence. His address was ill-advised because, if Sunalp had won the election, then many people would have discounted the result on the grounds that it was purely due to military pressure. If (as actually happened) Özal won, then the result could be seen as a serious snub for the President.

Fortunately for Evren, he had not committed himself so clearly to Sunalp that his subsequent position became untenable. Once the election results became known, the President accepted them with good grace, and congratulated Özal on his win. Though there have evidently been some points of disagreement between Evren and his Prime Minister, the President has usually confined himself to his neutral and relatively restricted Presidential role. An instance arose in January 1984, when the bill providing for municipal elections the following March was veteod by the President, only to be re-enacted by the Assembly with only minor amendments, and then accepted by the President. The constitutional machinery had been scrupulously adhered to.

This is not to say that conflicts could not develop in the longer term. In the spring of 1985, SDP and the True Path Party appeared to have reached a limited *concordat,* by which both parties would press for revision of the Constitution so as to remove the restrictions imposed on the old politicians and civil liberties in general. The True Path Party is also reported to favour removal of Provisional Article 15 which provides the former members of the NSC with immunity from prosecution for anything they may have done during the period of military government. This would allow investigation of alleged irregularities in the agreement with the Gen-

---

[39] Quoted, *Milliyet,* 5 November 1983.

eral Dynamics Corporation for the import and assembly of F-16 fighters. However, the President is known to oppose any such changes, on the grounds that they would "undo the work of 12 September."[40] Neither SDP nor the TPP were in any position to effect such amendments, which would have required the support of two-thirds of the Assembly. Moreover if the President refused to accept such amendments, but they were then re-passed by the Assembly, again with a two-thirds majority, then the President could submit them to a referendum. Nevertheless, the situation presented some unfortunate reminders of that of 1961-1965, when the question of an amnesty for the ex-Democrats preoccupied Turkish politicians to the exclusion of almost everything else.

4 Summing-Up

The first part of this chapter has attempted to show that there are a number of special features of Turkey's modern history and current situation which have had an important impact on the way the military regime conducted itself between 1980 and 1983. The Atatürkist legacy is an ambiguous one. On the one hand, it forbids serving army officers to play any part in the legislature; on the other, it encourages them to think of themselves as the ultimate guardians of the Atatürk revolution. Turkey's international situation is likely to wield an important, if unacknowledged, influence, since it makes long run military rule a much less acceptable option than it might otherwise be. Finally, the army's experiences since 1960 have demonstrated the need for agreement on a well-planned programme of action before power is seized, and the need to keep decision-making within as small and as senior a military circle as possible.

These factors seem to have been thoroughly appreciated by the makers of the 1980 coup. The main lines of what they wanted to achieve were agreed between them well before 12 September, and there was none of the diffusion of authority and the conflicts within their ranks which had been so evident in 1960-1961. They were determined to suppress anarchy, right the economy, and re-establish an elected civilian administration, and they achieved all three aims - no matter how elusive they may have seemed at the outset.

The army's greatest problem, it appears, was not in dealing with the terrorists, but with the politicians. Although this was not readily apparent at the time, the military had not originally proposed a total restructuring of the party system. In the event, they proved to have been too optimistic,

[40] *Ibid.*, 8 August 1985.

rather than too ruthless. Their hope was that the old party leaders (notably Demirel and Ecevit) would allow members of their parties to participate in the new government. If Demirel's version of events is to be trusted, then even as late as the summer of 1983 they had tried to persuade his followers to give support to Sunalp. What they failed to reckon with was the former politicians' fear that close association with the military regime would be the kiss of death in the long run. Faced with the opposition of the old parties, the military determined to kill them politically. Unfortunately, they refused to lie down and die. Once freedom to found parties was re-established, the old parties, who preserved their grass roots organizations largely intact, rapidly managed to insinuate themselves back into the political system. The re-incarnation was not complete, since the political mantle of the Justice Party was effectively inherited by both the Motherland and True Path Parties. On the left, Ecevit held himself aloof from SDP, and set up a rival left-wing party.

The military prevented SDP and the True Path Party from competing in the elections of 1983, but they could not legitimately abolish them as organizations, and were thus obliged to allow them to re-enter politics eventually. At the same time, their rather ambiguous attempt to encourage a new party, aligned to themselves, proved a dismal failure - as recent historical precedents had suggested it would. Fortunately, Evren himself preserved sufficient political neutrality and good sense to prevent this failure from damaging his own position. Whether potential clashes between the military and civilian political establishments can be held off for the rest of the decade remains to be seen.

Chapter 12
The Role of the Military in Turkey in the 1980s: Guardians or Decision-Makers?

George S. Harris

1 Introduction

Many years ago, the father of modern Turkey, Mustafa Kemal Atatürk, enunciated an important verity. He proclaimed of the new national state he was bringing into being: "We resemble ourselves."[1] By that, he did not intend to imply that Turks are inherently different from other peoples, or that the rules of political behavior in the world at large did not operate in Turkey. But he was calling attention to the undoubted fact that Turkish political experience was no carbon copy of that of other states. Following Atatürk's lead, one should be especially cautious in identifying Turkish political practice with models drawn from other societies and other times. The product of Turkish history, the changing constellation of international pressures, the impact of personality, and sheer chance combine to impart a uniqueness that cannot be completely comprehended in the shorthand of analogy to other countries.

Nowhere is this warning more apt than in considering the present role and future evolution of the Turkish military in politics. No matter how much the framers of the current constitutional system may have borrowed from European examples, Turkey today is far from resembling any of the various French republics, the Weimar regime, or any other external source of inspiration for Turkey's constitutional order. Likewise, to characterize

[1] Atatürk's speech analyzing the draft Fundamental Law bill being debated in Turkey's war-time parliament, December 1, 1921, *T.B.M.M.Zabıt Ceridesi* (Ankara: T.B.M.M.Matbaası, 1958), Devre 1, İçtima 2, vol.14, p.428. Atatürk was making clear that Turkey "does not resemble a democracy, does not resemble socialism, and does not resemble anything! Sirs, we must be proud not to resemble them! Because we resemble ourselves."

Turkish political experience under such rubrics as "ruralizing elections," the "functionalization of political voting patterns," or the "polarization of political competition" may convey a measure of truth; yet these formulations do not shed great light on the role of the military. Indeed, as Bülent Ecevit has recently made clear, it is even a mistake to focus so much on the wording of the constitution that one ignores the practice.[2] Hence, to derive from the constitutional language according general responsibility to the president to "insure the implementation of the constitution and the regular and harmonious functioning of the organs of state" the conclusion that he plays the leading role in the Turkish polity obscures the fact that the powers given him in this connection allow him only a narrow scope of action. In practice, it has turned out that the prime minister, using his peculiar constitutional prerogatives, and not the president, has set the tone for Turkish political practice.[3]

From the foregoing, it is evident that the role of the military in Turkish politics can best be understood by inspecting its own past, by analyzing the structure it left itself in the current regime, and by identifying the issues of possible controversy that could affect military interests. That is what the present chapter will attempt.

2 Importance of the Military

Little on the Turkish political scene can rival the potential importance of the military establishment. Yet little presents so many imponderables. To delve into the future course of the political role of Turkey's military is to leap into the unknown and even the unknowable. Clearly it involves the minds and reactions of actors whom we can scarcely yet identify to events that we are highly unlikely to be able to foresee with any accuracy. And over time, the uncertainty factor about who the actors will be as well as

---

[2] Bülent Ecevit told Henry Kamm, "Ex-Turkish Chief Says Democracy Is on Rise," *New York Times*, Aug. 11, 1985, p. 19: "'Before the military intervention, ... in many ways there were ample constitutional guarantees for democracy and freedom. Yet we felt a lack of deep-rooted democracy ... Now it's just the opposite ... Constitutional and institutional guarantees for democracy do not exist anymore, but the attitudes arising from accumulated experience with democracy have all of a sudden begun to assert themselves.' ... Despite what he called more police powers and more restrictive laws ..., Mr. Ecevit said there was a freer atmosphere."

[3] Article 104 enjoins the president to see that the constitutional machinery operates, but specifies powers to this end that relate merely to limited functions. The prime minister is charged in Article 112 with running the government with power to select and fire cabinet ministers. Relying on control of his political party and its parliamentary majority, Prime Minister Özal has been even able to override presidential vetoes of legislation.

the events that could set their political roles will certainly rise. In attempting to impose sense on a question with so many possible outcomes, therefore, it is necessary at the outset to lay out some assumptions underlying the analysis.

As a working hypothesis, it seems logical to assume that the major trends of the past will extend into the future. Turkish society has displayed striking conservatism. Atatürk himself was careful not to waste talent from the Ottoman regime. In the republican era, the patterns of politics have continued with remarkable consistency despite military interventions. In politics, the Third Republic in Turkey is very much like the Second in the quest for dominance between a right-of-center bloc and a left-of-center bloc which are continuing the long-standing rivalry between the Democrat/Justice Party and the Republican People's Party. If the leaders of these blocs have changed, the propensity to partisan wrangling between them has not; nor has the intramural factionalism that plagued these major formations in earlier times lessened. Even the relative size of the two constituencies has varied almost not at all over the decades.[4]

The consistency of the military actors, while not subjected to the precise measurement of elections, nonetheless can also be identified, at least in general terms. Such enduring traits as respect for hierarchy, devotion to the broadly secular modernizing reforms set in train by Mustafa Kemal Atatürk, and acceptance of the principle of the ultimate legitimacy of civilian rule have animated the officers in all periods of Turkey's republican history. Since Atatürk, the underlying motivations of successful military interventions have been to save the state, not to seize power for the benefit of a cabal.

But to gain reasonably strong purchase on the future role of the military we must penetrate deeper into why the officers moved. Those involved in intrusions into the political arena have been conscious of the experiences of their predecessors. Each set of military actors has clearly tried to avoid or correct the perceived mistakes of the past; indeed, they have all sought to derive lessons from previous operations. Almost certainly a future military group that intervened in politics would again look to the past for guidelines. Thus one of the keys to understanding possible military actions in future is to identify the motives and processes that brought the officers into political activity in previous periods.

If trends from the past will play a major role in the future, they will not of course be slavishly followed models to be repeated in substantially the same way. The rules of the political game have been altered by the new

---

[4] George S. Harris, *Turkey: Coping with Crisis* (Boulder, Westview Press, 1985), pp. 136–137, gives tables showing the constancy of left-of-center and right-of-center vote totals from 1961 to 1985

constitution and basic legislation, although the prerogatives of the military leadership have been adjusted but little. Moreover, the remedies for past political problems enshrined in the present legal and constitutional structure guarantee that the role of the military and the challenges it faces will not entirely resemble those of previous periods.

In this context, the question of whether the military establishment sees itself as "guardians or decision-makers" is likely to gain its larger significance. To integrate the trends of the past into the new environment to the extent possible involves both identifying possible threats to which the armed forces would react and estimating the strengths and weaknesses of the political system to deal with these challenges. Only on that basis will it be possible to give an answer, although perforce nuanced and tentative, to the question of whether a rough ten-year cycle for major military interventions in Turkey's politics is or is not likely to continue.

3 Trends

For the purposes of understanding the current position of the Turkish military establishment, little is to be gained by looking at Turkish experience before the latter nineteenth century. True, the standing of the officer corps as a most honored calling ran as a basic thread through all Ottoman and modern Turkish history. This attitude of respect for and confidence in the military commanders was in recent times to underlie their inclination to intervene when they saw threats to the state and to condition popular acceptance of a military move. But whereas the guardian role of the officers is deeply rooted in Turkey's past, until after the abolition of the Janissaries and the institutional reforms of the Tanzimat, military excesses by unruly troops eroded the bond of popular trust in the armed services. That confidence had to be reestablished by the patriotic service of the army during the struggle for independence under Atatürk before the modern role of the military could fully take shape.

The revolution of 1908 and the prominent part played by officers in the period of the Young Turk rule formed a backdrop for the republican era. The Young Turk experiences established precedents for military activism in politics that influenced the environment of the Republic to follow. They provided the example of military action against constituted authority on behalf of the welfare of the people. But in a more unfavorable light, they also showed lower-ranking elements of the army revolting in 1909, if unsuccessfully in the end, against the senior command; likewise they demonstrated that ambitious middle-grade officers (e.g., Enver and Cemal) could inject themselves into positions of political power with military backing. Thus, all in all, the lessons of the Young Turk period were mixed. They set no clear limits on military engagement in politics, beyond indicating that mutinies of the lower ranks were not a viable pattern of military intervention.

In terms of the connection of officers with political parties, the Young Turk experience provided a compelling example for Atatürk to follow. Officers were the heart of the Committee of Union and Progress, even though civilians played a continuing major part in this seminal political organization. This shared political involvement with civilian leaders was vital in nourishing the concept that the officers were responsible for the destiny of the state. And Atatürk persisted in fostering this role for the military establishment, however much he would work to establish the notion that elected government was the only legitimate system to run the state over the long run.

Atatürk's practice in governing the Republic provided patterns that could not be copied in their entirety by his successors. His military prowess formed a springboard to power. His charisma held his countrymen in a lasting grip, while he set up institutions intended to obviate the need for a personal hold on power and to remove the officers from day-to-day involvement in the affairs of state. Thus, on the one hand, he enunciated a litany of exhortations to the military to be the bulwark of the state against all enemies, domestic or foreign.[5] He indoctrinated them with the principles of his modernizing reforms. And he kept the military leaders attached to the office of the presidency. Yet after allowing them a political role in the independence movement, he took that away once independence was won.[6] They were even deprived of the right to vote. Moreover, he cut back on the influence of retired officers in parliament; their numbers declined significantly during his lifetime.

İsmet İnönü, although a former general, had become thoroughly civilianized during his decade and a half at the head of the governmental structure. Moreover, he operated to expand political competition by permitting rival parties and ending the vestiges of special status for the officers by finally moving the chief of staff out from under the personal aegis

---

[5] For example, Atatürk's speech on Feb. 22, 1931 said: "whenever the Turkish nation has wanted to take a step ahead, it has always looked to the army ... as the leader of movements to achieve lofty national ideals ... The Turkish nation ... considers its army the guardian of its ideals." *Atatürk'ün Söylev ve Demeçleri*, vol. 2, edited by Türk İnkılâp Tarihi Enstitüsü (Ankara, Maarif Basımevi, 1952), p. 266. In his speech opening parliament in 1937, Atatürk stated: "the army, which is the great school of national discipline, will help and assist especially in our economic, cultural, and social struggles." *Ibid.*, vol. 1 (İstanbul, Maarif Matbaası, 1945), p. 387.

[6] See George S. Harris, "The Role of the Military in Turkish Politics," *The Middle East Journal*, Winter, Spring (1965), pp. 54-66, 169-176.

of the president and by putting him under the defense ministry. But İnönü made these shifts without openly denigrating the honored status of the military profession. Nonetheless, military plotting against possible partisan abuses of the political system began during his era. The aim of these conspirators was to protect the nascent Democrat Party, not to institute a military regime. And had the elections of 1950 been attended with the blatant irregularities seen in 1946, a military intervention might have come a decade before it did.[7]

The Democrat Party's decade in power strengthened the interest of the officers in seeing the government abide by democratic procedure and provide nonpartisan administration. That consideration rose in importance as the Democrats, once in power, wasted no time in carrying out an extensive purge of the officer corps in a vain effort to weed out sympathizers of the Republican People's Party. The Democrat Party administration then used its government majority to threaten the continuing existence of Atatürk's reformist party, which formed its principal opposition. The strains of this intense political contest injected political considerations into the military as the Democrats turned to the armed forces to carry out this program. To make matters worse, the Democrats, who had no close ties to the military establishment, pointedly ignored the views of the military leadership, a humiliation all the more painful since members of the armed services were not eligible to vote. At the same time, squabbling among the politicians lowered their standing in the eyes of the officers. And as the political contest became increasingly embittered, the idea of the need to intervene to prevent a breakdown of the political machinery began to gain legitimacy within the officer corps.

4 The 1960 Precedent

Taking power in an environment where the military plotters felt great hostility against the majority party, but where many nourished a bond of sympathy for the reformist opposition, the new regime saw need to erect only a limited formal structure to defend the interests of the armed forces. Not surprisingly, they provided that members of the armed forces would have the vote. But the central element of the new system, which has endured in its essentials, was the creation of the National Security Council as a legal mechanism to assure a voice for the military profession. This body, established in the 1961 Constitution, was composed of the chief of

[7] For details of military plotting, see Abdi İpekçi and Ömer Sami Coşar, 'İhtilâlin İçyüzü,' *Milliyet*, May 27-July 10, 1962.

general staff and the force commanders meeting with the prime minister and ministers of defense, the interior, and foreign affairs under the chairmanship of the president. Its broad mandate to consider all matters of security concern guaranteed the continued involvement of at least the top ranks of the military establishment in political affairs.

In addition to the advantage of having this new institution, whose views were to be given consideration by the cabinet, the standing and influence of the military establishment gained from the recognition that the patience of the armed forces was not unlimited in political matters. No one could forget that under some circumstances the officers would order their troops to move. That realization added to the force of the pronouncements of the president, who was generally seen as speaking for the military establishment, but who lacked otherwise all constitutional sanctions to enforce his will. It also invested public statements of the top commanders or even to some extent those of the former junta with the aura of military pressure. That was to prove something of a waning consideration, as time and the success of the civilians in chipping away at prohibitions eventually served to dim the fear that the military might be able to intervene with force.

Also important to the weight of the military in politics was the continuing precedent that the presidency was reserved for a senior officer. This was an unwritten convention and one that depended on the acquiescence of the civilian politicians, who were formally free to vote for individuals of any background for president. Yet military pressure was evident in the election of General Cemal Gürsel in 1961 at the start of the transition back to civilian rule. The elevation of the chief of general staff, General Cevdet Sunay, to the presidency when Gürsel died in 1966 required little outside pressure by the soldiers, inasmuch as Sunay was such a commanding figure that the politicians themselves took the initiative to approach him.[8]

In some important respects, the military intervention of 1960, however, differed from military moves to come. It had been in essence a colonels coup with merely a façade of senior officers recruited by their juniors to take advantage of the strong hierarchical sense of the Turkish military profession. Only the widespread fear that the state was in danger from a breakdown of the constitutional process and that normal political rules were being or would soon be suspended led to general acceptance within the officer corps of the need to step in.

The military move of 1960 was also unlike succeeding military actions

---

[8] Former Air Force Commander Muhsin Batur, in his *Anılar ve Görüşler: Üç Dönemin Perde Arkası*, (İstanbul, Milliyet Yayınları, 1985) covers aspects of politico-military relations from 1960 to 1980. For the civilian invitation to Sunay to become president, see p.411.

in its diagnosis that excessive centralization of power had brought on the political problem which had to be solved. Hence, the officers in 1960 sought from their political and academic advisers constitutional precepts that would dilute government authority. Indeed, the system of checks and balances they erected was so effective in diffusing government power that henceforth at times the exercise of decisive rule to deal with crisis became all but impossible. Later military moves were thus perforce directed at redressing the imbalance introduced by the 1961 Constitution and at searching for a middle way between the permissiveness introduced after 1960 and the centralization of the 1924 Constitution.

The military rulers in 1960 conducted a much deeper purge of the officer corps than those attempted by later military actors. In comparison with the wholesale retirements of senior officers (some 90 percent of the generals to about 40 percent of the colonels and majors) in 1960, the moves of military leaders in following decades were minor indeed. In fact, by 1980 no need was perceived to clean out party partisans from the military establishment when the generals took power. In addition, the experience of 1960 left the commanders with an abiding concern to keep subordinates out of political roles and to confine dealings with politicians to the top-ranking generals.

Finally, the military rulers provided for the future security and status in a more permanent way than succeeding officers would find necessary. The Committee of National Unity members were accorded seats in the Senate with permanent tenure, provided that they did not join political organizations.[9] Moreover, initially the military leaders saw to it that the titular head of the junta became president for a seven-year term, although his appointment came not automatically, but through the votes of the newly elected parliament with the senior officers ostentatiously looking over the shoulders of the deputies as they voted. And President Gürsel used his commanding influence to secure the formation of a Republican People's Party/Justice Party coalition government under İsmet İnönü to provide additional reassurance that the former Committee of National Unity members would not be subject to retaliation. By contrast, in later instances of military intrusions in politics, the need for special protection when the leaders withdrew was either non-existent (as in 1971) or less long-lasting (as in 1983).

In these circumstances, the way back from military rule after 1961 saw the military establishment reduce its political activity only slowly and partially. In the period immediately after parliament reconvened in 1961, some field grade officers, who were disappointed by the results of the elections, resumed plotting. Indeed, the specter of renewed military inter-

[9] See Article 70 of the 1961 Constitution.

vention led the Republican People's Party to compose its differences with its new rival Justice Party sufficiently to form a coalition government led by İsmet İnönü, whose presence at the head of government was reassuring to most officers. But the danger of a new military move did not end with the formation of this unstable coalition. Continuing agitation by the Justice Party wing of the government for an amnesty for the members of the old regime led War School Commandant Talât Aydemir to attempt to take over the government in 1962. This uprising nearly succeeded, but attachment to the chain of command by most of the military establishment prevented its ultimate success. Aydemir, who was merely retired for this attempt, tried again the following year, again without success. This time he was executed with his principal collaborators. That ended the rash of plotting and the politicization of the middle and lower ranks of the officer corps which had continued unchecked after the return to civilian rule in 1961.

Yet political activities by the generals and by the president, ostensibly in the name of the armed forces, were not arrested by the fate of Aydemir's insurrections. Activist commanders such as Air Force commanders İrfan Tansel and Muhsin Batur as well as Ground Forces commander Cemal Tural, who was reputed to be an extreme conservative, persisted in following political activity with a close eye. Nonetheless, the intensity of military involvement in political matters fell off gradually during the 1960s as the civilians began to use the power of military assignment, for example, to shift General Tural to the relatively powerless Supreme Military Council (a body that merely ratified promotions) and to bring in as chief of staff General Memduh Tağmaç, who was thought to be politically relatively uninvolved.[10]

5 The 1971 Ultimatum: Way Station to 1980

The course of military disengagement from political affairs, however, was reversed by the growing challenge of violence which erupted in Turkey toward the end of the 1960s. This complex and stubborn problem proved difficult for civilian regimes to handle. After 1968, clashes between right-wing and left-wing students turned murderous. Killings spread to labor gatherings, and forceful disruption of extreme left and right political party meetings became common. Bank robberies to raise money for political extremist activities rocked Turkey for the first time. In addition, kidnap-

[10] Batur, *Anılar ve Görüşler,* p. 147. Ironically, Gen. Kenan Evren was also seen as non-partisan and essentially non-political when he became chief of general staff.

pings of members of the American military stationed in Turkey convulsed the Turkish political scene after 1970. These disorders and the reluctance of the civilian government under the Justice Party to take forceful action against them were powerfully felt by the generals.

Part of the problem was the ambiguous impact of the military move in 1960 on the civilian politicians. Party leaders like Demirel clearly misread the process that had propelled the officers into taking power a decade earlier: they assumed that the officers considered themselves the guardians of the students and had been drawn into political action in 1960 by the need to protect these youths from being manhandled by the police. While there was a kernel of truth to this assessment, for indeed the officers did sympathize with the students who were treated harshly by the Menderes regime, protection of those at civilian universities, as opposed to the cadets at the War School, had not been a major factor in the colonels' coup. Yet apparently overvaluing the affinity of students and officers led Demirel to be reluctant to move decisively against youthful terrorists at the end of the 1960s, when violence among the young became Turkey's principal political problem. He was thus late in ordering the security forces onto the campuses which had become veritable arsenals for the terrorists.[11]

The main commitment of the officers, however, was to the safety of the state. The military commanders were thus alienated by the disorder fomented by the young in the late 1960s. The generals had no wish to protect those who took advantage of the immunities granted universities from normal police procedure after 1960 to escape the laws that assured order and tranquility in the country. And when students fired on the gendarmerie troops finally sent onto university campuses toward the end of February 1971, the wave of revulsion among the senior commanders was almost tangible.

At bottom what brought the National Security Council's military members to issue their blunt demand in March 1971 for the government to be more decisive or step down was the failure of the Demirel regime to control political violence. Demirel, undoubtedly recalling the use to which martial law had been put by the military conspirators in 1960, had resisted imposing that extraordinary status in 1971 even after it was clear that the normal security forces could not keep order. The trouble was principally clashes between leftist and rightist student groups. But Turkish Labor

---

[11] *Ibid.*, p. 183, gives Batur's evaluation of why Demirel hesitated to declare martial law. Demirel told President Sunay, Apr. 24, 1970, that "the causes of the 1960 revolution were the radio administration and the university. If we take harsh steps ... we will act to justify revolution. Because these steps cannot be reconciled with democracy." Batur indicated (p. 185) that he "felt that Demirel might be sincere about democracy, but feared falling into the position of Adnan Menderes."

Party rallies and those of former Committee of National Unity member Alparslan Türkeş were also scenes of violence as were labor union gatherings. Powerfully disturbing to the generals as well were kidnappings of members of the American military serving in Turkey. Although Air Force Commander Muhsin Batur, for one, saw need for an economic agenda of reform to promote social justice, there was no unanimity among his fellow National Security Council members on such a reform program. Thus the principal matter on which the commanders could agree was simple: terror mounted by youths dedicated to upsetting the constitutional order had escaped the control of the Demirel government.[12]

The 1971 military ultimatum was not a full military intervention into the political arena. On its face, it was a declaration that the generals would use the authority vested in them to protect the state and would take power directly only if the civilians refused to provide more effective rule. And the top generals were careful not to dictate to the civilian politicians exactly how to proceed. They agreed on the choice of a non-partisan prime minister, but they apparently did not take the initiative to select him nor to dictate the composition of the cabinet.[13] And although they served as a watchdog behind the scenes, making clear their desire for martial law to be declared in the provinces principally beset with violence, they left the civilians considerable latitude to act through parliamentary procedure. Demirel and his party retained their majority in parliament, yet Demirel hastily resigned after prodding from the president, and he and his fellows made no open effort to challenge the procession of non-party cabinets that ruled until the 1973 elections.

Basically, therefore, there appeared to be some measure of popular acceptance of the government's claim that Turkey faced "a strong, active uprising against the motherland and the republic."[14] And as part of the justification for imposing martial law in a number of provinces, the new government cited the threat of "sabotage, subversion, and separatist movement" in eastern Turkey.[15] Thus there was little general protest when the authorities launched a broad wave of arrests of suspects, a number of whom had had no direct connection with violence. But even with this sweeping move against disorder, closing the Turkish Labor Party and

[12] On Batur's desire for social and economic reform, see Ibid., pp. 163 ff.

[13] *Ibid.*, pp. 306–307.

[14] Justice Minister İsmail Arar reported that martial law was necessitated by this "uprising." He noted that martial law would be conducted under art. 124 of the Constitution and Martial Law Act 3832. *Hürriyet*, April 27, 1971, reported that the martial law act would be amended to allow military trials to be continued even after martial law ended. The martial law commander could censor the press and radio.

[15] Nihat Erim gave his justification for martial law on May 1, 1971. See *Milliyet*, May 2, 1971.

shutting down leftist publications, order was not restored until after terrorists had kidnapped and murdered the Israeli Consul-General in Istanbul.

The non-party governments appeared less sure of their direction than did the National Security Council. The generals thus pinned their hopes on the lengthy constitutional amendment enacted in September 1971 as the principal vehicle for correcting the defects they perceived.[16] This bill of particulars provides useful insight into the direction and approach of the military commanders as well as into the role the armed forces saw required to assure sound political activity.

Basically, the changes in 35 regular articles and the addition of nine temporary articles to the Constitution took two general approaches: strengthening the powers of the government against threats to national unity, public order, and national security; and increasing the autonomy and freedom of action of the military establishment in more or less subtle ways. As regards the first, the changes sought to reinforce the powers of the authorities to prohibit the exploitation of "class, sect, religion, race, or language" to divide the nation; to restrict the press from promoting violations of "national unity"; to limit the right to form unions and associations; to give the cabinet power to issue decrees with the force of law when so instructed by parliament; to specify that university autonomy should not be allowed to shield perpetrators of crimes; to strengthen state control over radio and television; to extend the length of time that the cabinet could impose martial law without parliamentary approval; and to postpone elections due in October 1971 to October 1973. In terms of bolstering the position of the armed forces, the amendments provided authority to pass a law to adjust the powers of the minister of defense; specified that the National Security Council could present to the cabinet not merely its basic views on security, but its recommendations as well; increased the possibility that civilians could be tried in military courts; removed review of military personnel actions from civilian administrative courts; and increased the rank of members of courts martial.

This catalogue of concerns demonstrates that the generals still saw the problem in 1971 as relatively limited in scope. The commanders clearly did not see a need to throw out the existing system, but rather they agreed on a certain "fine tuning" that would promote more efficient and decisive government. To do so, they evidently concluded that somewhat greater direct involvement of the military establishment in dealing with such threats was required. But they made no basic change in the overall position of the military. And given the success of the Justice Party in attaining parliamen-

[16] For the text of the Sept. 20, 1971, constitutional amendment, see Tarhan Erdem, *Anayasalar ve Seçim Kanunları* (İstanbul, Milliyet Yayınları, 1982), pp. 114–127.

tary majorities in 1965 and 1969, there was no thought yet that the political system might not answer the need for orderly government or that partisan competition might stymie efforts within the cabinet to provide effective national leadership against domestic challenges.

6 To 1980: The Generals' Intervention

The course from the partial intervention of 1971 to the full takeover of 1980 was a complex one. Rivalries and dissension within the top ranks of the armed forces which eroded military prestige, on the one hand, combined with a general breakdown of the government's ability to confront its political challenges, on the other. The process ended in creating a sense of acute crisis which appeared to many officers as well as civilians to threaten the state.

The constitutional remedies enacted in 1971 conspicuously failed to serve the purpose. In the first place, they were by no means sufficient to assure military influence on government policy, even in the security area. In part, this result reflected the increasing opposition of the leaders of the major parties, Süleyman Demirel and Bülent Ecevit, who both saw the military move as directed against their personal and partisan interests. Inasmuch as the 1971 ultimatum had not restricted either figure from political activity or worked more than a temporary dimunition of his party standing, the two were well placed to undercut the bid for military influence in politics. And well aware of the partisan differences that divided the senior commanders, both these civilian political leaders were eager to find opportunities to downgrade the military's political role.

With the expiration of Sunay's term as president in the spring of 1973, the politicians saw their chance to weaken the hold of the commanders on the course of civilian politics.[17] In part their opportunity was provided by the senior generals themselves, for it was growing disunity among the ranking officers on partisan, interservice, and individual lines that sealed their inability to confront the civilians effectively. Maneuvering among the senior ranks of the officer corps for this important succession (by constitutional fiat the president could not succeed himself) began with the preparations for the annual round of promotions and reassignments to be

---

[17] Roger P. Nye, "Civil-Military Confrontation in Turkey: The 1973 Presidential Election," *International Journal of Middle East Studies* 8 (1977), pp. 209–228, discusses this important issue, but without fully recognizing the deep divisions within the military camp, or the ultimate significance of the crisis in making the soldiers appear to have returned to the barracks.

announced in August 1972. The split in party sympathies between Chief of General Staff Memduh Tağmaç, who leaned toward the Justice Party, and Air Force Commander Batur, who would later join the Republican People's Party, seems to have played a major part in preventing the extension of the term of the former. According to the inviolate rules of seniority, Tağmaç was retired, opening the way for Ground Forces Commander Faruk Gürler to succeed to the top military command.

This shuffle at the highest ranks and the retirement of the navy commander, whose term had likewise ended, did not repair military disunity. Gürler, who strongly aspired to the presidency, convened a special "Expanded Commanders' Council" of 52 top generals at the start of November 1972 to poll military support for the principle that the chief of general staff should accede to this office. Contrary to his expectations, about half of the generals in attendance indicated that they either did not want a senior officer to be elected or were indifferent to whether a civilian or a military figure were chosen.[18] It was clear, therefore, that Gürler's candidacy was not strongly favored within the armed services. The top ranks of the air force and the navy were especially alienated by the practice of drawing the chief of general staff from the ranks of the ground forces only, a practice that would have shut them off from the presidency in an automatic succession of the chief of general staff.

President Sunay himself added to the military disarray. He appeared to be maneuvering to have the constitution changed to extend his own term, although he depended on others to argue his case. And to the end, he seems to have hoped that the difficulties in agreeing on a successor would lead parliament to turn back to him. At any rate, despite his knowledge that General Gürler faced insurmountable civilian opposition, he offered to the chief of general staff a senatorial post in the presidential contingent in order to provide the parliamentary status then necessary for election as president.[19] Gürler had to retire from the army to accept a senate seat, thus breaking his active duty connections and effectively removing him from a position of influence once his candidacy failed.

Given this intrigue at the upper ranks of the armed services, the determined party leaders had no trouble turning back Gürler's bid in March 1973. Demirel considered it essential to do so because he hoped to gain the majority in the parliamentary elections set for October 1973 as he had done in 1965 and 1969. In order to make sure that the president at that time did not use the prerogative of unrestricted choice of members of parliament to deny him the prime ministry, Demirel wished to be sure that a signer of the 1971 ultimatum was not president. The Justice Party thus ar-

---

[18] Batur, *Anılar ve Görüşler*, p.377.

[19] *Ibid.*, p.415ff.

gued that the election of a military figure as president "would be considered a sign that democracy was not working" in Turkey.[20] For the same reasons, the Justice Party opposed changing the constitution to extend President Sunay's term. Ecevit too wished to break the precedent of the automatic succession of the chief of general staff. But he gave the impression to the officers who probed his views that he was more open to military pressure as regards extending Sunay's term. With these differences between the two main civilian protagonists, it was not possible to reach agreement on a purely civilian politician, and in the end, a compromise was worked out agreeable to both political parties and commanders: at the Justice Party's initiative, Admiral Fahri Korutürk, who had retired a decade earlier, was elected president.

This outcome significantly changed the relative weights of the civilian and military players. By appearing to give in to the civilian almost completely, the top generals lost their ability to threaten with words. Henceforth, the commanders would find that they had the option of acting or being ignored, but nothing in between. That guaranteed that the stream of warnings from the chief of general staff and other military leaders appealing for cooperation among the parties would not be heeded by the politicians. And as events turned out, that meant also that the civilians felt no compunction about trying to purge the officer corps to reinforce the impression that the military had returned to the barracks. In short, the retreat of the generals in the presidential election created a fatal disjunction between the real power of the military establishment and the illusion that it could be confronted with impunity by civilian politicians.

This disjunction might not have entailed such significant consequences if the politicians had been better able to cope with Turkey's political challenges. Indeed, the military leaders seemed prepared to accept a considerable level of political and social disorder, but only if those in charge of the political process showed themselves serious about tackling the problems. Clearly the generals were not thirsting for power, but were brought to this role by the evident disinclination of the political leaders to pull together instead of seeking immediate partisan advantage.

A detailed analysis of the failings of the politicians is not required to understand the concern of the generals. In brief, the problem revolved around the failure of any party after 1969 to win a majority in the lower house. Coalition politics enhanced the role of splinter parties which could use their bargaining positions to win concessions on political and social policies. The nearly equal strength of the two major political organizations encouraged a bidding war between them to entice the minor parties into coalitions. The resulting blocs were unstable as parties and individual

[20] *Ibid.*, p. 410 ff.

deputies shifted alignments. In this situation, governments focused more on maintaining their parliamentary majorities than on providing effective administration. And the evenness of the political balance led to complete parliamentary paralysis when in 1980 the term of President Korutürk ended. From March 1980 until the generals finally moved the following September, all parliamentary business was held hostage to the inability of parliament to elect a successor in over 100 rounds of inconclusive balloting.

Although political disarray prevented action on many pressing problems, it did not prevent the civilian regimes from at least addressing the mounting economic crisis. However disturbed the generals may have been by Turkey's economic performance, their own subsequent actions made clear that they did not regard military rule as the only solution to economic difficulties. Indeed, governments led by both major parties had, under strong IMF pressure, taken steps to reform the economy in the late 1970s.[21] Thus, though Turkey was buffeted by skyrocketing oil prices, declining demand for Turkish workers in Europe, and weakening markets for Turkish exports, the political ineffectiveness of Turkey's governments after 1973 did not stop them from increasingly firm economic response. In fact, by January 1980, even the minority Justice Party cabinet, on paper the weakest of the lot, was able to impose the most far-reaching economic reform program ever applied in Turkey.

It was the manifest *political* failings of the coalition governments that were most upsetting to the military leadership. On the one hand, the ability of the National Salvation Party to exploit its swing position as a necessary part of any viable coalition to extract concessions that appeared to compromise the secularist approach associated with Atatürk's reform program, powerfully disturbed the commanders. The National Salvation Party's success in shaping government policy toward education and even foreign policy was unacceptable to many generals. This unhappiness was sharply reinforced by the apparent insult to the armed forces from the failure of the National Salvation Party's leaders to come to congratulate the armed service commanders on the August 30 Victory Day celebration in 1980 and especially by the disrespect to the nation shown when that party's membership conspicuously sat silent during the playing of the national anthem at a televized local party gathering on September 6, 1980. This disturbing conduct also included the successful assault on the foreign minister, who was censured and forced out of the cabinet at National Salvation Party's behest on September 5, 1980, for failing adequately to defend Islamic causes.[22]

---

[21] For example, Ecevit reached two agreements for economic reform with the IMF, 1978/9.

[22] See General Secretariat of the National Security Council, *12 September in Turkey: Before*

While these anti-Atatürkist actions were powerfully undermining military confidence in the political structure, the government's inability to staunch violence and prevent separatist agitation in eastern Turkey created a widespread impression that the system could not respond to crisis. For the first few years after 1971, martial law had served to end violence. But after party politics resumed in earnest in 1973 and especially after the amnesty for political offenders returned many of those held for involvement in violence, the level of disorder began to rise. Partisan differences delayed the declaration of martial law in various provinces where the police had been overwhelmed by the magnitude of the problem. It was only after the large-scale communal clash in Kahramanmaraş in December 1977 that Ecevit changed his tune and declared martial law in 11 provinces. But to the end, the martial law commanders were under restrictions in their freedom to take decisive measures. And the chief of general staff complained with some bitterness that the civilians blamed the armed forces for the persistence of violence, while refusing to enact stronger legislation.[23] Thus the generals watched with mounting frustration as the political death toll rose with increasing velocity and attacks even turned against ranking officers. By early September 1980, it seemed clear that the system could not cope with this challenge inasmuch as partisan bickering prevented the politicians from cooperating on political remedies.

7 Remaking the System

When the generals moved to take power in this situation, they acted on the premise that the regime required more extensive adjustments than in 1971. Yet from their conduct as rulers, they demonstrated that they had not lost faith that with the proper rules a healthy democratic order could be devised. In short, they believed that they were acting to save Turkish democracy from itself.

To accomplish that result, the generals were convinced that the new order would have to rule out the political extremes of left and right which were seen as behind the upswelling of violence. Likewise they were concerned to guard against excesses by the politicians whom they saw as being too entrenched in their political positions to reflect popular will and popular desires. Indeed, judging that intense personal hostility between the political leaders had been in part responsible for their unwillingness

---

and After (Ankara, Ongun Kardeşler Printing House, 1982), pp.211, 215-217; "MSP Mitinginde Bir Grup 'İstiklâl Marşı' nı Söyletmedi," *Milliyet*, September 7, 1980.

[23] *12 September in Turkey*, pp.209-210.

to cooperate in the face of national disaster, the top commanders wanted both to remove these leaders from politics and to prevent new leaders from having a similar lock on the top party posts in the future. It was also important in the eyes of the generals to increase the chances that the party receiving the most votes secured a working majority in parliament. Hence they sought to reduce the checks and balances introduced in 1961, although they did not want to disassemble judicial controls on a wayward administration. And they wished to find ways to discourage a proliferation of parties.

The military leaders sought to carry out these aims by reworking the constitution and amending the political parties act and the elections law. It would be a mistake, however, to regard the 1982 Constitution as very much more authoritarian than the one enacted in 1961, for the 1961 document was the basic model for the new order. The adjustments embodied in the 1982 version were designed to provide ways to prevent parliamentary deadlock or to end it through such expedients as elections. The focus was on creating a system that would provide the voters effective government, not to restrict the options and ability of the electorate to express its desires. It was clear that the framers of the constitution considered anarchy a denial of democracy and hoped to inject greater discipline into society through such mechanisms as a more hierarchical educational structure under a centralized board of directors. Indeed, in exceptional circumstances of threat to the nation normal political rights could be curtailed. But the constitution made clear that even exceptional conditions could not be the pretext to destroy fundamental rights of citizens and that freedom of conscience was inviolate.

Significantly, the 1982 Constitution did not accord the military establishment important new powers. While it did add precision to the composition of the National Security Council and provide for a staff, the main change to previous practice was to specify that "decisions of the Council. . .are to be given *priority* consideration by the Council of Ministers" (Article 18, emphasis added). That strengthened the language inserted in 1971 providing merely for the National Security Council to "recommend" its fundamental views to the Council of Ministers (Article 111). The new language, however, was a far cry from giving the National Security Council any right to dictate to the Cabinet.

Beyond these essentially procedural changes regarding the National Security Council, the new constitution, if anything, decreased other powers associated with the armed forces in previous constitutions by depriving "privates and corporals serving in the armed services (as well as) students in military schools" of the right to vote. In fact, the only other category of those over 21 years of age barred from voting was that of "detainees and convicts in prisons" (Article 66).

Clearly the commanders were depending on some enhancement of the powers of the presidency to defend the rights of the armed services. While it was nowhere stated that the president should be drawn from a military background, he was to represent "the office of the commander in chief" on behalf of the parliament; and Article 104 gave the president the right to decide on the use of Turkey's armed forces, to appoint the chief of general staff, to convene the National Security Council, and to proclaim martial law. Yet although the president's powers of appointment were increased as compared with those granted to him in previous constitutions, he was not given specific mechanisms to prevent civilians from encroaching on the independence of the armed forces or indeed to impede civilian ability to run the day-to-day functions of government.

For the first seven years, however, the military rulers provided the president with special additional authority to protect the system they erected. By the very ratification of the Constitution, General Kenan Evren, chief of state during the period of military rule, became president. He was accorded the right to veto constitutional amendments, a veto which for the first seven years could be overturned only by vote of three quarters of the parliament (thereafter a simple majority could override his vetoes). Moreover, the four commanders who had served with him on the National Security Council during military rule were constituted as a Presidential Council to provide advice and assist in his functions until the end of his term. Thereafter, these special veto and Presidential Council provisions would lapse and the president would be left with less authority to defend military interests.

While a new structure to embody these alterations was being elaborated, the generals saw need of a cooling off period without civilian political competition and with severe measures to restore law and order. Their original intention to suspend, but not necessarily ban, the major parties of the past gave way to outright abolition of these organizations, after Ecevit and Demirel would not cooperate in the process of remaking the constitution. And in view of the suspicion with which the former civilian leaders regarded the transition to restored political life, the generals kept in their own hands far-reaching authority to limit both individuals and organizations that could compete in the first elections to the new parliament. They were clearly determined to avoid the possibility that a frankly revanchist party would come to power on a platform of restoring political rights to politicians of the past before the expiration of the five- and ten-year periods of ban on previous political leaders called for in provisional articles in the new Constitution.

The 1980 move was manifestly the work of the top commanders led by Chief of General Staff Kenan Evren. Evren had been favorably regarded by the politicians as a highly professional officer with no partisan leanings. He was brought to the top military post in 1978 by Ecevit who had maneuvered the retirement of General Semih Sancar for being suspected of sympathy for the Justice Party. Evren used the National Security Council as a base in futile attempts to call the civilian politicians to cooperate before the 1980 intervention. And he employed the expanded powers of the Council thereafter to personify the authority of the armed services. Although the generals named a prime minister to head a government of technocrats, Evren kept power firmly in his own hands, vastly overshadowing the force commanders with whom he shared responsibility on the National Security Council. Indeed, he showed himself to be a natural politician. Evren's frequent radio and television addresses and speaking tours made clear where the authority lay. And by the end of the military's tenure in power, he was well established as an attractive political leader in his own right, a standing reinforced by his accession to the presidency with the ratification of the 1982 Constitution.

The depth of the political crisis when the generals took over and the confidence inspired by the fatherly approach of General Evren assured that the populace at large accepted the military intervention as legitimate. As Bülent Ecevit told a group of visiting Americans during the second year of military rule, the people at large welcomed the end of political violence.[24] Unlike the aftermath of the 1971 ultimatum, when only the left was pursued with vigor, the generals after 1980 cracked down on the extreme right with evident impartiality. Thus, while more of those on the left of the political spectrum were detained than on the right, the disparity appeared roughly to mirror the difference in numbers between these two groups in society at large. The period of military rule would end, therefore, without leaving the residue of bitterness at partiality which the earlier experience had left. On the level of the leadership of the former parties, however, there was continuing unwillingness to accept the need for the far-reaching changes enacted by Evren and his colleagues. Demirel and Ecevit refused to cooperate in authorizing their followers to participate in making the new constitution. When time came to form new parties, Demirel all but openly sponsored a revival of the Justice Party in the quickly banned Great Turkey Party, while Ecevit's wife emerged as the leader of the Democratic Left Party in a bid to keep his family in politics despite the constitutional ban. Supporters of both leaders soon began to agitate for a formal return of their political rights. Moreover, the pressures from Demirel and Ecevit appeared to increase with time. In 1987 they regained their political rights.

---

[24] The author was present when Ecevit spoke to a group attending a conference on Turkey arranged by Georgetown University in 1982. Ecevit, however, expected that effect to wear off relatively quickly thereafter.

8 Transition Turbulence

The success of the generals in solving Turkey's political problems through legal and constitutional changes was called into question by events during the return to civilian rule. The desire of the generals to have three or four parties at most in the contest in order to avoid the need for coalition politics was frustrated. Only the forceful intervention of the commanders to use their veto rights limited the field to three parties in the 1983 elections. Thereafter, additional strong competitors have emerged: six parties competed in the municipal elections in 1984. The insistence of new and old personalities to vie for political dominance shows that the interest of the military leadership in diminishing partisan competition has not been and will not be realized. Moreover, from the vigor of the political contest it is apparent that the new politicians are no more disposed than their predecessors to eschew partisan advantage in the national interest.

Even the victory of the Motherland Party which bested its two rivals in 1983 by a large margin did not offer consolation to the generals. Evren himself had openly favored the conservative Nationalist Democracy Party led by a former general. In fact, Evren had made an election eve appeal steering voters away from the Motherland Party of Turgut Özal. To no avail. Voters disregarded Evren's suggestions and settled on the pro-private enterprise party of Özal, who had been the architect of the 1980 economic reform program. The Nationalist Democracy Party, with which Evren was identified, ran a poor last in the three-party field, a result that undermined Evren's prestige just at the key time when the precedents for the use of presidential power were being set.[25]

On this basis, the decline in military influence after the 1983 elections was precipitate. Özal came to office as prime minister neither beholden to the military for his election nor concerned that opposition from the generals would hurt him. His determination to be his own man was strengthened by his recognition that the Europeans nourished reservations about dealing with a continuation of military rule under a civilian guise. Thus he wanted to establish clearly the principle of civilian independence from the start, at least in the economic and political areas. On the other hand, he saw the value of sharing with the president responsibility for law and order, especially in the east, inasmuch as that was a continuing challenge that he could not be assured of handling adequately without military par-

[25] Evren's pre-election speech was carried on Ankara radio and television on Nov. 4, 1983. After sarcastically noting that the one "who claimed responsibility for improving the economy in 1980 and 1981" (i.e., Özal) now insists that he is the only one capable of solving Turkey's problems, Evren added: "I leave it up to you to decide what a person, who even before coming to power is capable of making such false statements, ... can do in the future."

ticipation. To make his point, Özal and his party overrode Evren's veto of the municipal elections bill, a move that was resoundingly vindicated by the strong showing of the Motherland Party in the March 1984 elections. Yet Özal strongly opposed agitation by the opposition and from within his own party for amnesty for those tens of thousands jailed for involvement in violence during the years of military rule. That stand served to keep the military content, despite their declining influence.

A final part of the legacy of the period of military rule was the effort to operate on the bureaucratic structure to instill discipline and combat partisanship. These were inherently controversial areas. Sharing the Atatürkist view that education was the cutting edge of reform and perceiving disorder among the student-age population to be at the heart of Turkey's troubles, the generals reformed the university system to centralize professorial promotions and assignments. They purged the ranks at the same time, leaving a residue of mistrust and frustration as younger elements faced a long wait for advancement. Thus the generals left power somewhat estranged from the reformist intellectual constituency that had generally been sympathetic to previous experiments in military rule.

Similarly, strong efforts to eliminate partisans from the civilian bureaucracy after September 1980 shook the confidence of that institution in the armed services. Extensive purges were directed at removing political partisans, reportedly up to 18,000 in number, who had infiltrated the ranks of the civil service during the 1970s. To prevent a recrudescence of the politicizing of the merit system, the generals saw to it that the president was given the authority to appoint some members of the Council of State, the top regulatory body for the bureaucracy.[26] Yet it was questionable whether such changes could long frustrate the normal political imperative to use government patronage as the staple of reward for party allegiance.

9 Outlook

Return to civilian politics thus left important unanswered questions about the ability of the officer corps and the politicians to coexist. Indeed, it is too early to tell with assurance whether the changes introduced after 1980 will be extensive enough to prevent the political problems they were intended to answer. How such looming issues as the succession to President

[26] See Metin Heper's "Bureaucrats, Politicians and Officers in Turkey: Dilemmas of a New Political Paradigm," in *Modern Turkey: Continuity and Change*, edited by Ahmet Evin (Opladen, Leske und Budrich, 1984), pp. 64–83.

Evren will be handled will clearly play a major role in the process. For if the political contest should stalemate as in 1980, requiring repeated national elections without a clear victor, or if the politicians should settle on a figure profoundly distasteful to the senior commanders, that development might elicit some sort of military response. While the president is at present overshadowed constitutionally and in practice by the prime minister, it is when and if the system runs into trouble that the personality of the president and his relationship with the top political leaders would become critical. Evren and Özal appear to have established good working relations after the contretemps on the eve of the 1983 elections. Moreover, Evren's powers authorized by the provisional articles of the Constitution could also be helpful in keeping the political scene on an even keel until near the end of the decade. But a ten-year cycle of crisis would almost certainly see another figure in the presidency and could well come when Özal too was no longer in office. Yet because Turks are conscious of the possibility of military intervention if relations between the politicians and the armed services were to sour significantly, military warnings about the need to cope with dangers to the system are not likely to be ignored as completely as they were in the buildup to 1980. Thus the auguries seem cautiously favorable for successful military and civilian coexistence, provided that economic or foreign policy disasters do not strike or political violence recur.

One of the reasons for confidence is the prospect that the military and the civilians will be able to divide responsibilities to provide for more harmonious cooperation than before 1980. The guardian role of the armed forces is well established. But the post-1980 pattern appears to be one of shared decision-making in security matters. President Evren was thus the point man in orchestrating the response to attacks on gendarmerie posts in eastern Turkey by guerrillas pursuing separatist goals in the fall of 1984. Indeed, should any widespread return to violence be discerned, he and the generals on the National Security Council (which has reverted to the limited authority of the pre-1980 period) would again take the lead in working out the response. It seems improbable that the civilian political leadership would seek to question that role. Indeed, the Motherland Party for one would certainly be happy to join with the senior commanders in taking whatever action was recommended. For a long time to come, politicians of all stripes will be sensitized to the need to cooperate with each other as well as with the generals to concert a response to violence.

The most favorable sign for the future of Turkish democracy is the persistence of almost all Turks in pursuing an elective parliamentary process. Although there have been several military interventions of a major sort into the political arena, they have all been brought to an end by the officers themselves. And soon after taking over, the military rulers have on each occasion begun to confront the problem of how to surrender power in an orderly way to leave behind a constitutional structure that would make future military intrusions into the political realm unnecessary. While the Turks have not in the past found the proper formula, they have undeniably gained experience in the various efforts. That too adds reason to hope that the present system will operate more successfully than the one just past and that consequently Turkish democracy will finally overcome the hurdles that have frustrated its smooth course. All indications are that the military as well as the civilians want that outcome.

Part V
The State and Democracy

Chapter 13
Changing Patterns of Cleavages Before and After 1980

Ahmet Evin

1 Introduction

Will the 1980 military intervention enter the annals of Turkish history as a fundamental turning point with regard to the role of the state in that polity? Or, with the passage of time, will it appear in retrospect merely as one of those periodic interventions which have characterized Turkish political life since the transition to the multi-party system? When the dust settles after a second round of elections and some of the principal actors of the 1980 regime are retired from political life, the latest intervention can be placed in a clearer perspective vis-à-vis its antecedents. Though without the wisdom of such hindsight it is a risky proposition to single out the 1980 intervention as being uniquely different from the preceding ones, certain trends that have emerged since the take-over do point to significant changes that have taken place with respect to the state and politics in Turkey.

At the outset one is tempted to distinguish the 1980 coup from the earlier ones, not so much in terms of its causes but certainly in terms of its effects. However, upon closer scrunity certain significant developments that have taken place since the 1983 elections appear to be unrelated to the constitutional and administrative changes made during the military regime. What immediately comes to mind is the contrast between the type of state elite traditionally chosen by the military to run the show and the new cast of actors who have appeared on the political stage since the closing of the political parties in 1981 and particularly after the formation of new ones in 1983.

On the surface this contrast can be easily explained in terms of the opposing characteristics of the state elites on the one hand and politicans on the other, a well-known phenomenon in recent Turkish politics and one which has been related to the cultural cleavage between the center and the periphery. In addition to politicans, who became the conveyors of the periphery's particularistic demands since the inception of competitive politics in the post-1950 era, some members of the center, notably those upholding the ideal of individual freedoms under the umbrella of a social welfare state, defected from the center and came to identify themselves with the periphery in the 1960s and 1970s. In the 1970s the civil bureaucracy, in the main, gradually lost its role and, hence, its outlook and status as part of the state elites. It can thus be argued that the military who acted as the sole representatives of the state in 1980 would stand in clear contrast to those who appeared in the political scene subsequently.

Still, the fact that the chief actors on the political scene now have, in the past, served in the high echelons of the civil bureaucracy, is a complicating factor. Moreover, Prime Minister Özal and most of his close associates can be categorized as members of both the bureaucratic and economic elite. Yet, despite the similarity of their background to the top-level personnel in the civil service, they display characteristics different from the type of bureaucrat one is accustomed to seeing. Moreover, they have actively opposed the traditional bureaucratic cadres.

The appearance of a new type of managerial elite in the civil bureaucracy certainly points to the weakening of bureaucratic culture as a socializing force. But the co-existence of two different types of governing elite and professional friction between them also reveal a certain type of fragmentation at the top levels of the government which is not politically based. Can this be symptomatic of secondary cleavages resulting from the differentiation of the elites? If so, a significant portion of the changes observed in the operation of the government since 1980 have little to do with the restructuring efforts attending the adoption of the new constitution, but have resulted from a process that was longer in the making. Also longer in the making but accelerated by the policies of the civilian government since 1983 has been a kind of vertical fragmentation in the bureaucracy, with increased distance between the top decision-makers and the civil servants of lower ranks.[1] The appearance of such cleavages in the central institutions shortly after the military intervention of 1980 is certainly ironic since the chief objective of its leaders was to establish uniformity and cohesion at the top to stem the tide of polarization at other levels.

Nevertheless, it can be said that the 1980 military intervention achieved its objectives in the short term, and the ballast it provided seems to be

[1] This is fully discussed in my forthcoming *Bureaucrats, Politicians and Managers*.

adequate to prevent violent pitching and rolling in the medium term. The aim of the military intervention was to put an end to the fragmentation in the political sphere and to devise a viable system of government with inbuilt mechanisms to prevent the recurrence of ideological polarization. As such, the military were chiefly concerned with restructuring the system around a new locus of authority, and in the process, eliminating the radical fringe. The corrective measures they chose to take resulted in a major transformation in the concept of state but only indirectly affected the formation of new cleavages in the central institutions. The following discussion will first attempt to underscore some salient features of the 1980 coup in the context of earlier military interventions and then to provide a map of the changes observed in the modus operandi of the state and government since the transition to civilian rule.

2 Military Intervention in 1980

Like all instances of military intervention into Turkish political life, the 1980 coup was, above all, a response on the part of the military to the crippling degree of fragmentation among the political elite. The reasons why the military stepped in on 12 March 1971 and 12 September 1980 were almost identical: stalemate in the parliament due to the inability of major parties to achieve consensus while those on the radical fringes hoping to make gains out of chaos, and as a result of this, a government rendered ineffectual in the face of increasing anarchy and violence. The fragmentation among the political cadres reflected to a large extent the fragmentation and polarization taking place in society at large; but what was particularly worrisome was the fact that the chaos on the street was being nurtured by the fragmentation at the top. Law and order had to be restored, but in the eyes of the military that could not be accomplished without resolving the conflict among the political actors in the first place.

Moreover, the anarchy stemming from the absence of governmental authority pointed to a greater menace, that of compromising the integrity of the state. If the government was indeed incapable of asserting any authority, then a means had to be found to restore and demonstrate the authority of the state, since by definition the state had authority in the deeply rooted patrimonialism of the Turkish political culture.[2] Thus, the military

[2] Metin Heper, "Center and Periphery in the Ottoman Empire with Special Reference to the Nineteenth Century," *International Political Science Review*, 1 (1980), pp.81-105; Şerif Mardin, "Turkey: The Transformation of an Economic Code," in *The Political Economy of Income Distribution in Turkey*, edited by Ergun Özbudun and Aydın Ulusan (New York, Holmer and Meier, 1980), pp.23-53.

would reason, persisting conflicts among politicians at the expense of the well-being of the system would be tantamount to the dissolution of the state itself since it reflected a contemptuous disregard for the state as a binding locus of authority. Politicians could be blamed as traitors since they were responsible for weakening the governmental institutions by persisting in their conflict, and these institutions had been conceived since the Ottoman times, as the very pillars on which the state rested.

Anarchy in itself was looked upon less as a syndrome of deeper cleavages in society than a reflection of the sad affairs of state. Some of the military commanders were certainly aware of the dissatisfaction among various segments of society with the economic situation, particularly the endemic frustration caused by the discrepancy between the actual situation and expectations of salaried workers and wage earners.[3] However, the prevailing perception was that the demands made on the system could not have escalated to such a degree and taken the form of anarchic violence without the introduction of nefarious ideologies. The lack of ideological consensus at the top was again a factor largely blamed for things getting out of hand. As the word for anarchy in Turkish, *başsızlık* (literally, "headlessness"), also implies, the cause of public disorder was ultimately the lack of authority at the top.

Contrary to popular beliefs held, the primary purpose of the military in intervening was not to take over policing functions to establish law and order. In any case martial law had already been declared by the parliament and imposed by the governments prior to the interventions of 1960 and 1971, as well as 1980, and the military had already been made to assume a policing role by the civilian governments. Rather, the chief concern of the military in undertaking all three interventions was to protect the state by reducing its vulnerability in the face of intra-elite conflict.

A second and equally important factor was the danger that the fragmentation and conflict within and among civilian institutions would adversely affect the military organization itself. In 1960 commanders were drawn into participation in a coup masterminded by junior and mid-level officers and the hierarchical organization of the system was disrupted.[4] It could be rescued with some difficulty from falling into total disarray by the last minute co-optation of a top-level commander to head the National Unity Committee. In 1971 unrest among junior commanders expedited the writing of the 12 March Memorandum.[5] A similar type of pressure

[3] Muhsin Batur, *Anılar ve Görüşler: Üç Dönemin Perde Arkası* (İstanbul, Milliyet Yayınları, 1985), passim.

[4] Feroz Ahmad, *The Turkish Experiment in Democracy, 1950-1975* (London, RIIA/C. Hurst, 1977), pp. 159-172.

[5] Batur, *Anılar ve Görüşler*, pp. 150-156.

from the lower echelons may well have contributed also to the comprehensive way in which the 1980 coup was planned and executed.

Apart from the fear of fragmentation within the military organization itself, which had been the major factor in moving the commanders to action, the cleavage that seems to have disturbed the military most was the one between the political elite and the top echelons of the civil bureaucracy, particularly the judiciary, whose decisions based on the 1961 Constitution were seen as obstacles in the way of the last Demirel government's resolve to establish law and order. Moreover, extreme polarization among the political leadership, preventing a parliamentary consensus in the absence of a majority government, precluded the possibility of a constitutional change to obtain greater executive power. From the viewpoint of the state elites both the legislative and executive branches would naturally make constituent parts of the realm of the state regardless of the individual association of legislators with different segments of the periphery. If, because of political polarization and intra-elite conflict these two branches were thrown into a crippling stalemate, then the state, too, with all its apparatus would be dragged into the same stalemate that arose in the political realm. This situation also led to a conceptual confusion concerning the *locus operandi* of the state on the one hand and whether the business of government fell within the realm of politics on the other. Hence, in seeking to establish the authority of the state, as Metin Heper has observed, all three military interventions since 1960 have displayed similar aims of delineating an arena for the state as opposed to the realm of politics.[6]

These confusions began after the adoption of the multi-party system, before which politics were not accorded a separate sphere but controlled directly by the representatives of the state. The period of the Democrat Party rule between 1950 and 1960 witnessed a transition of the governing elite from the realm of the state to the realm of politics. The chain of events leading to the undoing of the system began with the reaction of the ruling party to parliamentary opposition. As the conflict between the governing party and its political opponents escalated, the Democrat Party set out to crush the opposition, relying on their comfortable majority in the parliament. It soon became evident that they not only meant to protect their control of the political realm but the system theoretically allowed them to be able to do so. The parliamentary majority on which the government relied gave them power over all branches of the government including the judiciary which meant that they were in a position to control the state apparatus. Moreover, the president, who was supposed to represent the state, was also the leader of the political party elected. In its con-

[6] Metin Heper, "Introduction" in this volume.

test for political supremacy the Democrat Party was not only counting on the vote, representing "the national will" (expressed in large measure by the periphery registering its opposition to government by state elites during the single-party era), but also utilizing the very power it derived from the state, including the use of the state apparatus with impunity to wage its battle in the political sphere. It is not surprising, therefore, that resistance to the Democrats had begun early on among the higher civil service and the military, two groups with strong socialization into the state tradition, and that the military eventually stepped in.

The 1961 Constitution, which aimed to prevent the state from being manipulated by politicians, was drafted in such a way as to distinguish and separate the institutions of the state from the realm of politics. Accordingly the office of the presidency was redefined as being above politics and a series of checks and balances was introduced delimiting the power of the government over the judiciary, independent organizations such as the universities and even over the bureaucracy. Such a reorganization of the system did not so much aim to "carve" a distinct arena for the state as it hoped to create mechanisms with veto power over the realm of politics. It was thus tacitly acknowledged that a cleavage existed between the realm of politics and that of state. This, in effect, meant that the state, formerly associated with government, had been made more distinct (and sovereign), leaving room for politics at the top. The quid pro quo was envisioned to be the integrity of the institutions representing the state.

Although the 1961 Constitution clearly defined the locus of the state and its position above political competition, it failed to provide commensurate powers to the institutions representing the state in the face of political interference. What it provided instead was a means to resist, albeit passively, specific decisions or moves made by the political leadership representing the executive branch. The civil bureaucracy, for instance, could, and often enough would, resist a particular government's decision to appoint new personnel to key positions through appeal to the Council of State (Danıştay: the Turkish version of the French Conseil d'Etat). Although the Council of State had the authority to overrule appointments and transfers of civil servants to other positions to make room for new appointees, it did not have the power to enforce its decisions. The government, in turn, could dig its heels, too, while appeals and counter-moves could continue ad infinitum. Thus a series of constitutional provisions intended to help to maintain the separation of powers among the three branches came to be utilized in a negative fashion solely for the purpose of territorial protection, and the increased sensitivity with regard to territoriality helped to perpetuate the hostility between civil servants and political regimes, serving to deepen the cleavage between the institutions of the state and the realm of political decision-making.

Moreover, the late 1960s and the following decade witnessed a weakening of the state institutions as a result, among other things, of the declining status of the bureaucracy. Because civil service was gradually losing its appeal due to the limited economic opportunities it offered to the entry-level personnel, the quality at the lower ranks was rapidly declining, resulting in fewer qualified civil servants coming up the ranks to replace the retired ones. More importantly, as the functions of the bureaucracy were differentiated, requiring expertise in specific areas, the top level positions in agencies related to economic, industrial, and infrastructural activities were being staffed by technocrats brought from the outside who were not socialized as civil servants and therefore had no loyalty to the system. This development resulted in a cleavage within the bureaucracy. This cleavage was deepened because of the higher status and economic opportunities accorded to the technocrats while those assigned routine administrative tasks were demoralized.

It was not until the 1970s that political polarization and fragmentation seriously damaged the civil service. Government patronage to reward party supporters through civil service appointments became a frequent and widespread practice in the wake of constantly changing coalition governments. Moreover, the political parties of the radical fringe tried to exploit this mechanism to gain control of certain agencies to compensate for their weak position in the parliamentary representation. The ideological differentiation among what amounted to solidarity groups within the civil bureaucracy was completed with the radicalization of the left wing. The result was none other than the nearly total subjection of the bureaucracy to the political whims of competing groups.

Meanwhile, those transferred to passive positions or demoted by successive governments to make room for their own clients would seek restitution from the state through appeal to the administrative court. Government, however, would increasingly make a practice of turning a deaf ear to the injunctions of the administrative court. Once again a state institution could be ignored with impunity by political leadership.

The crisis that left no choice for the military but to interfere was of course the stalemate of the presidential election. The stalemate, which was symptomatic of serious cleavages throughout the system, reflected more than merely the inability of the political parties to function within a parliamentary system. The fact that the crisis was reduced to a central issue concerning "parliamentary arithmetic" revealed clearly where the priorities of the political leadership lay. The lack of consensus at the top compounded with the fragmentation of the officialdom could do nothing but provide additional fuel to the anarchy on the street. With no end in sight to political maneuvering, while the prestige of the state was at stake for want of a leader, the military took the helm.

3 The 1982 Constitution

The 1982 Constitution, which was to a large extent formulated according to specific demands made by the military leadership, is often described as the result of a reaction to the liberal Constitution of 1961. It is true that the 1961 Constitution has been made a scapegoat blamed for the destabilization of the country in the 1970s. Complaints about the Constitution in fact began in the late 1960s and the first one to describe it as being "unworkable" was Demirel, who wished to have amendments made prior to his first removal from office by the military in 1971. Significantly, the military commanders at the time did not believe that the Constitution was defective, but found fault with the political leadership and rivalry in the parliament.[7] The fact is they felt that a libertarian constitution was befitting a truly democratic system but that the enemies of democracy were politicians themselves – a train of thought that permeated the atmosphere after the 1980 intervention as well.

Though seemingly paradoxical, this train of thought is in keeping with the logic of patrimonial state tradition. It was the state in the first place which had provided the framework for a democratic system with all the freedoms associated with it. However, the politicians had been unable to appreciate the system, and moreover, had committed the sin of subverting it through manipulation for their own gains. The state giveth and the state taketh, too. What was seen to be the sin of the politicians was the fact that they were not content to operate within the perimeters defined for them, and as a result they would come to grief.

The 1982 Constitution has asserted the supremacy of the state over the realm of politics and placed constraints on the political system to prevent it from weakening the control of the state over the governing institutions. The pendulum seems to have swung in the opposite direction, away from the libertarian era opened up after 1961. The closing of the major political parties in 1981 and subsequent constraints placed upon political activity had already signalled that the military took the business of reducing the impact of political influence seriously. The fact that military interventions prior to 1980 have resulted in conditions favorable to civilian politics had made the 1980 intervention stand in sharp contrast with its antecedents. However, viewed from the standpoint of the patrimonial tradition, the objectives of the military do not seem to be widely divergent from what they had been all along, despite the fact that the means chosen to attain the ends have entailed greater resolution in 1980 than in the earlier interventions.

Nevertheless, there exists a consensus that the 1980 intervention has re-

---

[7] Batur, *Anılar ve Görüşler*, pp. 165–166.

vealed a fundamental change in the outlook and the ideological orientation of the military. One outcome of this reorientation are the far-reaching legal, procedural and administrative measures taken in the wake of the intervention. Particularly the measures that aimed to restrict the ways in which demands can be made on the system, such as the limitations placed on labor unions and voluntary associations, may be perceived as a swing toward enlarging the realm of the state. Among the recurring themes in discussions of the role of military in recent Turkish history are the elite status of the officers, their unflagging opposition to reactionary movements, their long-standing commitment "to raise the country to the level of contemporary civilization" and, in order to do so, to support a type of regime and defend the kind of governmental institutions that are befitting a modern state.

These themes constitute the normative base of the post-1980 realm of the state. Such a role had already been formulated for the military in the middle of the nineteenth century when the Ottoman state began to transform itself into a version of bureaucratic empire. The creation of a modern military corps earlier in the century (1826) was itself the major step towards the realization of subsequent reforms. In this respect, the military did not have to be co-opted into the role of guarding the reformist state, but they were conceived as an integral part of it in the first place. Moreover, they constituted an elite group not only by virtue of the fact that they were members of a central institution but also because of the fact that they received, especially in the nineteenth century, a superior education, and thus became a part of the intelligentsia as well.

During the century and a half following the establishment of a modern military institution, the armed forces have been identified as initiators and protectors of reform. To those who take progressiveness to mean the quest for increasing democratization in all spheres of public (and for that matter also private) life, the restrictive nature of the measures taken after the 1980 coup must have seemed somewhat of an aberration as compared to the changes previously brought by the military into the political sphere. If the military were responsible for the restoration of the constitutional regime in 1908, the supporters and protectors of all the reforms that shaped the modern republic, and furthermore, if they were the moving spirit behind the 1961 Constitution which provided greater freedoms than encountered ever before, then they were expected to find a solution to the political stalemate facing the country without veering from the progressive path followed in the past.

The logical fallacy in this kind of thinking partly stems from the ambiguity surrounding the concept of being progressive in the Turkish context. First, the concept is relative in respect to its antonyms, reactionary or backward. In the political sphere reformists have been called progressive in contradistinction to their opponents who resisted change. Because the change supported by the progressiveness has entailed the adoption of representative forms of government and equal protection under secular law, progressiveness has been identified with democratization and libertarianism. It is true that Turkish reforms since the nineteenth century have led, on the whole, to the establishment of representative institutions as befitting a modern state. But it must also be taken into account that the progressive elite cadres had to make sure that their opponents in the periphery did not gain the liberty to destroy these institutions. To put it bluntly, the establishment of representative institutions was a process distinguished from the democratization of public life if that meant unbridled freedoms in society.

A second point to clarify rests with the changing connotation of the word "progressive" in relation to political development over time. With the transition to multi-party politics, which was itself a reform conceived and executed by the state elite, the word gradually came to be associated more with participatory democracy, shedding its earlier connotations of reformist dirigisme. The social-democratic spirit of the 1961 Constitution, prepared under the auspices of a coalition of elites, including the military leadership involved in the 1960 coup, gave rise to the notion that progressive reformism by definition entailed a kind of liberalism with a left-of-center orientation supportive of pluralism. This was a remarkable transformation from the time when the word "progressive" was employed to describe the autocratic bureaucrat of the Tanzimat era. Yet in so far as the way in which the state elites have adopted the role of acting as enlightened leaders in the Turkish patrimonial system, there can be found no discrepancy between the stance of the Tanzimat reformer and later generations of reformist leaders. Just as the Tanzimat reformers willed and implemented a system of modernized secular bureaucracy, so, too, the coalition of military, bureaucracy, and intellectuals designed and put into effect a "libertarian" constitutional system in 1961.

What is significant is the fact that a radical change in the connotation of the word progressive was registered when its usage was transformed from the realm of the state into the realm of politics. Though in the latter context it has naturally emerged as an antonym to conservatism or retrogressiveness, it is nevertheless simultaneously taken with all of its significant historical connotations, thus creating a confusion through identifying progressive reformism with a progressive attitude toward the operations of a participatory democracy. In reality, the two have often pointed in somewhat different directions in Turkish political culture, although participatory democracy was achieved in the wake of a long tradition of reform, but one which aimed chiefly at modernizing the state rather than liberalizing political competition.

As these examples discussed from the viewpoint of semantics would indicate, it is misleading to evaluate the role of the state elites, particularly the military, in terms of criteria relevant to developments in the political realm only. The Turkish military have always acted within the realm of the state, and whenever they intervened in the realm of politics, it was done so on behalf of the state.

4 Changes Shown by 1980 Intervention

The fact that the military did not enter into any coalition with other elite groups is a second reason why the 1980 intervention is perceived to reflect a change in the attitude of the military. But unlike the situation in 1960, when the military intervened in 1980, the civil bureaucracy had been fragmented and the intelligentsia divided along ideological lines. They had no natural allies in any significant cadres. In fact they were the last homogeneous group left, defined along institutional lines. It is not surprising, therefore, that they acted as the sole representatives of the state. This, in fact, reinforced the impression that the 1980 regime was guided more by the objective of establishing a military authority over the state than restoring the authority of the state. The difference, in any case, is insignificant since the military were the only group which could be identified as the state elite. If in the absence of a broader coalition of elites committed to the tradition of patrimonialism the military felt an alineation as well (which may partially explain the defensive tone behind their severe statements), one would be tempted to seek a correlation between authoritarianism and the syndrome of being lonely at the top.

A similar argument could be made in trying to explain why such a emphasis was placed on Atatürk and in the way in which the emphasis was placed. An ideology was needed to battle all other ideologies which had led to the fragmentation and polarization of the polity.

Such an ideology had to be broadly acceptable by the citizens on the one hand and capable of playing a mediating role on the other. Traditionally the state elites in Turkey have refrained from ideological extremes and have taken great care to launch the promulgations of the center as having been conceived for the benefit of the public at large. The cultural cleavage between the center and the periphery necessitated translating the ideas of the center into a form acceptable by the periphery. Moreover, the periphery itself constituted a mosaic of culturally differentiated groups which would display different reactions to "hard" ideologies of one kind or another. Indeed, the adoption of certain "hard" ideological lines among several different types of groups and communities in the 1960s and 1970s had had the effect of reinforcing group solidarity and thus facilitating violence in the wake of political polarization.

It was natural, therefore, that the military would turn to Atatürk whose pursuit of national integration took precedence over ideological issues. Kemalism itself originated from and reinforced the state tradition but at the same time aimed to bridge the gap between the culture of the center and that of the periphery through socializing the people into being citizens of a modern nation-state. Yet Kemalism in its original shape was a program and not an ideology even if the program included certain clearly defined goals such as republicanism and secularism. Largely because it was an indigenous formulation even if it had originated from the center, Kemalism had become a key text which various groups strove to reinterpret and adopt in seeking to establish ideological legitimacy. If the military had to turn to Kemalism because they had no alternative ideology to offer, through this choice they also had a chance to correct the basic text and prevent it from being subjected to further subversion. However, the military, too, adopted a heavy-handed editorial policy in enunciating and reformulating Kemalism which, by official definition, emerged as Atatürkism. In the years following the military intervention, Atatürkism has been employed to serve as the guiding ideology but it has also been constantly reinterpreted so as to be relevant to each occasion that demanded an authoritative interpretation.

The fact that Atatürkism has been modified and reinterpreted after the 1980 military intervention may in fact be related to the syndrome of being lonely at the top. Pragmatism, a virtue of the military leadership, is not particularly compatible with analytical rigor in ideological interpretation. In the absence of intellectuals as coalition partners in the 1980–1983 regime, the military might have found themselves under pressure to develop an ideological construct as events unfolded. Parts of that construct had to be appended as the situation required. Not only was 1980 a time when the military faced, for the first time in modern Turkish history, a situation where no consensus existed among any substantial group of elites, but it also marked the end of a decade when social change had accelerated beyond the rate of political development. As a consequence, the military was put in a position to formulate the ideological premises of the center by themselves, utilizing a convenient text. Yet they had to do this at a time when received formulas were no longer relevant for spoon-feeding the virtues of the old étatist mode, particularly since social change had resulted in the rise of an entrepreneurial culture, reinforced by the increasing unemployment and decline in the status and income of salaried positions. In a situation where the periphery had come into its own by becoming viable economically, the center had to take a more pliable stand with respect to recognizing the culture of the periphery. As this situation bared itself gradually while the chaos of the 1970s slowly disappeared, the military leadership seem to have responded on every occasion to modify Atatürkism and make it relevant in a polity of cultural pluralism. As for the authority of the state, which used to be upheld at the ideological level and well understood on the cultural one, it was pragmatically relegated to the legal and administrative sphere by providing specific powers to the representatives of the state over and above those of the government.

The divergence between the intentions and results of the 1980 military intervention reveals, among other things, the enormous degree of social change which had been camouflaged behind the civil disturbances and political in-fighting throughout the 1970s. As the discussion attempted to underscore, the primary aim of the military leadership was to restore the authority of the state so as to counteract social conflict. Initially the military leadership had no plans to close down the major political parties, nor did they intend to have cadres other than experienced politicans to run the government. Shortly after the coup the leadership realized that they could not put together a coalition of politicians to run the show as had been the case in 1971. Later the intransigence of the major political parties also showed that competitive politics had been firmly established in the culture. In this respect, too, the state had to take into account the fact that the choices of the periphery would always be represented in the government. But a means had to be found to prevent the state being affected by the pluralism and lack of consensus in a parliament reflecting the conflicting particularistic and ideological demands made by groups in the periphery. As a result, the arena of politics was not only constrained but was placed under the control of the state.

The political situation in post-1980 Turkey reflects the disappearance of the chief cultural cleavage between the center and periphery. The reasons for the disappearance of this cleavage rest with socio-economic factors rather than political ones. As a result of a change in the economic principles, replacing a long tradition of distributive patrimonialism with market economy, a class-based society is in the making. Meanwhile the traditional state elites in the bureaucracy are being replaced by managerial cadres. The change in economic culture has not only resulted in the ascendancy of new cadres into positions of influence but has also led to a redefinition of status in society. Whatever final form the emerging pattern of cleavages will take, it is certain that it will reflect the range of choices in a pluralist society. However, in terms of the central institutions it would be safe to predict the continuation of two newly formed cleavages: those between the state and government, and those between political decision-makers and professionals in government employment.

Chapter 14
The Military, the Presidency, and the Constitution: A Comparative Approach to the Weimar Republic, France 1958, and Turkey 1982

Christian Rumpf

1 Introduction

It is well known that the ghost of the Weimar Constitution of 1919 and the still very much alive French Constitution of 1958 were selected as both positive and negative examples taken into consideration by Turkish legislators during the preliminary discussions in the course of making the 1982 Constitution.

The present chapter aims to describe and compare the circumstances and conditions obtaining in the Weimar Republic, France, and Turkey during the transitions from the collapse of the respective constitutional systems to the emergence of new ones, with particular emphasis on the military, presidency, and constitutions as well as the interrelations among these three institutions.

2 Weimar Republic[1]

"The army will march back home calmly and in order under their leaders and commanding generals, but not under the command of Your Majesty, for the army no longer stands behind Your Majesty."[2]

This remark by the quartermaster General Wilhelm Groener, uttered directly to the face of the Emperor William II in Spy, Belgium, marks the end of the Hohenzollern military monarchy. Groener thus rejected to comply with William II's order to march to Berlin after the armistice in order to suppress by military force what had begun as a sailors' revolt on November 4, 1918, and had reached a climax in Berlin on November 9 when a general strike was proclaimed and the workers' mob moved on to the center of the capital. Groener's argument that the field troops would not be willing to shoot at the revolutionaries was verified the same day when factions of the home troops in Berlin, after a short exchange of fire, fraternalized with the workers.

November 9 was to be the end of the old regime. In order to save the monarchy, the Imperial Chancellor Prince Max von Baden, proclaimed at noon, without any authorization, that the Emperor had abdicated and that his son had renounced the throne. Von Baden himself handed his office over to the leader of the majority Socialists, Friedrich Ebert. Ebert thus found himself, in one day, heading a bourgeois cabinet. The military, under the leadership of Groener and von Hindenburg, acknowledged this development as unavoidable, and for the sake of Germany, prepared itself for a peaceful transition to the new system.

In the late evening of the same day, Groener, as the representative of the still existing military power but at the outset without the formal consent of von Hindenburg, Chief of the General Staff, and Ebert, as the responsible representative of the civil power in transition, reached an agreement[3] which became the basis of a new legitimacy of power and which, as opposed to the old imperial one, unified the military and civil power. Be-

[1] Gordon A. Craig, *The Politics of the Prussian Army 1640-1945* (Oxford, Clarendon Press, 1955), pp. 342-467; Harold J. Gordon, *The Reichswehr and the German Republic 1919-1926* (Princeton, Princeton University Press, 1957); John W. Wheeler-Bennett, *The Nemesis of Power: The German Army in Politics, 1918-1945* (London, MacMillan, 1954), pp. 3-286; Karl Dietrich Bracher, *Die Auflösung der Weimarer Republik*, 5th edition (Villingen, Ring-Verlag, 1971); Ernst Rudolf Huber, *Deutsche Verfassungsgeschichte seit 1789*, vol. 5 (Stuttgart, Kohlhammer, 1978), pp. 673-1205; vol. 6 (1981), *in toto;* Otto-Ernst Schüddekopf, *Das Heer und die Republik* (Hannover, Norddeutsche Verlagsanstalt O. Goedel, 1955), *in toto.*

[2] Huber, *Deutsche Verfassungsgeschichte seit 1789*, vol. 6, p. 676.

[3] Craig, *The Politics of the Prussian Army 1640-1945*, pp. 342ff.; Wheeler-Bennett, *The Nemesis of Power*, pp. 20ff.; Huber, *Deutsche Verfassungsgeschichte seit 1789*, vol. 5, p. 752; and Brancher, *Die Auflösung der Weimarer Republik*, p. 21.

ginning the next day the latter was to be represented by the Council of the People's Commissionaries established as a revolutionary body.[4] The agreement contained the promise of each of the two parties to cooperate in restoring peace and order in Germany for the sake of the internal and external security of the nation. The next day Von Hindenburg gave his consent to the agreement, and the Council, presided over by Ebert, assumed sovereign power.

The significance of the agreement was evident: the military acknowledged the revolution as far as it had gone, and the civilians agreed to stop all further revolutionary movement. Thus, both parties recognized the legitimacy of the new system. The military looked with sympathy to the creation of the new (republican) constitutional order. The initiative nevertheless rested in the hands of the civilians, primarily in the hands of the majority Socialists under the leadership of Friedrich Ebert.

The provisional *Reichswehr* (Military Act) was promulgated by the National Assembly of Weimar which had been elected on January 19, 1919, and which itself elected Friedrich Ebert to presidency on February 11. Thus, the process of reconstructing the *Reichswehr* took place in a period when the civilians opted for the principle of the division of powers. Both the election of Ebert and the promulgation of the Provisional *Reichswehr* Act derived from a democratically legitimated civil power, and both decisions were of considerable significance with respect to relations that were to obtain between civil and military powers during the short-lived Weimar Republic. The military, i.e., the *Freikorps* (volunteer corps) and later the Provisional Reichswehr, did make occasional interventions under the central government's orders to suppress various revolutionary riots and disloyal movements in the federated states *(Länder)*, but it did not participate actively in the legislative process.

The only norm concerning the *Reichswehr* in the new Constitution of August 14, 1919, was the principle of unity in the *Reichswehr* (Article 79).[5] The rest of the rules governing the concept of the *Reichswehr* had to be laid down by law and not without due consideration for particular circumstances of each of the federated states. The lack of norm in the Constitution on this issue and the delay in promulgating the law on the *Reichswehr* which was supposed to follow the Provincial *Reichswehr* Act, may have been due to the fact that the new regime had to take into account the wishes of the Allies. The idea of the *Reichswehr* imposed by the dictates of

[4] See Gordon, *The Reichswehr and the German Republic in Politics,* p. 8, where he calls this council the "Council of People's Representatives." Also see Craig, *The Politics of Prussian Army,* p. 349.

[5] Gordon, *The Reichswehr and the German Republic,* pp. 151 ff.; Huber, *Deutsche Verfassungsgeschichte seit 1789,* vol. 6, pp. 592 ff.

Versailles was one of a professional army where, on the whole, traditionalism and the principle of efficiency were unified in an interesting amalgam that seems to be of some significance with regard to future developments.

According to Article 39 of the Weimar Constitution, soldiers were allowed to run as candidates in parliamentary elections. But in reality, this article had no practical consequences since the *Reichswehr* Act of 1918 prohibited any involvement in party politics, including membership in political clubs and parties. Furthermore, it denied soldiers the right to vote, as a result of the principle of the army's neutrality, propagated since the beginning of the Republic.[6]

But what was meant by political neutrality did not refer to political restraint as was understood by such significant figures in military politics as Noske, Ebert, von Hindenburg, Reinhardt, Heye, Gessler, von Seeckt, Groener, and Hasse. A telling example was provided by Hans von Seeckt,[7] who established military relations with Russia in 1921, without the government being informed beforehand.

This principle of political neutrality found its expression in the slogan: "The *Reichswehr* is an obedient instrument of the state." As von Seeckt, the successor of von Hindenburg, liked to point out, the main task of the army was to defend the Reich. Nevertheless, its political role in internal affairs was not to be overlooked. According to Article 17 of the Reichswehr Act, civil powers were allowed to call on the army in a state of emergency.

Such a situation arose in 1923, when the Reich was affected by a serious economic crisis while the French were occupying the Ruhr area. In the west there was a movement for establishing an independent state along the Rhine. In both Thuringia and Saxony, leftist coalitions rejected cooperation with the central government. Backed by radical rightists and those in the government as well as monarchist circles, the seccessionist movement in Bavaria culminated in the march on the Feldherrnhalle in Munich under the leadership of von Ludendorff and Hitler. Von Seeckt used his dictatorial powers given to him by Ebert. After he had restored order in the Reich, he withdrew to the barracks and thus once more proved the loyalty of the army to the republican civil power.

The Weimar Constitution was not clear in respect to the question of the competence to decide the state of war. On the other hand, Article 47 of the Constitution stated quite clearly that "The President of the Reich holds the supreme command over all armed forces of the Reich," a re-

[6] See *Ibid.*, pp. 626ff.

[7] Craig, *The Politics of the Prussian Army*, pp. 382ff.; Wheeler Bennett, *The Nemesis of Power*, pp. 83ff.

markable clause given the fact that the Constitution was formulated with a civilian president in office, and a Social Democrat at that.[8]

When von Hindenburg was elected President in 1925, some circles might have thought that the political role of the military would be considerably accentuated. But this was not true, since the old commander-in-chief made even less use than Ebert of his emergency powers and of the army as an instrument for maintaining domestic order. It was, instead, the civil power as embodied by the government which reinforced the political weight of the *Reichswehr* by the nomination of retired generals as *Reichswehrminister:* Groener in 1928 and von Schleicher[9] in 1932.

The importance of the position of the *Reichspräsident* (state president) was not only due to its democratic legitimacy but also to the political neutrality of the president. Both Ebert and von Hindenburg strictly adhered to this principle. The political neutrality of the president correlated juridically as well as politically with that of the *Reichswehr.* Both presidents saw to it that top-level officers were not shifted every time there was a change of government.

The Weimar Constitution defined the presidency primarily as an executive position. Among other things, the *Reichspräsident* had extensive emergency powers: Article 48 of the Constitution left it up to him to decide whether the conditions warranted the use of emergency powers and if so which measures to take. One of the means at his disposal was the *Reichswehr.* However, the powers of the president within the ordinary process of legislation did not go very far. He had to promulgate the laws passed by the Reichstag without the right to reject them by reasons of expediency. Instead, however, he could submit a law, the promulgation of which he considered otherwise doubtful, to a referendum (Article 73). Though he had the right to dissolve the Reichstag (Article 25), his significant power in this respect was bound to the consent of at least one minister or the *Reichskanzler* (state Chancellor).

The most important point is the emergency powers mentioned above.[10] Article 48, paragraph 2 gave the president the right to take measures by way of issuing normative decrees which were valid until the end of the state of emergency. But as there was no formal act of proclamation and of termination of the state of emergency, the validity of such decrees was of rather uncertain duration. The fact that at least one minister had to coun-

---

[8] Huber, *Deutsche Verfassungsgeschichte seit 1789,* vol. 6, pp. 610 ff.; Gerhard Anschütz, *Die Verfassung des Deutschen Reichs* (reprint of the fourteenth ed.) (Bad Homburg, Verlag Dr. Max Gehlen, 1968), p. 267.

[9] For the role of Kurt von Schleicher in the last years of the Weimar Republic see Wheeler-Bennett, *The Nemesis of Power,* pp. 182 ff.

[10] For the constitutional and legal aspects see Anschütz, pp. 267 ff. *Die Verfassung des Deutschen Reichs,* pp. 267 ff.

tersign the decree provided a certain amount of control. The parliamentary checks consisted of the right of the Reichstag to demand the derogation of such decrees, but given the force of Article 25 the influence of Reichstag was negligible. In fact, his extensive powers made the president a formidable rival of the original legislative body, the Reichstag.

Ebert, the Social Democrat, was loyally followed by the *Reichswehr*, but without any enthusiasm. Though the office of the president was accepted by all officers, including the commander-in-chief of the military hierarchy as defined by the Constitution, neither von Seeckt nor the majority of the older and conservative officers were willing to accept the Social Democrat Ebert, a former saddlemaker, as the supreme commander. Perhaps apart from the Kapp Putsch,[11] which under von Hindenburg might not have taken place or at least probably would have been suppressed by military force (despite von Seeckt's principle, "the *Reichswehr* does not shoot on the *Reichswehr*"), it was the mutual accommodation between the *Reichswehr* and Republic as well as the popularity of Ebert and the mutual respect between the President and von Seeckt which prohibited negative political effects on the relationship between the President and the *Reichswehr* as a whole.

It was the election of von Hindenburg[12] to the presidency in 1925 that finally led to a certain degree of satisfaction among the officers corps. To von Seeckt's regret as the commander-in-chief "only," the office and position of the president at the top of the military hierarchy gained influence through the person of the new President. The relationship between President and the *Reichswehr* became close at the expense of the political influence of the commander-in-chief. Unlike Ebert, von Hindenburg liked to deal with military problems; consequently, von Seeckt lost his dominant role in military politics.

To recapitulate, the defeat of the German Empire at the end of World War I and the multiple changes of organization and structure of the German army as well as its initial weakness toward the revolutionary movement in 1918-1919 forced the military not to play a strong political role and to ally itself with the moderate though dynamic forces of the Social Democrats instead of the exhausted forces of the Conservatives. This was, in terms of the state, the only way to face the revolutionary disposition of the domestic political atmosphere. Furthermore, the dictate of Versailles,

---

[11] Craig, *The Politics of the Prussian Army 1640-1945*, pp. 373 ff.; Gordon, *The Reichswehr and the German Republic 1919-1926*, pp. 90-143.

[12] For von Hindenburg and his role in the Weimar republic see, Andreas Dorpalen, *Hindenburg and the Weimar Republic* (Princeton, Princeton University Press, 1964); Walther Hubatsch, *Hindenburg und der Staat* (Göttingen, Musterschmidt-Verlag, 1966); Emil Ludwig, *Hindenburg* (Hamburg, Rütten and Loening Verlag, 1962).

which prohibited the creation of the material foundation of a new military power and thus prevented the *Reichswehr* from playing a significant role within state politics, helped to improve the smooth relations between the *Reichswehr* and the republican forces, despite the remaining monarchist attitude of the officers corps.

The traditional principles that "the *Reichswehr* is an obedient instrument of the state" and "there must be no party politics in the *Reichswehr*" resulted in the principle of civilian power, represented by the Social Democrat Friedrich Ebert, which dominated and imposed itself during the preparation of the Weimar Constitution, with the military playing a supportive but passive role.

The election of von Hindenburg to the presidency led to certain changes in the situation. The *Reichswehr* lost its independence which it had been able to conserve with regard to military politics. It led to a further instrumentalization of the *Reichswehr* within the framework of the emergency powers of the president, according to Article 48 of the Constitution. Since von Hindenburg accepted his role as the representative of the most important part of the civilian power within the republican constitutional system of Weimar with a grain of salt, his close relationship with the *Reichswehr* as his instrument within this framework seems to have had more the effect of paralyzing the *Reichswehr* as a political factor rather than of reinforcing it as a relatively independent power. This relationship thus prevented the military, which had not been totally imbued with a republican ethos, from playing a positive historical role in the face of the events of 1933.

3 France[13]

The political role of the military during the Fourth Republic was determined by the perpetual state of war in which France had been involved since its entanglement in Indonesia. The decisive defeat in Dien Bien Phu was followed by its engagement in Suez and then, above all, in Algeria.

---

[13] Antoine Azar, *Genèse de la Constitution du 4 octobre 1958* (Paris, Librairie Générale de Droit, 1961); Jean Barale, *La Constitution de la IV. République à l'epreuve de la guerre* (Paris, Librairie Générale de Droit, 1964); Raoul Girardet, "Pouvoir Civil et Pouvoir Militaire," *Revue Française des Sciences Politiques* 5 (1960), pp. 5ff.; Léo Hamon, *Une République présidentielle?* vol. 1 (Paris, Bordas, 1975); Dorothy Pickles, *The Government and Politics of France*, vol. 2 (London, Methuen, 1973); Roy Pierce, *French Politics and Political Institutions* (New York, Harper and Row, 1968); Gilbert Ziebura, *Die V. Republik* (Köln, Westdeutscher Verlag, 1960).

In Indochina the 100,000-men army lost the war as a politically neutral instrument for the sake of international politics: as the generals themselves noted bitterly, it had been used by a civilian government with no conviction and thus with no success. In Algeria, which was juridically not considered a colony but, with its four provinces, a part of the fatherland, the army became the protector of national interests. The activities of the Algerian Liberation Movement (FLM) urged the presence of larger contingents of French military forces, amounting to some 400,000 to 500,000 men, who had the task of protecting about one million French civilians, the *français de souche.*

Such deployment of the main forces of the army led to a certain territorial distance from the center of civil power. The government tried to compensate this fact by the nomination of a Minister of Algeria (since 1957, Minister of Algerian Affairs), who not only represented the interests of the central government in Algeria but also Algerian interests in Paris. Being at the same time governor general, he had the right to make use of the army in the case of emergency.

Another aspect of the situation of the military was the changing and confusing system of relationships between civilian and military power. As a rule, the supreme command and the defense policy remained in the hands of the prime minister (Article 47, paragraph 3 of the 1946 Constitution), but he could delegate these powers. The prime ministers of the time made use of this possibility in different manners. In 1954, General Koenig became the Minister of Defense and of the Army, although he was only given the task of organizing the military and looking after the military politics in terms of carrying the supreme command. The determination of the defense policy remained within the power of Prime Minister Mendes-France. At the beginning of 1955, the determination of the defense policy was delegated to a special Minister of Defense. In November 1955, Prime Minister Faure handed both the supreme command and the defense policy over to General Billotte who, until May 13, 1958, was followed by three civilian ministers of national defense and military forces.

In addition, given the powers of the Minister of Algerian Affairs as opposed to the larger part of the army, it is easy to see the institutional background of the scene in which the *état de siège* in Algeria, with its reinforcing effect on the position of the military, induced the army gradually to abandon its political neutrality and take on the rapidly increasing role of being the ruling power and most important social force in Algeria.[14]

The counterpart to the development of the role of the military was the growing confusion and debilitation of civil power, founded on a failing governmental system of the 1946 Constitution. According to this Consti-

---

[14] Barale, *La Constitution de la IV. République à l'epreuve de la guerre,* p. 504.

tution, the second chamber of the parliament, the Council of the Republic, and the President of the Republic were of no importance vis-à-vis the National Assembly. The executive power was held by a council of ministers, which was under the tight control of the National Assembly by virtue of the instrument of the "destructive vote of no-confidence." The National Assembly itself suffered under a permanent change of various party coalitions. The prolonged crisis in the colonial periphery of France easily spread to the fatherland. Because Algeria was considered part of the fatherland both in terms of the Constitution and in the eyes of most French people, the crisis there loomed large as it was taken to be a domestic matter. The quarrels between the defendants of *Algérie française* and others from all shades of the political spectrum resulted even in divided party fractions. These disputes concerning the status of Algeria, and the question of autonomy or secession rendered any political decision highly critical, even impossible. Unrest also spread to the army, penetrating even the highest ranks, among whom those stationed in Algeria and having effective ruling power under the *état de siège* identified themselves with the interests of the Algerians.

After the defeat of Dien Bien Phu, the majority of the higher-ranking officers pleaded for a strict policy to ensure the constitutional status quo of Algeria as part of the fatherland. They were not willing to accept the danger of being used as an instrument of weakening civil power, closely watching the events and snatching away any possible chance of a sound Algerian policy out of the hands of the civilians.

What took place in Algiers on May 13, 1958 was not a classic putsch, but a revolt by some French Algerians which was consented to and supported by the army.[15] Public Welfare Committees were established in the provinces, cities, and townships over the traditional administrative units. These Committees were mostly presided over by army officers. General Massu headed the general government in Algiers. (Since the beginning of 1957, he had been in charge of the maintenance of public order and security in Algiers.) Massu demanded that the President of the Republic, Coty, nominate a new emergency government. The same evening, the commander of the military forces in Algeria, General Salan, declared that he would take over for the sake of Algeria's destiny.

This set the stage for General de Gaulle. The question as to whether the revolt had been set up by the Gaullists[16] is of no particular importance. For several months already, de Gaulle, still well remembered as a crisis manager after the liberation of France following World War II, had re-

[15] Azar, *Genèse de la Constitution du octobre 1958*, pp. 194ff.; Pierce, *French Politics and Political Institutions*, pp. 45ff.

[16] This view is given by Azar, *Genèse de la Constitution du octobre 1958*, p. 195.

ceived several open calls for help in Paris. On May 15, 1958, after the revolt in Algeria, he officially declared his willingness to take over power. General Salan supported him by the first cry of *vive de Gaulle* in Algiers.

The Committees in Algeria increasingly grew independent. On May 24, Corsica was occupied with the support of the Algerian forces and a Public Welfare Committee was formed. Three days later, after a conference with Prime Minister Pflimlin, who himself had been in office for only two weeks, de Gaulle declared that the regular procedure for the formation of a republican government that would be able to guarantee unity and independence of the country had been initiated.

On June 1, despite the votes of quite a powerful opposition, de Gaulle became prime minister. Shortly thereafter, he obtained the full powers he had required for a fundamental reform of the political system of France.

During an open discussion, which evolved in keeping with the diffuse party and political structures of the Fourth Republic, de Gaulle was able to enforce his constitutional ideas; these were still well known from his famous speech of Bayeux in 1946,[17] where he had attacked the constitutional system of the Fourth Republic.

A referendum was held on September 28, with a participation rate of 84.9 per cent with 79.2 per cent in favor of the constitutional project, and the new Constitution was promulgated on October 4, 1958. The military had no influence on the working out of the Constitution itself, which lay in the hands of the transitional civil power under the leadership of de Gaulle.

The beginning of the second era of de Gaulle with the new Constitution meant, at the outset, the realigning of the military and civil powers. With de Gaulle there now existed a civilian regime with whose aims the military could identify.

This statement contains two different elements that nevertheless cannot really be separated from one another: the loyalty of the military to civilian power was again established. At the same time, the military no longer considered itself an instrument which had to reject all political thinking or party politics. Algeria and the weakness of the civil power during the crisis had politicized the military. It entered the new constitutional order without any important personal or structural change under the slogan, "conditional obedience,"[18] which was to cause de Gaulle some trouble in 1961 when he had to deal with the "revolt of the generals" in Algiers.[19]

After all, the new Constitution brought no direct juridical change with respect to the military, apart from the rules concerning the supreme com-

---

[17] For the text, see Ziebura, *Die V. Republik,* p. 31.

[18] Girardet, "Pouvoir Civil et Pouvoir Militaire," p. 32.

[19] Pickles, *The Government and Politics of France,* p. 45.

mand.[20] Civil liberties granted to soldiers in 1945 within the framework of military necessity and political neutrality did not gain any further importance. Formally, the soldiers had the right to vote, but they were not allowed to join any political party or association of a political nature and had to practice self-restraint with regard to freedom of speech. These restrictions aimed at making the military apolitical and neutral.

Only one article of the Constitution refers to the military. According to Article 15, the President holds the supreme command and presides over the National Defense Councils and Committees. This ended the dangerous confusion in relations between civilian and the military power under the 1946 Constitution. Both powers were thus integrated under the person and office of a powerful president. On the other hand the army was made free of parliamentary control.

Unlike the 1946 Constitution, the presidency was founded on a considerably stronger basis of legitimacy.[21] At the outset, he was elected by a body of electors. This body consisted not only of the two chambers of the parliament, but also of a large number of representatives from departments and townships (Article 6).

De Gaulle, however, initiated a referendum in 1962, through which he introduced the principle of a general and direct vote for the president. This referendum had the effect of offering a popular confirmation of his constitutional policy and increasing the basis of legitimacy of his own power as president.

During the preparatory work on the new Constitution, the notion of the "arbitrator-leader"[22] had already arisen, an element of de Gaulle's constitutional conception of 1946. The notion meant giving an eminent position to the president, whose functions were distributed to the three main powers of the state. The president could be considered the keystone, above legislative, executive, and jurisdictional powers. A small but meaningful sentence (Article 16) gave him dictatorial emergency powers including the right of the statement ("if") and the execution ("how") of the state of emergency.[23]

The legislature or the Assemblé Nationale can be replaced by the president only under the rule of Article 16. During normal times, the president

---

[20] For the juridical situation of the military see Jacques Robert, "Ethique Militaire, Condition Juridique et Libertées Publiques," *Annales de l'Université dés Sciences Sociales de Toulouse* 15 (1977), pp. 57 ff.

[21] Azar, *Genèse de la Constitution du octobre 1958*, pp. 211 ff.; Hamon, *Une République présidentielle?*, pp. 50 ff.; Pierce, *French Politics and Political Institutions*, pp. 49 ff.; and Pickles, *The Government and Politics of France*, vol. 1, pp. 99 ff.

[22] Hamon, *Une République présidentielle?*, p. 50.

[23] For Article 16 in the constitution see Benoit Jenneau, *Droit constitutionnel et institutions politiques* (Paris, Dalloz, 1978), pp. 261 ff.

has powers which ensure some influence over the Assemblé. First, he has to promulgate laws. At this stage of the legislative proceedings he can submit the law in question to a norm control by the Constitutional Council. Furthermore, the president can dissolve the National Assembly except during a state of emergency. Finally, on the request of the prime minister the president can convoke the Assemblé for extraordinary meetings.

According to Article 64, the president is the guarantor of the independence of the judiciary. In this respect the only concrete rule is that of Article 65, under which the president presides over the High Council of Judges. This Council is composed of - besides the president - the minister of justice and nine other members appointed by the president. The Council has to make propositions for the nomination of judges and has, under the presidency of the head of the Court of Cassation, to deal with disciplinary affairs.

The assignment of the supreme command over the military to the President of the Republic was the most important reaction to the alienation between military and civil power under the 1946 Constitution. Moreover, using the president as the guarantor of the continuity of the state, as understood by de Gaulle, meant avoiding having the military, the guardian of national security, submit to frequent changes in the chain of command between military and civil power. As a retired general with some experience and reputation as a civilian politician as well, and with his authority as a crisis manager, de Gaulle himself was the most suitable person for the role set by Article 15 of assuring concord between military and civil power.

Finally, it was due to this linkage through the supreme command that de Gaulle was later on able to manage the fundamental change - inevitable and foreseen by him - in his Algerian policy, which led to the independence of Algeria without any severe reaction or sign of disloyalty on the part of the military as a whole.[24]

In summary, the constitutional change-over in France in 1958 was the result of the growing weakness - encouraged by the 1946 Constitution - of the civilian power, which during the permanent colonial war situation from 1946 (Indochina) through 1956 (Suez) up to 1958 had not been able to make clear decisions to achieve the political aim of "victory."

The interior life of the state could not remain unaffected by the fact of constant external defeats. The army, which in Indochina had still considered itself the apolitical instrument of the politics of the civil power, was no longer willing to tolerate this situation. The crisis in Algeria and the

[24] Two attempts were of some importance but were not more than signs of the disloyalty of small groups - the revolt of the barricades in 1960 and the revolt of the generals in 1961. See Pickles, *The Government and Politics of France*, vol. 2, pp. 37, 44ff.

conflicts about the Algerian problem aggravated the discontent in the military. The military, which had won increasing de facto political power in Algeria via delegation, finally used its power on May 13, 1958, to bring down the Fourth Republic by a constructive vote of no-confidence in supporting the revolt and calling for de Gaulle to assume power.

Within a short time after assuming leadership, de Gaulle succeeded in restoring concord between the civil and military power by reconstituting the constitutional system in accordance with his own ideas and managed to persuade the military to identify with the political system.

4 Turkey[25]

Since the Korean War at the beginning of the 1950s, the Turkish army was only engaged in foreign combat once, in Cyprus in 1974. Generally, the role of the military during the 1961 Constitutional period was affected by internal politics.[26]

Two components determined the significance of military activity in Turkish politics: the historical-political guardianship in the Kemalist tradition of modern Turkey and participation in decision-making through membership in the National Security Council, which advises the government on matters of internal as well as external security.

The historical-political component, the guardianship of the Kemalist tradition, which was (and still is) an element of the spirit of the constitutional order, was connected with the considerable traditional social prestige of the army. The military considered itself not only an instrument of

---

[25] For general contributions with respect to this section of the chapter see the references given in this volume by Dodd, Harris, and Özbudun. Also see Heinz Kramer, *Das neue politische System der Türkei* (Ebenhausen, Report of the Stiftung Wissenschaft und Politik, September 1983); Heinz Kramer, *Die aktuelle politische Lage der Türkei* (Ebenhausen, Report of the Stiftung Wissenschaft und Politik, 1984); Jacob M. Landau, "Political Institutions," in *Südosteuropa-Handbuch, Band 4: Türkei*, edited by K.-D. Grothusen (Göttingen, Vandenhoeck and Ruprecht, 1985), pp. 248 ff.; Nicholas S. Ludington and James W. Spain, "Dateline Turkey: The Case for Patience," *Foreign Policy* 50 (1983), pp. 150 ff.

[26] Feroz Ahmad, *Military Intervention and the Crisis in Turkey*, MERIP Reports, 1981, pp. 93 ff.; Mevlut Bozdemir, *Le Rôle politique de l'armée en Turquie* (Grenoble, Service de Reproduction des Thèses de l'Université des Sciences Sociales de Grenoble, 1978), pp. 98 ff.; Ali Kazancıgil, "Die Türkei zwischen Demokratie und Militärherrschaft," *Europa-Archiv* 26 (1972), pp. 501 ff.; R. P. Nye, "The Military in Turkish Politics, 1960–1973," unpublished Ph. D. dissertation, Washington University, 1974; Gerhard Weiher, *Militär und Entwicklung in der Türkei 1945–1973* (Opladen, Leske-Verlag, 1978); Gerhard Weiher, *Die innenpolitische Rolle des Militärs*, in *Südosteuropa-Handbuch*, pp. 303 ff.; Horst von Zitzewitz, "Die türkische Armee und das Erbe Atatürks," *Außenpolitik*, 1964), pp. 338 ff. Also see Karpat in this volume and his references.

the civilian power but also a representative of the Turkish nation. The army had political weight - as proven on May 27, 1960 - which had its basis in its self-defined guardianship role along with a well-founded general social acceptance.

Military "participation" in solving the most recent crisis in 1980 derived from the extensive constitutional and legal reforms that were made between 1971 and 1973. The pressure of the military itself along with other pressures for reform led to a far-reaching legal provision of powers for the military in a state of crisis, making the military an effective element of internal politics. When the martial law was imposed, the military played a decisive role using its political weight in the National Security Council and in decision-making. It legally displaced civilian power in the provinces affected. Martial law in the last years before September 12, 1980 made the military a powerful political component of the government and an efficient part of the constitutional order.

The government, as established by the 1961 Constitution, was unable to reverse the disintegration of society and the bureaucracy, and the rise of social tensions, which were aggravated by the severe economic crisis.[27] There were several reasons for the weakness of the government. The various political parties were at odds with each other and the majority of the political elite was irresponsible. There were grave defects in the system of two parliamentary chambers which, under the last Demirel government, led to a virtual blockage of legislation. It proved impossible to elect within an appropriate space of time a person as president of the Republic, the last constitutional organ possessed of any real integrative capacity.

The integration of society and political power by democratic participation, as envisaged in the 1961 Constitution, was not realized and, instead, turned into a perversion of democracy, with everyone struggling against everyone else. The civilian power was dissolving itself as a consequence of these factors.

Before September 12, 1980, as the last political institution without obvious signs of dissolution,[28] the military had tried to play its role as a stabilizing factor, but within the framework of the existing constitutional and legal order, it was not able to stop the decline of the civilian power and the "rule" of the terror on the streets.

On September 12, 1980, the army as a whole under the leadership of

---

[27] For an outline of the 1961 Constitution, see Ergun Özbudun, "Constitutional Law," in *Introduction to Turkish Law,* 2nd ed., edited by Tuğrul Ansay and Don Wallace Jr. (New York, Oceana Publications, 1978), pp. 23 ff.; Ernst E. Hirsch, *Die Verfassung der Türkischen Republik* (Frankfurt, Alfred Metzner Verlag, 1966; Supplement 1973, Hamburg).

[28] Not "obvious," but nevertheless existing were the tendencies of political polarization within the military itself. This is supposed to be another argument for the seizure of power "within the chain of command."

the chief of the general staff and the four commanders of the main branches (air force, army, navy, and gendarmerie), by means of a bloodless coup, replaced the powerless shells of the legislative and executive organs by the transitional National Security Council. The basis of legitimacy of the government consisted of the force of arms and the supra-constitutional state of emergency, as well as the presumed silent consent of the people. After this coup, the military was successful in halting the symptoms of the disintegration of society as expressed in terrorist activities.

During the period of transition, all of the political power of the state was in the hands of the military.[29] Where civilians, such as members of the Ulusu cabinet, did have certain powers at their disposal, these powers were derived by delegation from that of the National Security Council. The Constituent Assembly one year later brought no change. The civilian part of that institution, the Consultative Assembly could do no more than consult while legal decisions, including those concerning the draft of the 1982 Constitution, were taken up by the National Security Council. Yet, although the Consultative Assembly was only charged with preparatory work, the impact of this Assembly on the legitimacy of the subsequent constitutional order cannot be denied. By holding a number of hearings with several interest groups and various representative bodies like professional chambers and universities,[30] the Consultative Assembly contributed significant input to the development of the new constitutional order.

The popular referendum of November 6, 1982, on the constitution did not add to the legitimacy of the new Constitution. It was a unilateral military decision to hold the referendum and to set the terms for the referendum.

Under the new regime the military is subject to quite a few constitutional rules.[31] The president of the Republic holds de facto the supreme command (Article 104b), which is nevertheless limited. In case of war (which is to be declared by the National Assembly, Article 92, paragraph 1) he decides on the use of military force; at times of peace the sending of mili-

---

[29] Harris in this volume; Ernst E. Hirsch, "Die einstweilige Ordung der türkischen Verfassung," *Orient* 22 (1981), pp. 431 ff.; Arnold Hottinger, "Die Türkei unter der Herrschaft des Militärs," *Europa-Archiv* 36 (1982), pp. 199 ff.; Otmar Oehring, "Die Verfassunggebende Versammlung in der Türkei," *Orient* 22 (1981), pp. 611 ff.

[30] See for example the drafts and commentaries in the collection by Yaşar Gürbüz, *Anayasa-Görüşler-Taslak* (İstanbul, Ekin Yayınları, 1982).

[31] For the new constitution see Feyyaz Gölcüklü, "Notes on the Turkish Constitution," *Foreign Policy* (Ankara) 10 (1983), pp. 40 ff.; Abdullah Ş. Gözübüyük, *Anayasa Hukuku* (Ankara, Genel Dağıtım, 1986); Ernst E. Hirsch, "Die Verfassung der Türkischen Republik vom 9. November 1982," *Jahrbuch des öffentlichen Rechts der Gegenwart - Neue Folge* 32 (1983), pp. 507 ff.; Otmar Oehring, "Die Verfassung der Dritten Türkischen Republik," *Orient* 24 (1983), pp. 301 ff.; Christian Rumpf, "Verfassung und Verwaltung," in *Südosteuropa-Handbuch*, pp. 169 ff.

tary forces to foreign countries needs the consent of the National Assembly. The president also nominates - on the basis of a proposal by the Council of Ministers - the Commander-in-Chief.

As in the 1961 system, military influence is guaranteed by having the five chief commanders serve as members of the constitutional National Security Council, which advises the Council of Ministers on items concerning internal and external security (Article 118). The military is, by its numbers, the dominant element in the Council, and its influence is further reinforced by the power of President Evren until at least 1989.

Here it is vital to mention the law No. 1402 which, even if it is not formally part of the Constitution itself, has since 1971 established the guidelines for the implementation of the state of emergency rules. In a state of martial law executive powers are transferred to military emergency administrations in the provinces and some judicial functions are transferred to military courts.

The legitimacy of the present President of the Republic, Kenan Evren, is a special case.[32] As the Head of State during the transitional period his legitimacy is derived from a mixture of military support and of tacit consent by the majority of the people. The 1982 constitutional referendum, in which the fate of the new Constitution and of Evren himself were determined by one single vote, did not strengthen the basis of legitimacy. Evren's tightly controlled propaganda apparatus in the weeks before the referendum had presented the referendum as a "choice" between *this* new constitution ("yes") and "anarchy" ("no"). It was not clear if the high positive vote was for the Constitution or for Evren personally.*

The president of the Republic is elected by the National Assembly (Article 108) for a single period of seven years. The legitimacy of the next president, the successor to Evren, will in accordance with the Constitution be based on that of parliament. The constitutional principle of the sovereignty of the National Assembly, which derives from the sovereignty of the nation, means that in the future any executive power including the presidency will derive from the power of parliament.

These provisions of the Constitution lead to quite an interesting problem. In case the National Assembly should fail to elect a President according to the procedure and within the time specified by the Constitution, the Assembly will be dissolved. The neutrality of the president in party politics, which should be seen as a constitutional principle, will then be in danger. The candidates for the presidency and for the prime minister will become tools for propaganda by the competing political parties in the new elections.

---

[32] See also Özbudun in this volume.

* Editors' note: Cf. Özbudun and Karpat in this volume.

The president of the Republic enjoys many powers: the nomination of the prime minister; on the suggestion of the prime minister, the nomination and dismissal of ministers; the right to call meetings of the Council of Ministers and to preside over them; the ratification and promulgation of international treaties; the chairmanship of the National Security Council; the adoption of ordinances together with the prime minister and the minister concerned; the right of grace in single cases on humanitarian grounds; and several other powers of appointment (Article 104a).

With regard to legislation, the power of the president has, in comparison to the 1961 constitutional system, been strengthened. He has the right to convoke the National Assembly and he promulgates laws. He can refuse to promulgate laws for legal reasons or other doubts and can send laws back to the National Assembly (Article 89, paragraph 2). But if the National Assembly insists on retaining the law, he is obliged to promulgate it unchanged. He may then apply to the Constitutional Court for a ruling. The draft of an amendment to the Constitution can be submitted to a referendum if the National Assembly insists on its text after it has been rejected and returned by the President (Article 175, paragraph 3). Finally, the President can dissolve the National Assembly, if the prime minister who is nominated by him, fails to win a vote of confidence (Article 111) or if he falls by a vote of non-confidence (Article 99) and if a new council of ministers fails to be approved by the National Assembly within 45 days. The same applies, after the prime minister's resignation or after a new election, if a council of ministers cannot be formed due to a lack of the necessary support from the National Assembly (Article 116).

Even in a state of emergency there is no significant increase in the president's powers. As chairman of the council of ministers, he participates in the adoption of ordinances with the force of law, a process which itself is controlled by the parliament (Article 122, paragraph 2; see also Article 91: ordinances with force of law during normal times).

Regarding the judiciary, including the Constitutional Court, too, the president of the Republic has some powers of appointment. However, the candidates for positions in the upper levels of the judiciary are nominated by the Supreme Council of Judges and Prosecutors. These levels include positions in the Court of Cassation and the Council of State, the supreme administrative court. The president's choice, is therefore limited. Only three of the eleven members of the Constitutional Court, whom the president can choose from among the ranks of high functionaries or lawyers, are appointed subject only to the discretion of the president.

The notion that the president is the "guardian of the constitution," often asserted in Turkey,[33] is not totally incorrect. But, one must be aware

[33] See, inter alia, *Milliyet*, 8 August, 1985.

that the president has no power or right to play the role of a "guardian of the constitution" in the sense of Carl Schmitt's *Hüter der Verfassung:* the guardianship of the latter stems from his dictatorial powers, which he can utilize in times of constitutional crisis when the parliament or the executive power fails. This same notion is now used in the Federal Republic of Germany for the Federal Constitutional Court.

The only areas where the president can play such a role are in applying for a ruling from the Constitutional Court, and in the submission to a referendum of a proposed amendment to the Constitution. There, the final decision is not made by the president but by the people.

Apart from Celâl Bayar, every Turkish president to date has been a former general. Before 1980, the question of the loyalty of the military to the president, which was due to this fact, had little political significance because of the constitutionally weak position of the president. After Atatürk, Kenan Evren became the first president to establish a direct relationship between the presidency and the military. As the chief of the general staff he became the natural chairman of the transitional National Security Council and, as such, head of state on September 12, 1980. Finally, in contrast to Cemal Gürsel in 1961, Evren became president not by a constitutional procedure but as a consequence of the above-mentioned referendum on the new constitution and the presidency. Thus, Evren embodies a model of a *rapprochement* between civilian and military power. Through his person the military may perhaps exert its stabilizing influence on the civilian power within the constitutional system.

Though the new constitution may be considered as the pure product of the military, only in one point does it lead to modification of the political role of the military within the legal framework of the constitutional order. The reinforcement of the presidency leads to a realignment of military and civilian power, this fact being of special weight due the personality of the current president, Kenan Evren.

5 Some Comparisons

The historical situations in which the constitutional change of the three countries took place differed from one another. Germany had lost a world war and also its position as a world power. This had severe social and economic consequences, which also affected the long-term repercussions of the October Revolution on the social movement. One could say that Germany owed its constitutional change to its defeat in World War I and that the defeat limited the role of the military during the period of change that followed the war.

France owed the change in its constitutional system mainly to internal forces. It is true that France suffered from its defeats in foreign wars as well, and above all, from the effects of the decolonization process. However, it was the weakness of its own constitutional regime that finally brought about an internal crisis.

In the case of Turkey, there were national and international economic factors which, despite a stable situation in foreign political relations, led to social unrest and the eventual breakdown of the constitutional system. The inability of the regime to pursue an efficient economic and social policy aggravated the situation.

Besides the different international contexts, we must also consider the different internal situations. Germany in 1918 had a constitutional monarchy. There was a strong executive power which had the Emperor at the head, while the princes headed the *Länder* governments. These were at the same time the holders of sovereignty and were represented in the second important legislative organ in the Reich, the Federal Council (Bundesrat). Only in the Parliament (Reichstag) was the ruling power democratically legitimized.

France in 1958 (Fourth Republic) was a parliamentary democracy in which the executive power was narrowly circumscribed by the legislative power of the Assemblé Nationale. The president of the Republic played a relatively unimportant role. The principle of the people's sovereignty was upheld, an undivided ruling power was - through the Assemblé Nationale - democratically legitimized, while the existence of a second chamber was of no importance.

In Turkey in 1960, there was a parliamentary democracy in which the executive power was narrowly circumscribed by the Grand National Assembly. Besides the National Assembly there was a second chamber, the Senate, which had considerable weight in the process of legislation. The president of the republic played a relatively unimportant role. The principle of the people's sovereignty was upheld, while the divided ruling power was legitimized democratically in the Assembly and, to a lesser extent in the Senate.

In Germany in 1918-1919, the system was overthrown by a joint action of the civilian power and the military forces that had just returned from the battlefield. The leading force was the Social Democrats, who succeeded in marshaling the greater part of the revolutionary potential of the worker's movement and in winning the military's loyalty.

In France in 1958 the system was overthrown following the initiative of some rebellious civilians in Algeria by the open pressure of the military on the civilian central power, which was then forced to give way to de Gaulle.

In Turkey in 1980 the system was overthrown by a simple and efficiently organized military coup through which all ruling power was turned over to the army.

In Germany in 1918-1919 those who managed the transition to the new constitutional order were the same as those who had overthrown the old one, with a tendency on the part of the military to keep itself out of the actual constitution-making. The transition took place - with some difficulties caused by the struggle against unruly revolutionary forces - under the dictatorship of the Council of the People's Commissaries, which was legitimized by the revolution and which could rely on military loyalty. A few months later, in February 1919, the Council handed power over to the democratically legitimized National Assembly of Weimar. This Assembly gave way to the first Reichstag in June of 1920, one year after the new Constitution of August 14, 1919 had come into force.

In France in 1958, the Committees of Public Welfare in Algeria, which were dominated by the military, stopped their pressure on the central power in Paris when the civilian powerholders resigned and made way for de Gaulle. Political institutions at the outset remained unchanged. Within the framework of these institutions, de Gaulle was granted full power, which enabled him to carry out fundamental changes in the constitutional order within a few months. Both civilian and military forces remained mostly loyal.

The transitional period ended with the election of de Gaulle as President of the Republic. The final date of the transition was that of the elections to the Senate in April 1958. The military played no active role in the working out of the new Constitution.

In Turkey in 1980-1983, the transition was managed by the military alone. For the maintenance of the transitional order and for the definition of the new Constitution it made use of civilians of its own choice. The new Constitution was produced at a time when the military was exercising full power, during the three years of well organized transition to a new constitutional order. With the first meeting of the new National Assembly in November of 1983, the transitional period approached an end. The final phase of this period should coincide with the end of the state of emergency in all of Turkey's provinces, the first elections to the National Assembly without any unconstitutional restrictions on the participation of political parties and with the end of the term of office of the current president and his Presidential Council.

Germany in 1919 had a system with a democratically elected parliament (Reichstag) and a less important federal chamber of representatives of the *Länder (Reichsrat)*, on the one side, and a president, who himself was democratically elected and played the constitutional role of a fairly powerful head of the executive branch, on the other. The Weimar Constitution thus tried to follow the principle of the balance between the legislative and executive powers. With both powers being democratically legitimized, the new Constitution brought the principle of the people's sovereignty into full effect.

In France in 1958–1959 there existed a new Constitution which provided for a powerful president as the head of the executive branch, elected by the people, vis-à-vis a parliament with two chambers, one of them being of lesser weight and importance. This balance is at least on the surface, quite similar to that of the Weimar Constitution.

In 1982 Turkey obtained a parliamentary regime without the sort of balance of powers seen in Germany in 1919 and France in 1958. The National Assembly is a unicameral legislative body. There is also a president with a strengthened position in comparison to 1961 but without the important powers of the presidents of Germany in 1919 and France in 1958. The National Assembly, democratically elected and legitimized, is an important embodiment of the principle of people's sovereignty.

The Weimar conception of the presidency was that of the "guardian of the constitution" which, as noted, should not be confused with the same term as used in Turkey. It cannot be separated from its historical context, the need for an *Ersatzkaiser* and a certain lack of confidence in a parliament as sole representative of the people's sovereignty and holder of all the ruling power in the polity. Guardianship of the constitution meant power. In the Weimar system there was in Article 48 an implied constitutional dictatorship. The Weimar Constitution was an attempt to deal with the lack of confidence in a system that would be solely in the hands of a parliament, where many different political tendencies would be represented and which could thus threaten stability. To check this, confidence was placed in a single man as a counterpart to the parliament. In this system there were two problems. The president had to be in a position to judge reasonably *if* there was a need for measures to secure the functioning of the system in case of emergency (Article 48), and to judge, as well, *which* measures would be necessary and reasonable. The other problem was the parliament itself which could reverse the measures taken by the president. In a state of emergency where the parliament might not be stable enough to manage the crisis itself, it nevertheless had the power to interfere with the efforts of the president to stabilize the situation.

In this context the constitutional role of the military was very limited. Being an army of a mere 100,000 men, its main role was, aside from national defense, to remain at the disposition of the president in the case of emergency (Article 48). Thus it was, constitutionally, only an auxiliary factor of stabilization, and the effective role of the military in politics did not go further than this.

Editors' note: Cf. Heper in this volume.

With Friedrich Ebert, the new Republic had a man who was able to play the role of a stabilizer. In the first place he was a man with plenty of parliamentary experience. In the second place he knew how to make a reasonable but also courageous use of his emergency powers and of the army, which was loyal to him. In the case of von Hindenburg, the situation was not the same. First, von Hindenburg was no republican at heart. Secondly, instead of making reasonable but determined use of his powers as the counterpart of the multi-party parliament, he let the parliament play during the last few years of the Republic a disruptive and destabilizing role. Thirdly, as the former commander-in-chief, he exerted certain controls over the army by virtue of which the military lost more of its political power than under Ebert, but, due to his age and his lack of sense of power politics, he himself was not able to play the role of a stabilizer or to motivate the army to serve as an instrument that could stabilize the new system.

De Gaulle's conception of the presidency was quite similar to that in the Weimar Constitution. Developments after 1945 had shaken confidence in the parliament as a sole representative of the people's sovereignty and holder of all ruling power. Whereas the presidency of the Weimar Constitution was partly to fill the vacuum left behind by the Emperor, the presidency in the French 1958 Constitution is the result of a crisis within a previous parliamentary system. But in both there is the idea of stability through one reliable person, the *capitaine arbitre* who should stay above the various political groups. De Gaulle went a step further; the veiled dictatorship implicit in Article 16 of the Constitution was not under the control of the parliament. Although the president did not have the right to dissolve the parliament in a state of emergency, he still had more power than the president of the Weimar Republic. The president of the Republic had the power to decide *if* the conditions for the state of emergency were given and *which* measures were to be taken, and neither decision was subject to parliamentary or judicial control. Thus, the stabilizing measures taken by the presidency could not be disturbed by the parliament. With respect to normal constitutional life, the stabilizing character of the presidency seemed to be evident, too. The constitutional conception of the presidency secured a powerful executive vis-à-vis the parliament and enforced cooperation between the parliament and the president, who, formally, seemed to be independent from the parliament as a consequence of their separation. If cooperation was not possible, the president could use his own powers, since he had the right to dissolve the National Assembly under certain conditions or to dismiss the prime minister.

In comparison to the president of the Republic, the army played no important constitutional or political role. After its experiences in Indochina and Algeria and under the presidency of the respected former general de

Gaulle, the army concentrated on reforming the national defense program. After the last attempt by some generals to seize power in 1962, the military remained in the background of the political scene in France, without any obvious positive or negative influence in politics. Up to now, France has been lucky enough to have presidents with personalities that fit the expectations raised by the constitutional conception of the presidency. Even de Gaulle made use of Article 16 of the Constitution only once.[34] It might be due to the political culture in France as well as to de Gaulle's sense of power that in the internal crisis of 1968 de Gaulle made no use of Article 16, and finally resigned under the pressure of public opinion. His successors had nothing further to do than to fulfill their presidential functions within the framework of their office, which has been well defined via political practice. All of them also had the luck to have stable and friendly parliamentary majorities and relatively quiet times in terms of domestic social and political life.

The conception of the presidency in the 1982 Turkish Constitution is somewhat different from that of the 1961 Constitution, but it is nonetheless hardly comparable to the Weimar and French models. To deal with aspects of the 1961 Constitution that are supposed to have caused instability and, thus, the breakdown of the constitutional system, remedies have been included. Changes have been made in the parliamentary structure itself, such as the reduction of the parliament to one single chamber and by reforms in the electoral and political parties systems. Certainly, there are additional powers attributed to the president now, above all his ability to play a role in the process of legitimation. Yet, it is still the parliament which has the last word, unless a law passed by it is annulled by the Constitutional Court, which has the power to make binding interpretations of the Constitution and thus an effective control over the legislature.

The president's functions mostly involve diverse powers of appointment. His influence on the composition of the Council of Ministers is limited. Once the prime minister and his cabinet have obtained a vote of confidence, the Council is only subject to the control of the parliament. The Turkish president has no emergency powers; there are no provisions such as Article 16 (France) or Article 48 (Weimar) in the Turkish constitutional system to make him the "master of the state of emergency." The "ifs" and "hows" in a state of emergency are controlled by parliament. The participation of the president in the decision-making process in the Council of Ministers or in the National Security Council is of no decisive character. The *constitutional* role of the president is thus remarkably less important than that of the presidents of the Weimar Republic or of France under the 1958 Constitution.

---

[34] Pickles, *The Government and Politics of France*, pp. 122ff.

In practice, this view is verified by political life in Turkey since 1983. After the retirement of the transitional National Security Council, the parliament regained its traditional control role in constitutional life. The government under Turgut Özal exercises executive powers through the majority of Özal's Motherland Party in the parliament, an important influence on the process of legislation. The limitations on presidential powers have become obvious, too. Kenan Evren is not the *capitaine arbitre,* but, instead, a formal head of state who tries to take initiatives which might have some moral, if no political or legal force. Even the fact that Evren is a former general does not have a decisive influence on his ability to exercise power.

The role of the military under the new Turkish Constitution has not changed. Its role cannot be described by constitutional norms. As the guarantor of national security, both external and internal, and with its traditional position within society and political life in Turkey, it can be considered an informal constitutional and political institution of great importance. It has never declared itself able to solve all the problems which led to September 12, 1980, and in spite of some poor decisions taken during the transitional period, it has saved its reputation by retiring in time. It has thus kept intact its political position within the constitutional system.

At this moment, it is still too early to judge how political dynamics are developing under the new Constitution. The balance of power as provided by the Constitution depends much more on the actions of the parliament and the political parties than on the president. This might change if Turkey has a civilian president with more personal influence on his (former) party colleagues. Evren makes uses of his limited powers quite often, as he has the right of veto over the process of legislation and can contest legislation at the Constitutional Court. However, his personal influence seems to be on the decline. It is neither the former general and president nor the military, but, rather, Özal and his government who determine the course of politics in Turkey.

Chapter 15
Transitions to Democracy: Turkey's Experience in Historical and Comparative Perspective

Dankwart A. Rustow

1 Introduction

Democracy means government by the people, or, more specifically, by representatives elected by popular majorities in free and competitive elections. And this implies two essential requisities: (a) a settled sense of national identity ("The people cannot decide until somebody decides who are the people," as a British constitutional lawyer remarked - cuttingly but accurately enough - in commenting on the recent quest of colonies for self-government)[1] and (b) a self-reinforcing pattern of political and social competition providing constant pressure for political equality. Two major patterns of democratic evolution may thus be distinguished, depending on the sequence in which these two requisites of identity and equality were attained.

In much of Western and Northern Europe, the achievement of national identity preceded the struggle for equality. In the thirteenth to sixteenth centuries, dynastic wars and marriages fixed the boundaries of such European nations as France, Britain, and the Scandinavian countries; and, within such stabilized boundaries, the use of a single standardized language by the expanding royal bureaucracies helped to solidify the linguistic identity of the populations. Then, a number of sharp internal contests - in Britain from the English civil war to the class conflicts of the nineteenth century, in France the violent regime changes from 1789 to 1870, in

[1] Sir Ivor Jennings, *The Approach to Self-Government* (Cambridge, University of Cambridge Press, 1956), p. 56.

Sweden the lesser upheavals from 1718 to 1905 – completed the transition to democracy.[2]

In sharp contrast to this pattern of democratization of bureaucratic monarchies stands the evolution of democracy in immigrant countries such as the United States, Australia, New Zealand, or Israel. Here equality was guaranteed, by and large, by the equal experience of persecution or suffering in the old country and political and social competition in the new. (If the elders of a first immigrant community such as Massachusetts Bay proved too autocratic, the dissidents could always move on to new locations such as Providence.) Meanwhile, the task of building and defending the new communities strengthened the immigrants' common sense of identity.

Germany and Italy offer an important variant of the first pattern. Here modern linguistic identity developed in the train of Dante's and Luther's achievements in the fourteenth and sixteenth centuries; yet there was no monarchic-bureaucratic centralization. The stirrings of egalitarian sentiment in the wake of the French Revolution were soon overshadowed by the military threat from outside and the quest for national unification within – this being the tragedy of the abortive German and Italian revolutions of 1848. And when the merger of the petty principalities into a linguistic nation-state was brought about through aggressive wars (1860–1861, 1866–1871) launched by the largest of them, it would serve to emphasize the conservative and antidemocratic elements in the political tradition – from Cavour and Bismarck to Mussolini and Hitler. In sum, whereas countries such as Britain, France, and Sweden achieved national identity first and equality next, the struggle for both at once delayed the advent of German and Italian democracies until after their military defeats in World War Two.[3]

Turkey offers yet another variant of the basic Western European pattern, one where democracy was delayed not by the problems of a multi-

---

[2] See Dankwart A. Rustow, "Transitions to Democracy: Toward a Dynamic Model," *Comparative Politics* 2 (1970), pp. 337–363. For a more recent discussion see Samuel P. Huntington, "Will More Countries Become Democratic?" *Political Science Quarterly* 99 (1984), pp. 192–218. For a specific application to Israel, Turkey, and other Middle Eastern countries, see also Dankwart A. Rustow "Elections and Legitimacy in the Middle East," *Annals of the American Academy of Political and Social Science* 482 (1985), pp. 122–146, from which the opening five paragraphs of this essay are adapted. On Sweden cf. Dankwart A. Rustow, *The Politics of Compromise: Parties and Cabinet Government in Sweden* (Princeton, Princeton University Press, 1955).

[3] In the Middle East, the Arab experience after 1945 offers some significant analogies to this German-Italian theme. Gamal Abdul Nasser, however, never achieved his ambition to become an Arab Cavour or Bismarck, and since Sadat the trend in most Arab countries has been toward national consolidation within the existing boundaries.

state nation; but of a multinational state caught up in the throes of defensive modernization.[4]

2 Modernization in Turkey

In Turkey, modernization in its defensive phase was initiated in late Ottoman days and continued through more than a century of defeat and secession (1789-1918). Modernization was pushed ahead with great vigor and as an integral program by Kemal Atatürk, and, lately it has been embraced by Turkish men and women both as voters at the polls and in their search for better jobs in villages, cities, and abroad. Today many aspects of Turkish everyday life indicate the striking success of that program of modernization: universal schooling in villages and towns, religion as a matter of private choice, the growing social equality of women, and Turkish scientists and artists receiving international recognition.

The typical sequence of change in Turkey has been (1) a political decision, perhaps taken reluctantly or under duress, sketching out new cultural goals; (2) a program of education instituted to move toward them; and (3) the beneficiaries of that education giving growing momentum to change far beyond those original goals.

Just so, a mid-nineteenth century sultan sent some young officers of his military forces to Paris for training in French, mathematics, and the arts of artillery; and one of the young trainees, named İbrahim Şinasi returned to Istanbul, imbued with enthusiasm for European romantic poetry, and ready to start the first Turkish-language private newspaper. A generation later, his disciple, Namık Kemal, was to join a conspiracy that forced on the then sultan's successor the adoption of the Ottoman Empire's first written parliamentary constitution.

In the same vein Mustafa Kemal, the later Atatürk, broke with the imperial Ottoman tradition itself. He announced that break as he launched a desparate defense of the empire's Turkish core region after its final military defeat in 1918: "Today the nations of the whole world recognize only one sovereignty: national sovereignty."[5] Following the brilliant victory of

---

[4] On that concept see Cyril E. Black, *The Dynamics of Modernization* (New York, Harper and Row, 1966); *Political Modernization in Japan and Turkey,* edited by Robert E. Ward and Dankwart A. Rustow (Princeton, Princeton University Press, 1964); Dankwart A. Rustow, *A World of Nations: Modernization and Leadership* (Washington, Brookings, 1967).

[5] This was Mustafa Kemal's statement in a programmatic speech given as he first arrived at Ankara, his later headquarters and capital, in December 1919; cf. Dankwart A. Rustow "Atatürk as Founder of a State," in *Philosophers and Kings: Studies in Leadrship,* edited by Dankwart A. Rustow (New York, G. Braziller, 1970), p. 214.

his nationalist movement, he proceeded to build a new structure of government and a Western-style system of popular education. And very soon this new Turkish national identity was fully accepted, while the dynamic of mass education began to revolutionize the towns and villages of the country.

Just so, Atatürk's successor İnönü decided in 1945 that the logic of Atatürk's political system and the need for closer relations with the West required a transition from one-party rule to competitive, democratic elections. And despite a number of temporary reverses through political deadlocks or military coups, that commitment to democracy was resoundingly vindicated by Turkey's mass electorate in 1983.

And so, most recently, Prime Minister Turgut Özal has launched his liberal revolution of competition, free enterprise, and open economic bridges to Europe and Asia - a bold decision that may well be vindicated by Turkish factory workers returning from jobs in Germany and Turkish businessmen returning from their construction contracts in the Middle East.[6]

3 Turkey's Difficulties with Democracy

The difficulties that Turkish democracy still faces are well illustrated by the periodic interventions of the armed forces at roughly ten-year intervals, in 1960-1961, in 1971-1973, and most recently in 1980-1983. Yet there is a fundamental contrast between these temporary interventions in Turkey and the long-term interventions by the military in other Third World or Mediterranean countries, such as Korea, the Philippines, Argentina and Brazil in the 1960s, Chile in the 1970s, Nasser in Egypt, Reza Shah in Iran, Franco in Spain, or the 1967 colonels' junta in Greece. Whereas those other coups established repressive authoritarian or personalist regimes, the Turkish military on each occasion assumed power for a strictly limited period, relinquishing it as soon as law and order were restored and democratic institutions strengthened. Turkey's soldiers, that is to say, aside from serious excesses during each of their three interventions,[7] on balance have acted as a temporary and progressive political

[6] Cf. Dankwart A. Rustow, "Turkey's Liberal Revolution," *Middle East Review* 17 (1985), pp. 5-11.

[7] Among these, I would list the hanging of Menderes and two of his associates in 1961; serious human rights violations in the treatment of political opponents after 1971 and 1980; the arbitrary aspects of the university reform after 1980 (ideological interference in the curriculum, dismissals of faculty, and arbitrary regulations on personal appearance - no

force, taking seriously their self-chosen role as guardians of the constitutional order.

The pre-1960 Constitution and election law had allowed Prime Minister Adnan Menderes to exercise quasidictatorial powers. By contrast, the regimes of the 1960s and 1970s, particularly the former, erred on the side of excessive checks and balances, and their electoral laws virtually guaranteed stalemate in the face of mounting violence. It was not until the basic laws adopted during the most recent military intervention of 1980-1983 that Turkey was at last able to achieve a workable balance between executive and legislative powers, avoiding the earlier dangers of extreme majoritarianism and excessive party splintering.

This constitutional balance was reinforced by the political events of 1983-1984. The electorate, by solidly rallying behind Özal's Motherland Party in the national and local elections, restrained the military's over-ambitious attempt to prescribe the personnel as well as the institutions of the new regime. And, in a true test of their constitutional commitments, President Kenan Evren and his colleagues (the members of the junta who now make up the Presidential Council, an advisory body to the president) promptly accepted the voters' verdict, no matter how distasteful at the moment. In the meantime, Özal's liberal revolution is releasing unprecendented social and political forces, symbolized by the rise of a new business class and the concerted attack on the entrenched bureaucracy. In sum, it is this maturity of the Turkish electorate, the resourcefulness of its economic and political leadership, and the generals' readiness to bow to the voters' verdict that are likely to make further military interventions unnecessary. And it is those same innovative and conciliatory attitudes that furnish the best long-term guarantee for Turkey's constitutional stability and democratic future.

4 Influence of Atatürk

In setting the cultural policy of the Republic of Turkey which he founded in 1923, Atatürk followed the dictum of a writer of the preceding Union-and-Progress period: "There is no second civilization; civilization means European civilization, and it must be imported with both its roses and its thorns."[8] The Kemalist revolution of the 1920s and 1930s extended to

---

headscarves, no beards); and the attempt, by now clearly futile, to prescribe the character and personnel of the post-1982 political parties.

[8] Abdullah Cevdet (1913) quoted in Bernard Lewis, *The Emergence of Modern Turkey*, 2nd edn. (London, Oxford University Press, 1968), p. 236; cf. Dankwart A. Rustow "Turkey

both social fundamentals and emotion-laden cultural symbols: secular Western instead of Islamic education, European law codes instead of Islamic jurisprudence, emancipation of women, the Latin instead of the Arabic alphabet, Sunday holidays and the Christian (or "international") calender, Western hats instead of fezzes or turbans, and European-style family names.

One ardent personal concern of Atatürk's was the transplantation to Turkey of Western music. In the course of the thorough reorganization of higher education which he undertook in the early and mid-1930s, one of his most cherished projects was that of a Music Teachers' School. Like other branches of the new university system, this one was staffed for a start in part with German refugee professors who, voluntarily or under duress, were leaving Nazi Germany. Thus the composer Paul Hindemith became one of the first musicology professors in Ankara - until his further emigration to the United States, where he became a professor at Yale.[9] And it is due to his influence and that of his successors that Turkish composers are making contributions to twentieth century electronic music as important as those of their scientific colleagues in their respective disciplines.

To ensure the acceptance of that social and cultural revolution, Atatürk proceeded to rule the Turkish Republic as a benevolent one-party dictatorship. He briefly allowed an opposition party in 1924-1925 and encouraged the formation of another in 1930, but soon called off the experiments when they gave rise to strong expressions of traditionalist Islamic sentiment or seemed to threaten his personal stature. The sustained effort to make the transition to democracy came later, when a new generation of leaders had been educated along Atatürk's Western, secular, nationalist principles. Specifically, Atatürk's successor İsmet İnönü in 1945 allowed a free press and the formation of opposition parties, and by 1949 committed the bureaucracy to scrupulous fairness as between government and opposition.

Once again - as in the days when the sultans' military reforms hastened the transformation of their traditional, dynastic empire into a modern, republican nation-state - developments soon ran ahead of the cautious intentions of the original sponsors. Atatürk had consolidated Turkey as a

and Europe: The Roses and the Thorns," in *Turkey and the Community,* ("Sussex European Papers," No. 10; Brighton, University of Sussex, 1981).

9 German refugees were in a majority in most of the faculties of the Universities of Istanbul and Ankara from about 1933 to the mid-1940s. It is a pleasure to acknowledge with gratitude that among these was my father, Alexander Rüstow. See my biographical introduction to the English translation of his opus magnum, written in his years of Turkish exile: Alexander Rüstow, *Freedom and Domination* (Princeton, Princeton University Press, 1981).

nation by creating a parliamentary machinery within a one-party state. İnönü, in allowing an opposition, intended to bring Turkey closer to the Western powers.[10] More immediately, he hoped to relieve the accumulated dissatisfaction of six years of full mobilization and wartime economic dislocations - while securing his party's further stay in power. But, to İnönü's own surprise, the voters eagerly seized the opportunity to change governments as soon as it was offered in the first free and honest election in May 1950. And it is that very process of competitive elections since 1950 that has provided the major mechanism by which Atatürk's cultural and educational reforms have been spread from a small urban elite to the Turkish people as a whole.

5 Political Parties and Living Conditions in Turkey

It has been widely, and somewhat smugly, assumed among Western social scientists that such social accomplishments of advanced industrial countries as urban residence, universal literacy, and a high standard of living are among the essential preconditions for a smoothly functioning democracy.[11] Turkish experience, instead, confirms the possibility of the reverse causal nexus: political parties competing for the ballots of an illiterate peasantry will soon be forced to offer their constituents more schools as well as better roads and other economic amenities. And soon those roads may be facilitating the peasantry's mass migration toward the greater economic opportunities of the cities.

In Turkey's first free election in May 1950, the voter turnout was an astonishing 89 per cent, illiterate voters being helped by the presence of pictorial symbols on the party ballot; average participation in national elections since then has been well over 70 per cent. The resulting social transformation has been truly remarkable. In 1935 only one Turkish child out of three went to elementary school; by 1950, it was two out of three; and today schooling is virtually universal. Similarly, the proportion of lit-

[10] During a lengthy private interview in Ankara in 1954 İnönü at first angrily denied my suggestion that foreign policy considerations had influenced his decision: "All that slander spread about me, as if I had been swimming with the stream!" Then he visibly relaxed, and with a shrewd smile added: "And suppose I had been swimming with the stream, that, too, is a virtue - *o da bir meziyettir.*" Once again he grew bitter in recalling the 1950 election defeat: "I never expected to see so much ingratitude - *bu kadar nankörlük göreceğimi hiç beklemezdim.*"

[11] See, e.g., Seymour M. Lipset, *Political Man* (Garden City, N.Y., Doubleday, 1960), and W.W. Rostow, *The Stages of Economic Growth* (Cambridge, Cambridge University Press, 1966).

eracy, which was 20 per cent in 1935 and 32 per cent in 1950 has jumped to 67 per cent in 1980, with four out of five men and half the women now literate; and, in view of current school attendance rates, literacy will be near-universal by the end of the century. Attendance at high schools (or *lycées*) since 1950 has increased tenfold; and more Turks now go to college than went to primary school at the beginning of the Republic.

The ratio of urban population (inhabitants of cities and towns over 10,000 to the total) was virtually unchanged during the one-party period - 16 per cent in 1927, 19 per cent in 1950 - but since then has jumped to nearly half. And in the remaining rural half of the population, by 1968, every other village (49.6 per cent) had sent some of its residents to work abroad, mostly in West Germany; and, remarkably, the women among the Anatolian migrants, in their prevalent occupation as dressmakers, seem to adapt faster to the German scene than do their husbands, who may be sitting between a Yugoslav and an Italian guest worker at the assembly line.

Throughout Turkey, newspaper circulation has quadrupled since 1950; and, although television was not introduced until 1970, there now are more television sets in town and country than there are printed copies of daily newspapers in circulation.[12]

6 Post-1983 Reforms

Taken together, the Ottoman legacy and its peaceful transformations - in Kemal Atatürk's national revolution, in the transition to multi-party politics brought about by İnönü in the late 1940s and reconfirmed by the voters in 1983, and in the economic program initiated by Turgut Özal which places emphasis on market forces - have given Turkey a uniquely favorable climate for the achievement of a stable and thriving democracy. And the importance of each of these three fundamental changes becomes clearer when Turkey's situation is compared, point by point, with other developing countries of the Third World as to governmental tradition, national identity, and the social basis of political competition.

Most Third World countries have had much difficulty in training a governmental bureaucracy; and only a few, such as India, embarked upon political independence with a functioning, indigenously staffed civil service bequeathed by their colonial rulers. Turkey inherited its governmen-

---

[12] For data through the late 1970s see the convenient statistical summaries in Walter F. Weiker, *The Modernization of Turkey: From Atatürk to the Present Day* (New York, Holmes and Meier, 1981), p. 144 (voting), pp. 154ff. (schools and literacy), p. 65 (urban residence), p. 56 (workers abroad), pp. 166ff. (media).

tal tradition, including sizable cadres of a civilian and military bureaucracy, from the Ottoman Empire; indeed, upon the collapse of that Empire in 1918, over half of the civilian bureaucrats and nine out of ten of the trained military staff officers continued their service in the Turkish Republic, with only a small minority serving in other successor states such as Syria, Iraq, or Libya.[13] This uninterrupted Turkish tradition of government responsibility is especially notable in the moderation and continuity of Turkey's foreign policy.

Throughout most of the Third World, the present borders of would-be nation-states were drawn by European colonial rulers and do not coincide with any spontaneous sense of national identity. Only in Southeast Asia do those boundaries include solid, homogeneous ethnic communities. For the Arabs, the problem is one of a single language spoken in a score of countries from Oman to Morocco, and hence the aspiration of pan-Arab nationalism actively competing with a sense of loyalty within existing state borders - Egyptian, Syrian, Iraqi, Saudi, Jordanian, etc. In India and in most of tropical Africa, the post-colonial borders bring together many different ethnic and linguistic groups. Typically there is no linguistic majority, so that the language of the outgoing colonial rulers (English or French) must continue to serve as a *lingua franca*. Not surprisingly, political parties tend to divide along ethnic-linguistic lines, and democratic institutions often mask the reality of rule by one of the ethnic minorities over the rest. Too often, the heavy inflow of arms to the Middle East and Africa has reinforced this pattern of domination by tribal or sectarian minorities, such as the Alawites of Syria or the Sunni Arabs in Iraq.

Turkey, by contrast, never was a colony. Her army is one of the few in the Third World recruited by universal conscription, and its officer corps has long been one of Turkey's chief avenues of social mobility.[14] And it was this national citizens' army that under Atatürk's leadership established the boundaries of the Turkish Republic by averting the threat of colonial partition. Specifically, the regions that Atatürk set out to defend in the war of independence (1919-1922) correspond to the Turkish-speaking heartlands of the former Ottoman empire, so that, within those national borders, over 90 per cent of the population speak Turkish and over 98 per cent are Muslims.[15]

---

[13] See Dankwart A. Rustow, "The Army and the Founding of the Turkish Republic," *World Politics* 11 (1959), pp. 513-552.

[14] For example, in the 1970s farmers constituted 64 per cent of the gainfully employed population but only 7 per cent of the membership of parliament; yet 14 per cent of military officers and as many as 38 per cent of the non-commissioned officers were the sons of farmers. See Weiker, *The Modernization of Turkey*, pp. 22, 38.

[15] The remainder are Muslim Kurds and Arabs in the Southeast of the country who are be-

In short, Turkey offers the phenomenon - exceptional among non-Western countries - of an almost complete coincidence of national and state identities. As a result, democratic competition has been according to social divisions and over economic policy issues - town vs. country, business vs. agriculture, military vs. civilians, rich vs. poor - and those divisions have been attenuated by the processes of economic development and social mobility which democracy itself has done so much to accelerate.

---

ing gradually assimilated by an organic process of social mobility; and a small Greek, Armenian, and Jewish minority mostly in Istanbul.

Chapter 16
Conclusion

Metin Heper

The significant point that "the stamp left on Western society by feudal conflicts and by the struggles of the bourgeoisie has no Islamic equivalents" (Mardin),* goes a long way to explain the particular difficulties that are faced in transition or re-transition to democracy in polities with such heritage. The Ottoman-Turkish case has not been an exception to this general phenomenon.

The Ottoman "tacit contract" (Mardin) has little resemblance to a "feudal" let alone a "national contract."[1] Alien to it are the notions of near equal powers recognizing the rights and privileges of one another, which elsewhere contributed to the emergence of a liberal political culture. Rather, the Ottoman "contract" contained strong elements of a resistance on the part of the periphery to the official sphere and a search for a "seamless society" through resort to esoteric knowledge (Mardin). As such the opposition in the Ottoman context, and, later, during the Republic, emerged primarily as a protest movement.

Under the circumstances the "obstinacy with which the Turkish population of all walks of life has continued to define politics as an arena which belongs to it" (Mardin) was hardly an endeavor to widen political participation and to engage actively in the affairs of the political center. In the Ottoman context it was an effort to carve out a sphere of influence at the local level. Albert Hourani has shown that this style of political activity or the "politics of notables" as he referred to it, entailed a two-way intermediation between the "government" and the people.[2] The intermedia-

---

* Here and below references in parantheses refer to the chapters in this volume.

[1] I take "national contract" here as in Reinhard Bendix, *Kings or People: Power and the Mandate to Rule* (Berkeley, University of California Press, 1978), pp.193–195.

[2] Albert Hourani, *The Emergence of the Modern Middle East* (Berkeley and Los Angeles, University of California Press, 1981), pp.36–66.

ries, i.e., the local notables, were interested in protecting their (what often turned out to be) *de facto* privileges from the *encroachments* of the center.[3]

In contrast to the Tanzimat period (1839-1876), during the republican regime the centralization policy had been carried out more effectively. Consequently transformations in the polity could no longer be "segregative" but had to be "coalescent." Except for the initial decades it was now impossible for the periphery to isolate itself from the affairs of the center - politics could not be conducted in a departmentalized fashion. As has already been suggested, however, the integration of the two worlds proved very problematic. In a lingering crisis of legitimacy the political system could easily be fragmented and polarized, as indeed it was particularly during the 1960s and 1970s.

The antecedents of the crisis of legitimacy in question could be found in the Ottoman past: The folk experience was centered around a collectivistic understanding of freedom and was not conceived as the defense of individual rights; rather it was "keeping the right sort of society, the *nizam-ı İslami,* functioning" (Mardin). The "political" agenda centered on the substantive issue of whether the high culture informed by the orthodox Islam or the little culture shaped by the folk Islam[4] should carry the day.

Within Ottoman patrimonialism, however, no mechanisms existed for resolving, or even ameliorating, the crisis in question. The collectivistic understanding of freedom did not lead to the establishment of estates through which the members of the periphery could "voice their protests, restate their rights, formulate their advice, establish the terms of their collaboration with the ruler, and shoulder their share of the burdens of rule."[5] This was because the Ottoman officials had only suspicion and scorn for any privilege which was obtained by powers which were not integrated with the machinery of the state. They constantly rescinded or abolished privileges obtained when the state was weak (Mardin).

Not much has changed during the republican period. For the 1965-1975 period G. Bingham Powell, Jr. found very weak linkages between political parties and social groups in Turkey.[6] This must be primarily due to

---

[3] This point is taken up at greater length in Metin Heper, "Center and Periphery in the Ottoman Empire with Special Reference to the Nineteenth Century," *International Political Science Review* 1 (1980), particularly p.97.

[4] Şerif Mardin, "Power, Civil Society and Culture in the Ottoman Empire," *Comparative Studies in Society and History* 1 (1969), pp.258-281.

[5] For the role of the estates in the polity as mentioned here, see Gianfranco Poggi, *The Development of the Modern State: A Sociological Introduction* (London, Hutchinson, 1978), p.44.

[6] G. Bingham Powell, Jr., "Party Systems and Political System Preference: Voting Participation, Government Stability and Mass Violence in Contemporary Democracies," *American Political Science Review* 75 (1981), pp.866-867.

what İlkay Sunar has observed even in Turkey of the 1980s - a very low level of civil societal integration, with horizontal ties.[7] The end result has been a "party-centered" polity. The political parties have become a means of elite conflict. They have hardly functioned as bodies responsible for aggregating demands, interests, and beliefs. Continuing emphasis on "cultural" rather than "functional," i.e., socio-economic, cleavages provided a conducive environment for fragmentation and polarization.[8]

While there continued to be an absence of horizontal ties at the level of political class, the Ottoman collectivism did linger as an important datum of republican political life. The collectivistic attitude in question was bound to develop a sensitivity toward the general (as against particularistic) interest(s). Further, this attitude had been reinforced by a particular conception of the state-society relationship common to both the Tanzimat period and the republican regime: a direct relationship between the state and each of its subjects where the state is responsible for the welfare of the citizens, who, in turn, are members of an homogeneous entity - the nation. Closely related with this approach is, of course, a monistic conception of public interest. In the absence of institutionalization of intermediary structures with political power - be it an aristocracy and/or an entrepreneurial middle class - and in the presence of state welfare policies (*hisba,* populism/étatism) the state came to be respected as well as feared. It is perhaps for this reason that "in Turkey ... political culture is much less hostile to the state than in France" (Dodd).

It is also possible to explain the "constitutional" (as against "political") voting in the 1982 constitutional referendum in terms of this collectivistic legacy: By acting in a bi-partisan manner the people seem to have given their overwhelming support for a constitution that attempted to "carve up a greater sphere for the state" (Karpat) and which aimed at "protecting the state by reducing its vulnerability in the face of intra-elite conflict" (Evin).[9] The charisma of Kenan Evren (Özbudun, Karpat) should also be at least partly due to the same legacy.

However, for those elites who registered their opposition to the 1982 Constitution and for everything that it symbolized, an approach that em-

---

[7] İlkay Sunar, "Dünya'da ve Türkiye'de Demokrasiye Geçiş Sorunları," *Ekonomi ve İdari Bilimler Dergisi* (Istanbul) 1 (Winter 1987).

[8] This view is elaborated in Metin Heper, *The State Tradition in Turkey* (Walkington, England, Eothen Press, 1985).

[9] If the present thesis has validity, the obvious question is why in the constitutional referendum of 1961 did only two-thirds of the voters come up with a yes-vote? A plausible explanation may be that as compared to the 1970s, to many people society in 1961 did not seem to be coming apart at the seams, and, that as a consequence the voting was "political" rather than "constitutional." The present argument may also shed some light on why in Turkey the "right" as compared to the "left" kept garnering more votes at the polls.

phasizes the collectivistic legacy, cannot be satisfactory. In fact as a consequence of efforts at Westernization during the Republic an individualistic, or rather personalistic, orientation had been superimposed upon the collectivistic legacy. However, it is important to recall here that in the Ottoman-Turkish context "individualism" did not develop as a result of multiple confrontations between social groups, and, thus, through conflict. Rather, "individualism came from reading about the West" (Mardin). As a consequence, it has remained alien for the masses. It was for this reason that "Namık Kemal, the proponent of a libertarian stance, ended up swimming outside the mainstream of Ottoman culture" (Mardin).

On the other hand, the fact that an individualistic conception of freedom has not taken hold at the level of civil society, permitted the elites to juggle such concepts, and twist them in ways convenient for their own purposes. Thus, a concept like "rule of law" quickly gained not only *Reichstaatist* but also patrimonial qualities: Not only has the legitimacy of the basic rules not been derived solely from popular mandate, but the intellectual-bureaucratic elite at times took a cavalier attitude when they themselves were supposed to conform to those rules.[10]

The tug-of-war between the state and political elites that ensued, made highly unlikely the success of the attempts on the part of the state elites of the 1960s and 1970s to moderate conflict. The political life under the 1961 "mixed-Constitution" which was overly detailed on the substantive as well as procedural rules of politics and stacked the bureaucratic elite against the representatives of the people, quickly degenerated.

"There was no major realignment of electoral behavior in the decade and a half prior to the 1980 military take-over. Rather, there was a complex process of deterioration in system capacity" (Ergüder and Hofferbert). Thus, the main target of the 1982 Constitution were the pre-1980 politicians. The post-1980 state elites in Turkey no longer trusted the politicians for internal as well as external security of Turkey and for related matters, including the socialization of the young. In the "hybrid system of government" (Özbudun) that has been launched, the military became the ultimate guardian of the Republic. There was now an enlarged role for

[10] I have in mind here the partisanship that is claimed to have spread in the 1960s and 1970s to the higher tribunals such as the Council of State (the Turkish version of the French *Conseil d'Etat*) and the Constitutional Court. See Geoffrey Lewis, "Political Change in Turkey since 1960," in *Aspects of Modern Turkey*, edited by William M. Hale (London, Bowker, 1976), p. 18 and C. H. Dodd, *The Crisis of Turkish Democracy* (Walkington, England, Eothen Press, 1983), pp. 25-26. For some street-level examples see Metin Heper, "Urban Migrants and their Plight: Dynamics of Service Procurement in a Squatter Area," in *Sex Roles, Family and Community in Turkey*, edited by Çiğdem Kağıtçıbaşı (Bloomington, Indiana, Indiana University Turkish Studies 3, 1982), pp. 249-267.

the military in the form of the National Security Council, which came to have greater powers than under the earlier regimes.[11, 12]

More immediately, however, the office of the presidency has become the locus of the state. Following the 1980 military intervention General Kenan Evren (then the head of the military junta, now the president) stated: "We cannot ... reduce the state to a petty entity subservient to the law of associations. The office of the head of the state cannot be relegated to that of a master of ceremonies."[13] Later, Article 105 of the 1982 Constitution stipulated that, "No appeal shall be made to any legal authority including the Constitutional Court against the decisions and orders signed by the president of the republic at his discretion." That the Turkish constitution in contrast to the French constitution did not enumerate the occasions on which the president is authorized to act alone (Özbudun), indicates that in Turkey more scope of action was granted to the president.*

On the other hand, in France the president of the republic normally presides over the Council of Ministers while the Turkish president does so only when he deems necessary (Özbudun). This must be due to the fact that there is now a division of labor between the state and political elites (Karpat). In the new regime, the state elites are expected to be strictly non-partisan concerning "political" (particularly economic) issues. On this matter Evren himself observed that the strict impartiality of the President is an integral part of the new political regime. He added that it is for this reason that he has been provided with extensive powers.[14] The President's functions include safeguarding the security and independence of the country, the indivisibility and integrity of the nation, and the secular republic guided by the tenets and reforms of Atatürk (1982 Constitution, Article 103). It must be added that not only his responsibilities but his charisma (Özbudun, Karpat) are also circumscribed by these functions.

---

[11] Under the 1961 Constitution the National Security Council provided 'information' to the Council of Ministers; following the Constitutional amendments of the early 1970s it offered "advice" to the Council of Ministers; now the Council of Ministers have to give "top priority" to the suggestions coming from the National Security Council. The National Security Council comprises the chief of general staff, top commanders of army, navy, air force, and gendarmerie, the prime minister, and the ministers of foreign affairs, defense, and the interior. When he deems necessary the president heads the Council. Otherwise the Council convenes under the chairmanship of the prime minister. As is apparent, the military is in the majority in the Council.

[12] That as compared to France the regime in Turkey under the 1982 Constitution is closer to parliamentarism rather than a presidential system of government (Özbudun) may be explained by the fact that the state elites in Turkey, when necessary, "act" not through the executive but through the National Security Council.

[13] Quoted in Heper, *The State Tradition in Turkey*, pp. 140-141.

* Cf. Özbudun in this volume.

[14] *Ibid.*, p. 204.

When he gives the impression that he is intruding in the "proper sphere of politics" the people tend to turn a deaf ear to him. A well-known example was his statement on the eve of the 1983 general elections in which he seemed to accuse Turgut Özal of engaging in the type of political behavior which the military condemned after the 1980 intervention; nevertheless, Turgut Özal's Motherland Party went on to capture the majority of the seats in the parliament. As time went by President Evren himself seemed to realize that his charisma, and therefore authority, is conditional upon his observing the division of labor between the state and the political elites.

"Özal's liberal revolution" (Rustow) was thus possible because of the division of labor in question, and because the new state elites no longer took Atatürkism as an ideology in the Shilsian sense. The definition of the general interest was not viewed as an all-embracing task. The drawing up of the economic policy was left to the political elites. Atatürkian thought was not regarded as a source for all public policies.[15]

The new state elites, however, have tried to inject into Turkish politics greater doses of "rationality" and have endeavored to lower the degree of politicization. In this vein an attempt was made to accomplish two things: First, to "improve" the individual qualifications for membership in the political parties and in the Turkish Grand National Assembly (TGNA). Second, attempts were made to tighten the procedural rules of politics. Hence the legal provisions inserted into the relevant laws (Turan, Özbudun), with the best of intentions.

It is apparent that some of these provisions *would* contribute towards the establishment of a smoothly functioning democracy. One example here is the arrangement for the election of the president by the TGNA (Özbudun). Also, some of the provisions intended to increase "rationality" in Turkish politics may be seen to have worked *in the direction that the new state elites had in mind:* (1) Those in official positions in the parliament have increased to the highest level since 1946; (2) religious functionaries have almost disappeared from the 1983 TGNA; (3) the proportion of former military officers appears to have arisen in the 1983 TGNA; (4) the proportion of members with secondary or less education has fallen; (5) the average number of children per family has fallen back to its lowest, 2.4; (6) the proportions of engineers and business and commercial elements have increased, and the like (Tachau). To what extent such and

[15] The president's responsibility for safeguarding "the secular Republic guided by the tenets and reforms of Atatürk," should be interpreted with regard to this new approach. The new state elites do not take Atatürkian thought as a political manifesto; but Atatürkian thought does serve as a justification for rejecting radical ideologies of both the left and the right. Heper, *The State Tradition in Turkey,* p. 143.

similar developments would indeed increase the level of "rationality" in Turkish politics is, of course, an open question.

On the other hand, the efforts to inject greater doses of "rationality" into Turkish politics has had some adverse consequences, too. The attempt to depoliticize the polity (by not allowing the political parties to have auxiliary organizations and preventing interest groups from articulating their views on matters not immediately related to their concerns) led to a situation where some interests are not represented; the ban on changing one's party during a given term of the parliament added a further inflexibility to the system (Turan). As an outcome of restrictions placed on the candidates, in the 1983 TGNA only 5 per cent of the MPs had previous parliamentary experience (Tachau). Despite the provisions in the new Political Parties Law for bringing about greater democracy within the political parties this low level of political experience on the part of the most party members is claimed to have contributed to the authoritarian atmosphere of the post-1983 TGNA (Tachau). The lack of parliamentary experience may also hasten the unruly behavior against the members of the other parties within the TGNA that seems to start after a certain period of time following each major realignment of forces in the polity (Kalaycıoğlu). And, perhaps most important, the last factor may interrupt the learning process and the development of a capacity to take lessons from the past mistakes (Ergüder and Hofferbert).

The very last point seems to be crucial for the future of Turkish democracy. As has already been suggested, while earlier some false starts seem to have been made, on the whole the president representing the state, has been successful in not meddling with the "political sphere." The people for their part, still drawing upon the collectivistic legacy but also having lived through the tumultuous decades of the 1960s and the 1970s, do not support those who would like to keep the "cultural" at the expense of "functional cleavages," alive. The constitutional referendum, the local elections of March 1984, and the 1987 general elections in which the True Path Party openly ran as the direct representative of the closed Justice Party and failed, are testaments to this particular orientation on the part of the people.[16]

As far as the performance of the political elites is concerned here evidence is mixed. Are the new political elites no more disposed than their predecessors to eschew partisan advantage in the national interest, as Harris suggests in this Volume? Or, do they try to be different since they resent being referred to as "politicians" (Kalaycıoğlu)?

[16] In 1984 a municipal election was held; the candidate for mayor from the True Path Party who lost in the elections, claimed that he lost because in his propaganda campaign he made numerous references to Süleyman Demirel, who used to be the chairman of the Justice Party as well as prime minister before the 1980 military intervention.

At the present time, everything may depend on whether efforts to revive in a new form the "cultural" in place of "functional cleavages," will succeed. The reference here is to "the civilian versus the military cleavage" that was claimed to best define the present-day configuration of Turkish polity. In this new reformulation, the civilians were presented as "democrats" who were intent on establishing in Turkey a "genuine democracy." The military, of course, was perceived as a bottleneck in the way of establishing such a democracy. This "movement" was said to be spearheaded initially by Süleyman Demirel and supported by the "democratic elites" on both the left and the right.

As already noted, the extremely instrumentalist tendencies of this movement did not seem to be shared by the majority of the electorate. Also, these tendencies were shared neither by Aydın Güven Gürkan and Erdal İnönü who jointly led the Social Democratic Populist Party, the main opposition party on the left, nor by Turgut Özal of the Motherland Party. Erdal İnönü gave up his chairmanship of the Social Democracy Party so that a merger could take place with Gürkan's Populist Party. Gürkan in turn agreed that in about six month's time the party congress would elect a new leader. These moves were seen as sacrifices on the part of both leaders so that fragmentation on the left would be avoided. On the other side of the fence "Özal's Motherland Party may have provided a broadly acceptable, pro-system alternative, neutralizing (for the time being at least) and reintegrating, if not eliminating, the anti-systemic tendencies on the right and the periphery" (Ergüder and Hofferbert).

The Social Democratic Populist Party and the Motherland Party competition may be said to primarily reflect a "functional cleavage," while the democratic elites and the military (or the state) elites confrontation may be said to primarily represent a "cultural cleavage." The former cleavage may move the regime towards moderate instrumentalism, or a "sensible society" in a Lockean sense, the latter cleavage would move it towards extreme instrumentalism, or a debilitating pluralism. The indications are that the electorate will not allow the latter eventuality to materialize.

Perhaps a better guarantee for a smoothly functioning democracy, where "functional" rather than "cultural cleavages" would dominate the polity, does not consist in elite realignments and voter preferences but in horizontal integration at the civil societal level and organic-institutionalized links between the civil societal groups and the political elite,[17] and the autonomy, in some measure, of the latter from the former so that coherent and prudent policies may be pursued. Özal's liberal revolution

[17] For the absence in Turkey of such links and their adverse effects on democracy in Turkey, see note 7 above.

(Rustow) *may* bring about such a development. Some of the conditions for such a structural change in Turkish politics are spelled out by Ergüder and Hofferbert in this volume: "If he and his colleagues sustain the perception of putting Turkey back on the slope of economic growth, with reasonable domestic tranquility, and if they are not derailed by international economic shocks, Turgut Özal may be facing an historic opportunity to umpire Turkey's entry into the community of democratic, materially prosperous nations."

Selected Bibliography

Abadan-Unat, Nermin (1981) "Major Issues of Turkish Political Parties Under The Light of Structural Change," in *Die Türkische Krise*. Bonn: Friedrich Ebert Stiftung.

Abadan-Unat, Nermin (1979) "Patterns of Political Modernization and Turkish Democracy," *The Turkish Yearbook of International Relations*, 18: 1-26.

Ahmad, Feroz (1981) "Military Intervention and the Crisis in Turkey," *MERIP Reports*, 93: 5-24.

Akarlı, Engin D with Gabriel Ben-dor (1975) *Political Participation in Turkey: Historical Background and Present Problems*. Istanbul: Boğaziçi University Publications.

Alkan, Türker (1986) *12 Eylül ve Demokrasi*. Istanbul: Kaynak Yayınları.

Anderson, James, ed. (1986) *The Rise of the Modern State*. Brighton, Sussex, England: Wheatsheaf.

Arcayürek, Cüneyt (1986) *Oniki Eylül'e Doğru Koşar Adım*. Istanbul: Bilgi Yayınevi.

Atalay, Sırrı (1986) *Bir Ömür Politika: Kars'tan Zincirbozan'a*. Istanbul: Milliyet Yayınları.

Badie, Bertrand and Pierre Birnbaum (1983) *The Sociology of the State*. Trans. by Arthur Goldhammer. Chicago: University of Chicago Press.

Batur, Muhsin (1985) *Anılar ve Görüşler: Üç Dönemin Perde Arkası*. Istanbul: Milliyet Yayınları.

Bazin, Marcel and Contributors (1986) *La Turquie en Transition. Disparités, Identités, Pouvoirs*. Paris: Maisonneuve et Larose.

Berki, R.N. (1979) "State and Society: An Antithesis of Modern Political Thought," in *State and Society in Contemporary Europe*. Edited by Jack Hayward and R.N. Berki. Oxford: Martin Robertson.

Bianchi, Robert (1984) *Interest Groups and Political Development in Turkey*. Princeton, N.J.: Princeton University Press.

Birand, Mehmet Ali (1986) *Emret Komutanım*. Istanbul: Milliyet Yayınları.

Birand, Mehmet Ali (1984) *12 Eylül: Saat 04.00*. Istanbul: Karacan Yayınları.

Cem, İsmail (1984) *"Geçiş Dönemi" Türkiyesi, 1981-1984*. Istanbul: Cem Yayınevi.

Cemal, Hasan (1986) *12 Eylül'ün Günlüğü, Tank Sesiyle Uyanmak*. Ankara: Bilgi Yayınevi.

Cemal, Hasan (1986) *12 Eylül'ün Günlüğü: Demokrasi Korkusu*. Ankara: Bilgi Yayınevi.

Dodd, C.H. (1983) *The Crisis of Turkish Democracy*. Walkington, England: Eothen Press.

Dodd, C.H. (1983) "Revolution in the Ottoman Empire and Modern Turkey," in

Revolutionary Theory and Political Reality, edited by N. K. O'Sullivan. Brighton, England: Harvester.

Doğan, Yalçın (1985) *Dar Sokakta Siyaset: 1980-1983*. Istanbul: Tekin Yayınevi.

Donat, Yavuz (1987) *Buyruklu Demokrasi, 1980-1983*. Ankara: Bilgi Yayınevi.

Dyson, Kenneth (1980) *The State Tradition in Western Europe*. Oxford: Martin Robertson.

Evin, Ahmet (forthcoming) *Bureaucrats, Politicians and Managers in Turkey*.

Evin, Ahmet, ed. (1984) *Modern Turkey: Continuity and Change*. Opladen: Leske Verlag and Budrich.

Grothusen, Karl-Detlev, ed. (1985) *Südosteuropa-Handbuch*, Band 4: *Türkei*. Göttingen: Vandenhoeck and Ruprecht.

Güneş, Turan (1983) *Araba Devrilmeden Önce*. Istanbul: Kaynak Yayınları (Posthumously published).

Hale, William (1981) *The Political and Economic Development of Modern Turkey*. London: Croom Helm.

Hall, John A. (1986) *States in History*. Oxford: Basil Blackwell.

Harris, George (1985) *Turkey: Coping with Crisis*. Boulder: Westview Press.

Held, David and Contributors (1983) *States and Societies*. Oxford: M. Robertson.

Heper, Metin, ed. (1987) *The State and Public Bureaucracies: A Comparative Perspective*. New York · Westport, Connecticut · London: Greenwood Press.

Heper, Metin, ed. (1987) *Democracy and Local Government: Istanbul in the 1980s*. Walkington, England: Eothen Press.

Heper, Metin (1987) "The State, Military and Democracy in Turkey," *Jerusalem Journal of International Relations*, 9: 52-64.

Heper, Metin, ed. (1986) *Dilemmas of Decentralization. Municipal Government in Turkey*. Bonn: Friedrich Ebert Stiftung.

Heper, Metin (1985) *The State Tradition in Turkey*. Walkington, England: Eothen Press.

Heper, Metin (1984) "A Weltanschauung-turned-Partial Ideology and Normative Ethics: 'Atatürkism' in Turkey," *Orient*. 1: 83-94.

Kalaycıoğlu, Ersin and Ali Yaşar Sarıbay, eds. (1986) *Türk Siyasal Hayatının Gelişimi*. Istanbul: Beta.

Kalaycıoğlu, Ersin (1985) "The Turkish Political System in Transition: Multi-Party Politics in the 1980s". *Current Turkish Thought*. (Istanbul) 56: 2-38.

Karpat, Kemal H. (1981) "Turkish Democracy at Impasse: Ideology, Party Politics and the Third Military Intervention." *International Journal of Turkish Studies*, 2: 1-43.

Karpat, Kemal H. (1981) "The Military and Its Relation to the State and Democracy," in *Die Türkische Krise*. Bonn: Friedrich Ebert Stiftung.

Kazancıgil, Ali and Ergun Özbudun, eds. (1981) *Atatürk: Founder of a Modern State*. London: C. Hurst.

Kazancıgil, Ali (1986) *The State in Global Perspective*. Aldershot, England: Gower.

King, Roger (1986) *The State in Modern Society. New Directions in Political Sociology*. London: Macmillan.

Kongar, Emre (1987) *12 Eylül ve Sonrası*. Ankara: Say Yayınları.
Kramer, Heinz (1983) *Das neue politische System der Türkei*. Ebenhausen: Stiftung Wissenschaft und Politik.
Kramer, Heinz (1984) *Die aktuelle politische Lage der Türkei*. Ebenhausen: Stiftung Wissenschaft und Politik.

Landau, Jacob M., ed. (1984) *Atatürk and the Modernization of Turkey*. Boulder: Westview Press.
Landau, Jacob M. (1982) "The Nationalist Action Party in Turkey," *Journal of Contemporary History*, 17: 587-606.
Landau, Jacob M. (1981) *Pan-Turkism in Turkey: A Study in Irredentism*. London: Hurst.
Landau, Jacob M., Ergun Özbudun and Frank Tachau, eds. (1980) *Electoral Politics in the Middle East: Issues, Voters and Elites*. London: Croom Helm.

Mackenzie, Kenneth (1981) *Turkey Under the Generals*. London: Conflict Studies, No. 126.
Magnerella, Paul J. (1982) "Civil Violence in Turkey. Its Infrastructural, Social, and Cultural Foundations," in *Sex-Roles, Family and Community in Turkey*, ed. by Çiğdem Kaçıtçıbaşı. Bloomington, Indiana University Turkish Studies, No. 3.
Mango, Andrew (1983) "The Third Turkish Republic," *The World Today*, 39: 30-38
Mango, Andrew (1982) "Understanding Turkey," *Middle Eastern Studies*, 18: 194-213
Mango, Andrew (1980) "Managing the Turkish Crisis," *The World Today*, 36: 259-265
Mardin, Şerif (1983) "Religion and Politics in Modern Turkey," in *Islam in the Political Process*, ed. by James A. Piscatori. Cambridge: Cambridge University Press.
McFadden, John H. (1985) "Civil-Military Relations in the Third Turkish Republic," *The Middle East Journal*, 39: 69-85.

Nettl, J. P. (1968) "The State as a Conceptual Variable," *World Politics*, 21: 559-592.

Özbudun, Ergun (1985) "Political Parties and Elections," in *Südosteuropa-Handbuch*, ed. by Klaus-Detlev. Grothusen, Göttingen: Vandenhoeck and Ruprecht.
Özbudun, Ergun (1981) "Turkey: The Politics of Political Clientelism," in *Political Clientelism, Patronage and Development*, ed. by S. N. Eisenstadt and René Lemarchand. Beverly Hills, California: Sage.
Özbudun, Ergun (1981) "The Turkish Party System: Institutionalisation, Polarisation and Fragmentation," *Middle Eastern Studies*, 17: 228-240.

Pevsner, Lucille W. (1984) *Turkey's Political Crisis. Background, Perspectives, Prospects*. New York: Praeger.
Poggi, Gianfranco (1978) *The Development of the Modern State: A Sociological Introduction*. London: Hutchinson.

Rustow, Dankwart A. (1987) *Turkey: America's Forgotten Ally*. New York: Council of Foreign Relations.
Rustow, Dankwart A. (1985) "Turkey's Liberal Revolution," *Middle East Review*, 17: 5-11.
Rustow, Dankwart A. (1970) "Transitions to Democracy: Toward A Dynamic Model," *Comparative Politics*, 2: 337-363.

Sayarı, Sabri (1985) *Generational Changes in Terrorist Movements: The Turkish Case*. Santa Monica: Rand Paper Series, P-7124.
Singer, Morris (1981) "Turkey in Crisis," *Current History*, 80: 27-31, 39-40.
Skocpol, Theda (1979) *States and Social Revolutions. A Comparative Analysis of France, Russia and China*. Cambridge, etc.: Cambridge University Press.
Soysal, Mümtaz (1982) *Demokrasiye Giderken*, Istanbul: Hil Yayın.
Sunar, İlkay and Sabri Sayarı (1986) "Democracy in Turkey: Problems and Prospects," in *Transitions From Authoritarian Rule: Experiences in Southern Europe*, ed. by Guillermo O'Donnell, Philippe C, Schmitter, and L. Whitehead. Baltimore and London: Johns Hopkins University Press.

Tachau, Frank (1984) *Turkey: Authority, Democracy and Development*. New York: Praeger.
Tachau, Frank and Metin Heper (1983) "The State, Politics and the Military in Turkey," *Comparative Politics*, 10: 17-33.
Tamkoç, Metin (1983) *Inconsistency Between the Form and the Essence of the Turkish Political System*. Salt Lake City: University of Utah, Middle East Center Research Monograph No. 8.
Toprak, Binnaz (1981) *Islam and Political Development in Turkey*. Leiden: Brill.
Turan, İlter (1986) "Stability versus Democracy: The Dilemmas of Turkish Politics," Paper delivered at Colloque sur les Groupes d'Interet d'Europe du Sud et leur Insertion dans la Communauté Européennes, Université de Genève, April.
Turan, İlter (1984) "Cyclical Democracy: The Turkish Case," Paper delivered at the Annual Meetings of the Midwest Political Science Association, Chicago, April.
Turan, İlter (1983) "Stages of Political Development in the Turkish Republic," Paper delivered at the Third International Congress on the Economic and Social History of Turkey, Princeton University, August.
12 September in Turkey: Before and After (1982). Ankara: General Secretariat of the National Security Council.

Vincent, Andrew (1987) *Theories of the State*. Oxford: Blackwell.

Weiher, Gerhard (1978) *Militär und Entwicklung in der Türkei, 1945-1973*. Opladen: Leske Verlag und Budrich.
Weiker, Walter F. (1981) *Modernization of Turkey: From Atatürk to the Present Day*. New York: Holmes and Meier.
Weiker, Walter F. (1981) "Democracy and the 1980 Military Intervention in Turkey, Problems and Prospects," Paper presented at the Annual Meetings of the Middle East Studies Association, Seattle, Washington, November.

Contributors

C. H. Dodd is Professor of Politics at the University of Hull, and Professorial Research Associate in the School of Oriental and African Studies, University of London. A past president of the British Society for Middle Eastern Studies, his publications include *Politics and Government in Turkey, Political Development, Democracy and Development in Turkey,* and *Crisis of Turkish Democracy.*

Üstün Ergüder is Professor of Political Science at Boğaziçi University. Author of two books in Turkish, he has contributed to several scholarly journals such as the *Journal of Public Policy.*

Ahmet O. Evin works on cultural projects at the Secretariat of His Highness the Aga Khan. Formerly Director of the Middle East Center at the University of Pennsylvania, Professor Evin's publications include *Modern Turkish Architecture* (co-editor), *Modern Turkey: Continuity and Change* (editor), *The Origins and Development of the Turkish Novel* and *Bureaucrats, Politicians and Managers in Turkey* (forthcoming).

William Hale is Senior Lecturer in the Politics of the Middle East and Chairman of the Board of Studies in Politics at the University of Durham, England. Dr. Hale's publications include *Four Centuries of Turco-British Relations* (co-editor), *Aspects of Modern Turkey* (editor), and *Political and Economic Development of Modern Turkey.*

George Harris is Director of the Office of Analysis for Near East and South Asia in the Department of State, Washington, D.C. Dr. Harris has been a Professorial Lecturer at George Washington University and Johns Hopkins University and is the author of *The Origins of Communism in Turkey, The Troubled Alliance: Turkish American Problems in Historical Perspective, 1945-1971,* and *Turkey: Coping with Crisis.*

Metin Heper is Professor of Political Science, Chairman, Department of Public Administration, at Boğaziçi University, Istanbul, and editor of *Journal of Economics and Administrative Studies* (Istanbul). Among his books are *Islam and Politics in the Modern Middle East* (co-editor), *Dilemmas of Decentralization: The Municipal Government in Turkey* (editor), *Democracy and Local Government: Istanbul in the 1980s* (editor), *The State and Public Bureaucracies* (editor), and *The State Tradition in Turkey.*

Richard I. Hofferbert is Professor of Political Science and Director of Graduate Studies in Political Science at the State University of New York, Binghamton. He is the author of *The Study of Public Policy* and *The Reach and Grasp of Policy Analysis.*

Ersin Kalaycıoğlu is Associate Professor of Political Science at Boğaziçi University. He has contributed to several scholarly journals including *Comparative Political Studies, Legislative Studies Quarterly* and *International Journal of Political Education,* and is the author of two books in Turkish.

Kemal H. Karpat is Distinguished Professor of History and Chairman of the Middle East Studies Program at the University of Wisconsin, Madison. Professor Karpat is the editor of *International Journal of Turkish Studies;* among his books are *Political and Social Thought in the Contemporary Middle East* (editor), *Social Change and Politics in Turkey* (editor), *Turkey's Politics: The Transition to Multi-Party Politics, The Gecekondu: Rural Migration and Population,* and *The Ottoman Population 1830-1914.*

Şerif Mardin is Professor of Sociology and former Dean of the Faculty of Economics and Administrative Sciences, Boğaziçi University. A founding member of the Turkish Social Science Association, Professor Mardin is the author of *The Genesis of Young Ottoman Thought* as well as several volumes in Turkish.

Ergun Özbudun is Professor of Government and Constitutional Law at Ankara University. He is co-editor of *Electoral Politics in the Middle East, The Political Economy of Income Distribution in Turkey, Atatürk: Founder of a Modern State,* and *Competitive Elections in Developing Countries,* and the author of *The Role of the Military in Recent Turkish Politics, Party Cohesion in Western Democracies: A Causal Analysis,* and *Social Change and Political Participation in Turkey.*

Christian Rumpf is a Research Fellow at Frankfurt University and the Max Planck Institute for Comparative Public Law and International Law at Heidelberg. Mr. Rumpf has contributed to several scholarly journals such as *Europäische Grundrechte Zeitschrift* and *Rabels Zeitschrift* and collected work such as *Südosteuropa-Handbuch* and *Encyclopaedia of Public International Law.*

Dankwart A. Rustow is Distinguished Professor of Political Science at the City University of New York and editor-in-chief of *Comparative Politics.* His publications include *Turkey: America's Forgotten Ally, Oil and Turm-*

oil: America Faces OPEC and the Middle East, OPEC: Successes and Prospects (with J. F. Mugno), *Middle Eastern Political Systems,* and *A World of Nations.*

Frank Tachau is Professor of Political Science, a Faculty Fellow of the Honors College, and former Chairman of the Department of Political Science at the University of Illinois at Chicago. Among Professor Tachau's books are *Political Elites and Political Development in the Middle East* (editor), *Electoral Politics in the Middle East* (editor), and *Turkey: The Politics of Authority, Democracy and Development.*

Binnaz Toprak is Associate Professor of Political Science at Boğaziçi University, Istanbul. Professor Toprak is author of *Islam and Political Development in Turkey.*

İlter Turan is Professor of Political Science at Istanbul University. Professor Turan is the co-author of *The Legislative Connection: The Representatives and the Represented in Kenya, Korea and Turkey.*

Bei Fragen zur Produktsicherheit wenden Sie sich bitte an:
If you have any questions regarding product safety,
please contact:

Walter de Gruyter GmbH
Genthiner Straße 13
10785 Berlin
productsafety@degruyterbrill.com